More Praise for *Rethinking Teacher Supervision and Evaluation*

"Kim has written an important book, a must-read for anyone who believes that school can be and must be greatly improved. His argument is clear, cogent, and buttressed by endless practical ideas borne of his long work on the front lines of urban education. But his message applies to all educators: pay attention to what does and doesn't work; build upon a rich curriculum; and most of all redefine supervision and evaluation to ensure that it is ongoing, efficient and always focused on staff learning about learning. Marshall has written a thoughtful, practical and hopeful book that should play a vital role in ending the fatalism that is a cancer in American education."

— *Grant Wiggins, president, Authentic Education, Hopewell, New Jersey*

"Every principal continuously grapples with the question 'How can I most effectively improve instruction in my school?' Kim Marshall provides a set of powerful answers to that question by seamlessly weaving together his personal experiences as an accomplished Boston principal, insightful analysis of educational research, and countless conversations with expert researchers and practitioners. This is an excellent guide to instructional leadership for both new and experienced principals."

— *John King, senior deputy commissioner for P–12 education, New York State*

"Kim Marshall is quickly establishing himself as a pre-eminent voice in the field of school leadership. He does what few authors have done before: integrate the critical tasks of observation, curriculum planning, and data-driven instruction to drive real student achievement. His combination of real-world experience and visionary thinking creates a roadmap that has the potential to alter the national landscape on teacher supervision."

— *Paul Bambrick-Santoyo, managing director, North Star Academy Network, Uncommon Schools*

"Classroom teachers and principals alike will decorate the pages of this insightful book with notes and underscored passages that offer inspiration and the kind of down to earth advice you seek from the best teacher you know. Kim Marshall is a visionary thinker with his finger right on the pulse of how good teaching transforms thinking, and how deep concern for students transforms teaching; in direct, compelling language, he describes the magical synergy that happens when educators at all levels work together to prepare students for life—not just for tests."

—*Vicki Spandel, author,* **Creating Writers** *and* **The 9 Rights of Every Writer**

"Kim Marshall brings the wisdom of a seasoned principal and the insights of a scholar/researcher to this analysis of instructional leadership. His work is practical, smart and most of all clear and accessible. Any educational leader seeking to find ways to improve the quality of instruction will find in this book an invaluable resource. Marshall writes with the authority of someone who understands what needs to be done to create successful schools because he has already done so himself."

—*Pedro A. Noguera, Ph.D., Peter L. Agnew Professor of Education,*
Steinhardt School of Culture, Education and Development
Executive Director, Metropolitan Center for Urban Education,
New York University

"Kim Marshall's invaluable book is more than a new view of supervision and evaluation—it offers a broad-based map of the multiple paths that a principal must consider if teaching and learning is to be improved deeply."

—*Jon Saphier, author of* **The Skillful Teacher**

Rethinking Teacher
Supervision and Evaluation

Rethinking Teacher Supervision and Evaluation

HOW TO WORK SMART, BUILD COLLABORATION, AND CLOSE THE ACHIEVEMENT GAP

Kim Marshall

JOSSEY-BASS
A Wiley Imprint
www.josseybass.com

Published by Jossey-Bass
A Wiley Imprint
989 Market Street, San Francisco, CA 94103-1741—www.josseybass.com

Library of Congress Cataloging-in-Publication Data
Marshall, Kim, 1948-
  Rethinking teacher supervision and evaluation : how to work smart, build collaboration, and close the achievement gap / Kim Marshall.
     p. cm.
  Includes bibliographical references and index.
  ISBN 978-0-470-44996-7 (pbk.)
  1. Teachers—Rating of. 2. Teachers—In-service training. 3. Performance standards. I. Title.
  LB1728.M26 2009
  371.14'4—dc22
                                 2009035516

Printed in the United States of America
FIRST EDITION

PB Printing   10 9 8 7 6 5 4 3 2 1

CONTENTS

For Lillie and David,

skillful and intrepid teachers

ACKNOWLEDGMENTS

First and foremost, I am grateful to my wife, Rhoda Schneider, for her support, wise counsel, and keen eye, and also to Lillie Marshall, David Marshall, Katherine Marshall, and Laura Marshall.

Christie Hakim at Jossey-Bass believed in this book from the beginning and persuaded me to write it, and she and her colleagues contributed mightily to the final product, including Leslie Tilley (special thanks for helping reformat the rubrics), Julia Parmer, Hilary Powers, Kate Gagnon, and Pam Berkman.

Loyal friends and thought partners have helped encourage and shape this book over the years: Jon Saphier, Mike Schmoker, Doug Reeves, Roland Barth, Paul Bambrick-Santoyo, Larry Cuban, Jay McTighe, Grant Wiggins, Jeff Howard, John King, Rick DuFour, Dylan Wiliam, Charlotte Danielson, Mike Lupinacci, Mark Jacobson, Jenn David-Lang, Andrew Bundy, Andy Platt, John Dempsey, Mary Scott, Barney Brawer, Barry Jentz, Mary Ellen Haynes, Lorraine Cecere, Dick Best, Lois Jones, Bill O'Neill, Bill Henderson, Bob Weintraub, Doug Lemov, Ellie Drago-Severson, George Hill, Gerry Degnan, Vikki Ginsberg, Jay Heubert, Joan Dabrowski, Karen Drezner, Kathleen Flannery, Mairead Nolan, Mark Roosevelt, Mary Grassa O'Neill, Mary Russo, Maureen Harris, Michael Fung, Emily Cox, Sandi Kleinman, Pamela Seigle, Pedro Noguera, Vicki Spandel, Penny Noyce, Pete Turnamian, Jamey Verilli, Rick Weissbourd, Sandy Mitchell-Woods, Ted Dooley, Diane Lande, Toni Jackson, Lisa Pacillo, Gary Gut, Maria Palandra, Pamela Pelletier, Betsey Useem, and Mike Useem.

Finally, I am grateful to the teachers at the Mather School, who tutored me as these ideas germinated, and to the budding principals, seasoned coaches, and honchos in New Leaders for New Schools who have contributed in ways they cannot imagine: Jon Schnur, Monique Burns, Ben Fenton, Cami Anderson, Jann Coles, Kris Berger, Stephanie Fitzgerald, Vera Torrence, Mark Murphy, my coaching colleagues in New York, Washington D.C., Chicago, and the Bay Area, and all New Leaders principals, and Gerry Leader and the ELI program's budding school leaders.

Finally, my thanks to Athie Tschibelu, who went above and beyond the call of duty to help launch one of the first components of this book.

INTRODUCTION

Principal evaluation of teachers is a low-leverage strategy for improving schools, particularly in terms of the time it requires of principals.

—Richard DuFour and Robert Marzano

Write-ups have low to medium leverage on influencing teaching practice.

—Jon Saphier

These quotes from three of America's leading authorities on instructional improvement are shocking and counterintuitive to many educators. For decades, the assumption has been that if we want to improve teaching, one of the best ways is to supervise and evaluate teachers. Surely, the argument went, inspecting classroom performance and giving teachers feedback and formal evaluations would make a positive difference.

But when educators are given a few minutes to reflect on what DuFour, Marzano, and Saphier are saying, it begins to ring true. I frequently ask groups of administrators to think back to when they were teachers and raise their hands if an evaluation ever led them to make significant improvements in the way they taught. Typically, I see around 5 percent of the group raise a hand. When I ask if the evaluations that principals themselves have written produce significant classroom improvements, I get a similar response. Most principals sheepishly admit that after all the work they put into all those pre-observation conferences, classroom visits, write-ups, and post-conferences, they rarely see much difference in what teachers do—much less in student achievement.

This is disturbing. It means that school leaders are spending huge amounts of time on a process that rarely improves classroom teaching. And teaching, after all, is the heart of the matter. Recent research has shown that the quality of instruction is the single most important factor in student achievement (Fergusson & Ladd, 1996; Sanders & Rivers, 1996; Haycock, 1998; Rivkin, Hanuschek, & Kain, 2005; Whitehurst, 2002; Hattie, 2002; Rice, 2003; Nye, Hedges, & Konstantopoulos, 2004; Clotfelter, Ladd, & Vigdor, 2007).

GOOD TEACHING REALLY MATTERS

This was not always the conventional wisdom. For years, factors outside the schoolhouse were believed to be the main determinants of student achievement—social class, innate intelligence, family background, community dynamics, negative peer pressure, or racism and discrimination. But now we know that good classroom teaching can overcome the disadvantages with which many students enter school, and that children who grow up in poverty are not doomed to failure. Figure I.1 shows the dramatic difference in the achievement of students who have three years of effective, mediocre, or ineffective teachers.

Good teaching helps all students, but it turns out that it makes a bigger difference for some than for others. Figure I.2 shows the results of a study that compared the impact of effective and ineffective teachers on students as they moved from fifth to seventh grade. Students who had effective teaching for three years in a row achieved at almost identically high levels, even though some started with much lower achievement than others. But a matched sample of students who had three years of ineffective teaching fared quite differently: those who started out with high and average achievement were still doing quite well at the end of

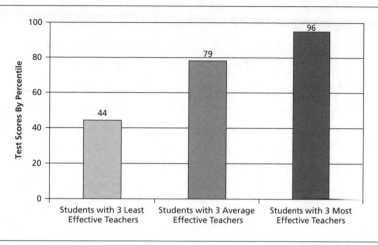

Figure I.1
Fifth-Grade Math Scores on Tennessee Statewide Test:
Based on Teacher Sequence in Grades 3, 4, 5

Source: Sanders & Rivers (1996)

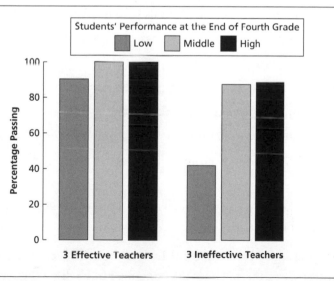

Figure I.2
The Impact of Effective and Less Effective Teachers on Grade
5-7 Students With Different Levels of Entering Proficiency

Source: Bracey, 2004

seventh grade, but students who started out with low skills did poorly. This study and others like it show that low-achieving students benefit disproportionately from good teaching.

All this points to a conclusion with which almost every parent would agree: the principal's most important job is getting good teaching in every classroom. The achievement gap widens every day that children are subjected to an ineffective or mediocre teacher, and good teaching has the potential to narrow it.

But what is the best way to get effective teaching for every child? For starters, removing *in*effective teachers. Hiring is also key, since each vacancy is a golden opportunity to upgrade the team. But the vast majority of teachers are not candidates for dismissal, and vacancies don't occur that frequently. So while hiring and firing are tremendously important, this book will focus on strategies for supporting and improving the teachers (ranging from excellent to mediocre) who are in classrooms now.

In recent years, schools and districts have tried a variety of approaches for improving teaching:

- More aggressive supervision and evaluation
- Using test scores to evaluate teachers
- Merit pay for high-performing teachers
- Revamping the teacher evaluation forms that principals fill out
- Doing "learning walk" tours of schools with feedback to the staff
- Getting teachers to visit exemplary classrooms and schools
- Having teachers analyze student work
- Requiring teachers to use highly scripted curriculum programs
- Providing laptop computers for every student
- Encouraging teachers to use the Internet to find effective ideas and materials
- Setting up "critical friends groups" in which teachers read and discuss articles and books
- And the old stand-by, getting teachers to attend workshops and courses inside and outside their schools

Each of these approaches can contribute to the quality of instruction under the right conditions, and they all have proponents. But I believe there is a much more powerful way to improve teaching and learning and close the achievement gap. This book will present four closely linked strategies for principals: making short, unannounced classroom visits followed by one-on-one feedback conversations; participating much more actively in the curriculum planning process; working with teacher teams to analyze and follow up on interim assessment results; and using rubrics for end-of-year teacher evaluation. I believe these are the most effective ways for a principal to exercise instructional leadership and make a real difference at the classroom level. Figure I.3 is a diagram that will evolve through the book, showing how the four strategies interact.

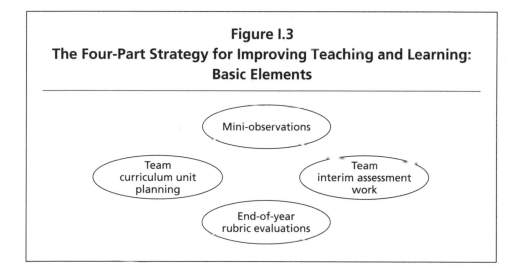

Figure I.3
The Four-Part Strategy for Improving Teaching and Learning: Basic Elements

Mini-observations

Team curriculum unit planning

Team interim assessment work

End-of-year rubric evaluations

Implementing these four strategies involves fundamental changes in the way principals handle supervision and evaluation and the professional dynamic within schools. Chapters Three through Eight will show how school leaders can shift:

- From periodically evaluating *teaching* to continuously analyzing *learning*
- From occasional announced classroom visits to frequent unannounced visits
- From taking extensive notes on one or two lessons to extracting key "teaching points" from portions of multiple lessons
- From guarded, inauthentic communication with teachers to candid give-and-take based on authentic classroom observation

- From formal yearly or twice-yearly evaluations to continuous suggestions and redirection
- From inadvertently sowing envy and division among teachers to empowering and energizing teacher teams
- From teachers saying "Let me do it my way" to everyone asking "Is it working?"
- From administrators doing most of the work to teachers taking on real responsibility for improving teaching and learning
- From evaluating individual lessons to supervising the effectiveness of curriculum units
- From one-right-way evaluation criteria to constantly looking at new ideas and practices
- From focusing mainly on ineffective teachers to improving teaching in every classroom
- From cumbersome, time-consuming evaluations to streamlined rubrics
- From being mired in paperwork to continuously orchestrating schoolwide improvement

This book grew out of my own experience, extensive research, and close observation of scores of effective and ineffective schools. My thirty-two years as a Boston teacher, central office administrator, and principal were the starting point. Since leaving the Boston schools in 2002, I have continued to develop my initial insights and practices and have presented them in scores of workshops and consultations in a wide variety of schools and districts. These ideas have been adopted in part by a number of schools, but there is no pure exemplar and, to date, no definitive research on what happens when all four components are implemented together.

I believe strongly, however, that the combination of all four elements is the key to dramatic gains. Mini-observations have a powerful logic, and I challenge readers to present a better system for seeing what is really going on in classrooms on a daily basis. Curriculum unit planning has a strong track record all over the world, thanks to the work of Grant Wiggins, Jay McTighe, and their colleagues. Interim assessments have robust research support and a number of successful practitioners. And teacher evaluation rubrics, while lacking a research track record because they are so new, just make sense.

So what you are reading is a combination of personal experience, research, and theory. I hope it will be provocative and helpful. Here is a chapter-by-chapter overview:

- Chapter One tells the story of my fifteen-year Boston principalship, during which my colleagues and I struggled against some significant obstacles and realized quite late in the game that major gains in student achievement are difficult without external standards linked to good assessments.

- Chapter Two shows how supervision and evaluation ideally *should* improve teaching and learning, and then presents twelve reasons why, in most schools, they don't.

- Chapter Three describes my initial failure with supervision and evaluation as a principal and my discovery of mini-observations—an effective way of getting into classrooms and giving teachers feedback.

- Chapter Four is a set of best practices for using mini-observations, drawn from my own experience and the wisdom of other educators.

- Chapter Five broadens the usual definition of supervision to include principals' working with teacher teams as they clarify learning goals and "backwards design" curriculum units—all of which can make the principal a more perceptive and helpful thought partner during and after classroom observations.

- Chapter Six broadens supervision further still, describing how principals can direct and support teacher teams as they look at interim assessment results, figure out learning problems, help struggling students, involve students in improving their own performance, and continuously improve teaching.

- Chapter Seven returns to a major flaw of year-end teacher evaluations—how time-consuming and disrespected they often are—and presents a set of evaluation rubrics that are more time-efficient and give teachers succinct, detailed, and constructive end-of-year feedback.

- Chapter Eight deconstructs the time management challenge that all principals face and suggests ten ways they can survive, do first things first, and get the engine of improvement humming in their schools.

- Chapter Nine sums up, describing how mini-observations, curriculum planning, interim assessments, and teacher evaluation rubrics interact and build on each other. By successfully orchestrating these four components, principals can build collaboration with and among teachers and foster continuous improvement of teaching and learning aimed at closing the achievement gap.

- Appendix A is a model of a slim curriculum outcomes booklet—a clear statement of what students need to know and be able to do by the end of the year.

- Appendix B is a set of rubrics for evaluating the performance of a principal. Like the teacher evaluation rubrics in Chapter Seven, these rubrics are "open source" and can be downloaded from the *Marshall Memo* website.

Throughout this book, the word "principal" is used as shorthand for school leaders. Readers should take this to include assistant principals, deans, department heads, and all school-based administrators who supervise and evaluate teachers.

Rethinking Teacher
Supervision and Evaluation

The Challenge

Closing the Achievement Gap

Knowledge powers a global economy that is utterly unforgiving
to the unskilled, uneducated young adult.

—Joel Klein, New York City Schools Chancellor

I became principal of Boston's Mather Elementary School late in the summer of 1987, absolutely determined to boost achievement and convinced that supervising and evaluating teachers was at the core of my role as an instructional leader. But had I reflected more carefully on my seventeen years as a teacher, graduate student, and central office administrator, I might have anticipated some of the bumps that lay ahead.

SUPERVISION AS SEEN BY A ROOKIE TEACHER

Fresh out of college in 1969, I began my career at Boston's Martin Luther King Jr. Middle School. Supremely ill-equipped to handle a class of twenty-five energetic sixth graders, I had a rough first year. A supervisor from Boston's central office visited several times and was highly critical, so my first exposure to teacher evaluation was one in which my job was on the line. I was one of several first-year teachers at the King, and we all regarded this man with fear and loathing. We muttered about how the only thing he cared about was quiet students, a clean chalkboard ledge, and window shades pulled down at exactly the same height. Disdain for this vision of good teaching was fiercest among those of us who were having the most trouble with classroom discipline. Imagine our glee when students turned the supervisor's Volkswagen Beetle upside down in the parking lot one spring afternoon.

But the supervisor was right to criticize my teaching, and the point was driven home when I invited a professor from Harvard's Graduate School of Education to observe. He sat patiently through a couple of lessons and said afterward that he had not seen "one iota of learning" taking place. This was not exactly what I wanted to hear, but again, the criticism was on target. One of the school's assistant principals was assigned to the sixth-grade corridor, and he knew I was struggling. But there were so many other crises in the building that he wasn't able to give me detailed feedback or substantive help.

Somehow I got through the year without being fired—perhaps an acute teacher shortage in Boston helped—and spent the beginning of the summer writing an article vividly describing my experiences ("Law and Order in Grade 6E," published a little later in the *Harvard Alumni Bulletin*). After it came out, I received perhaps the most devastating evaluation an idealistic young urban teacher could receive:

> Your article clearly shows that whites do NOT belong in Black schools. With all your woes and problems, you forget that the 25 Black students you "taught" have had another year robbed from them (and people wonder why when they become adults they can't "make it" in society). It is unfortunate that you had to "gain your experience" by stealing 25 children's lives for a year. However, Honky—your day will come!
>
> —From one Black who reads the Harvard Bulletin

In my second year, I implemented "learning stations"—a decentralized style of teaching with students working on materials I wrote myself—and right away things were calmer and more productive. The principal was quite supportive of my unconventional teaching style, even bringing visitors up to my classroom from time to time. But I rarely got any direct evaluative feedback. Did my students learn a lot? I believed they did, judging from weekly tests I created, but I was never held accountable to any external standards. These were the 1970s, there was no state curriculum to speak of, and measurable student outcomes weren't part of the conversation.

During these years, I operated very much as a loner, closing my classroom door and doing my own thing. At one point I actually cut the wires of the intercom speaker to silence the incessant schoolwide PA announcements. Here was teacher isolation at its most extreme; if World War III had broken out, my students and I might have missed it.

OUT OF THE CLASSROOM

After eight years of teaching, I stepped out of my classroom to act as the King's "education coordinator"—a grant-funded curriculum support role that allowed me to work on curriculum improvement but barred me from evaluation because I was still in the same bargaining unit as my colleagues. As I moved around the school, I noticed that the curriculum was highly fragmented, with teachers covering a wide variety of material without a coherent sequence from Grade 6 to 7 to 8, and the quality of teaching varied widely, with no agreed-upon definition of best practice. I saw all this clearly, but my "soft" administrative status prevented me from making much of a difference. After two years as education coordinator, I returned to the classroom, believing that I could have more impact teaching a group of twenty-five students.

But it wasn't the same. I had definitely been bitten by the administrative bug, and this was reinforced as I pondered a series of *New York Times* articles about a new wave of research on schools that somehow managed to get very high student achievement in tough urban neighborhoods. One prominent exponent was Harvard Graduate School of Education professor Ronald Edmonds, who boiled down the formula for effective urban schools to five variables: strong instructional leadership, high expectations, a focus on basics, effective use of test data, and a safe and humane climate. A 1978 British study, *Fifteen Thousand Hours* (Harvard University Press), had much the same message, describing the "ethos" and expectations that made some schools much more effective than others. All the effective-schools research emphasized the importance of the principal going beyond routine administrative functions and being an instructional leader, and I began to think seriously about becoming a principal.

The problem was that I didn't have administrative certification, so in 1980, I bid an emotional farewell to the King School, where I had spent eleven formative years, and enrolled in Harvard's Ed School. I had the good fortune to study with Ronald Edmonds himself, and his searing comment on failing urban schools became my credo:

> We can, whenever and wherever we choose, successfully teach all children whose schooling is of interest to us. We already know more than we need in order to do this. Whether we do it must finally depend on how we feel about the fact that we haven't so far [1979, p. 23].

But the voters of Massachusetts passed a tax-limiting referendum in 1980, sending Boston into a budget tailspin and forcing the district to close twenty-seven schools. There was no way I was going to be a principal in the near future, and I prepared to return to the classroom.

Then, through a chance connection, I was recruited to serve on the transition team of Boston's new superintendent, Robert Spillane, a forceful advocate of high student achievement and school accountability. He and I hit it off immediately, and I ended up spending the next six years in the central office, first as a speechwriter, policy adviser, and director of curriculum, then, under Spillane's successor, Laval Wilson, as director of an ambitious system-wide strategic planning process. The "Nation at Risk" report of the National Commission on Excellence in Education dominated the national discourse during this period, and I found myself in the thick of Boston's response to the "rising tide of mediocrity" acerbically described in the report.

My central-office colleagues and I did some useful work, producing a set of K–12 grade-by-grade learning expectations and aligned curriculum tests, but throughout my six years as a district bureaucrat, I felt that our efforts to improve schools were like pushing a string. There weren't enough like-minded principals at the other end pulling our initiatives into classrooms, and we didn't make much of a dent in Boston's student achievement. I was more convinced than ever that the real action was at the school level, and I hankered to be a principal.

MY OWN SHIP

In 1987, I finally got my chance. Laval Wilson put me in charge of the Mather, a six-hundred-student K–5 school with low achievement and a veteran staff. As I took the reins, I believed I was ready to turn the school around after having seen the urban challenge from three perspectives: as a cussedly independent teacher, as a student of effective urban schools, and as a big-picture central office official. I firmly believed I was finally in the right place to make a difference for kids.

So how did I do? During my fifteen years as Mather principal, the school made significant gains. Our student attendance rose from 89 percent to 95 percent and staff attendance from 92 percent to 98 percent. Reading and math scores went from rock bottom in citywide standings to about two-thirds of the way up the pack. In 1999, the Mather was recognized in a televised news conference for making the biggest gains in the MCAS (Massachusetts Comprehensive Assessment System, the rigorous statewide tests introduced the year before) among large elementary schools statewide. And in the spring of 2001, an in-depth inspection gave the Mather a solid B+. I was proud of these gains and of dramatic improvements in staff skills and training, student climate, philanthropic support, and the physical plant.

However, these accomplishments came in agonizingly slow increments, and were accompanied by many false starts, detours, and regressions. Graphs of our students' test scores did not show the clean, linear progress I had expected. Far too many of our students scored in the lowest level of the 4-3-2-1 MCAS scale, too few were Proficient and Advanced (the top two levels), and our student suspension rate was way too high. Serious work remained to be done. In 2002, I decided to move on, hoping that my vigorous young successor would take the school to the next level.

Why didn't Mather students do better? It certainly seemed that we were pushing a lot of the right buttons, and if the Mather's student achievement had been extraordinary, outside observers would have pointed to a number of "obvious" explanations: my seventy-eight-hour workweek, the arrival of a number of first-rate teachers, frequent classroom supervision, extra funding and other resources, major improvements to the building and grounds, a daily memo communicating operational matters and research findings to all staff (dubbed the *Mather Memo*), and more. But our student achievement was not extraordinary. Why?

Looking back, I can identify a number of factors that made it difficult for me to get traction as an instructional leader. Teacher supervision and evaluation was the hardest of all, and Chapter Two will describe my struggle to get into classrooms and give teachers meaningful feedback. Others included staff expectations, the school's unique culture, teacher isolation, curriculum fragmentation, poor alignment of teaching and assessment, and unclear goals. Let's examine these challenges (which were hardly unique to the Mather) and an external event that finally began to break the log-jam.

Low Expectations

From the moment I arrived at the Mather, I was struck by the staff's unspoken pessimism about producing significant gains in student learning. Teachers had never seen an urban school with really high achievement, were depressed by the poverty and crime around the school (85 percent of our students qualified for free and reduced-price meals), and had internalized U.S. cultural beliefs about the innate ability level of students like ours. As a result, many staff members saw themselves as hard-working martyrs in a hopeless cause; they loved their students (at least most of them) and did their best, but really high achievement was not in the cards. As for the new principal's starry-eyed speeches about the "effective schools" research, teachers were highly skeptical.

Sensing this ethos, I took a big risk and brought in Jeff Howard, the charismatic African American social psychologist, to explain his "Efficacy" philosophy to the whole staff at an all-day professional meeting in the fall of 1987. Howard held teachers spellbound as he argued that people are not just born smart—they can *get smart* by applying effective effort. He said we could dramatically improve our results by directly confronting the downward spiral of negative beliefs about intelligence and effort. Over lunch, most of the staff buzzed with excitement.

But that afternoon Howard had to leave for another speaking engagement and the Efficacy consultant he left in charge was peppered with questions from the most skeptical members of the staff. Was he saying that teachers were racist? Was he implying that teachers were making the problem worse? And what did he suggest they do on *Monday*? As the meeting wore on, it was clear that my gamble to unite the staff around a novel approach to higher expectations was going down in flames. As teachers trooped out that afternoon, even those who were sympathetic to the Efficacy message agreed that the day had been a disaster.

In the months that followed, I licked my wounds and took a more incremental approach. In private conversations, team meetings, the staff memo, and clipped-out research articles, I tried to convey the message that higher student achievement was doable at schools like the Mather. I sent small groups of teachers to Efficacy training and eventually brought in one of Howard's colleagues to do a three-day workshop for the whole staff. It was an uphill battle, but Efficacy beliefs gradually found their way into the school's mission and it became taboo to express negative expectations about students' potential.

A Resistant Culture

The Mather's staff had been dominated for years by a small group of very strong personalities, and they did not take kindly to my idealistic approach to urban education or to the fact that I had gone to Harvard (twice!) and had worked in district's central office. The "Gang of Six," as I dubbed them privately (a reference to the Gang of Four, China's maligned leadership team during the Cultural Revolution), began to undermine my agenda with a vehemence that was unnerving. Monthly confrontations with the Faculty Senate, the forum used by the resisters, invariably got my stomach churning. A parody of the *Mather Memo* ridiculing me was slipped into staff mailboxes: "For Sale: Rose-Colored Glasses! Buy Now! Cheap! Get that glowing feeling while all falls apart around you."

I tried to keep up a brave front, but I could not hide my dismay when I heard that on the day of the Efficacy seminar, one of these teachers was overheard to say in the bathroom, "If I had a gun, I'd shoot Jeff Howard dead." At another point, one of these teachers put a voodoo doll likeness of me in the teachers' room and stuck pins in it. Others were so spooked that they didn't dare touch it, and the doll stayed there for several days until a teacher finally had the courage to throw it away.

Unprepared by my upbringing and lack of leadership experience for this kind of behavior, I was sometimes off balance, and every mistake I made became a major crisis ("People are outraged! Morale has never been worse!" said one of the leaders). One such kerfuffle was provoked by the ratings I gave teachers in the initial round of performance evaluations I was required to do in the fall. At this time, Boston's teacher evaluation system had three ratings: Excellent, Satisfactory, and Unsatisfactory. I felt that I hadn't been in teachers' classrooms enough to give them Excellent ratings, and not wanting to devalue the currency, I gave Satisfactory ratings to almost everyone. Although I explained this decision carefully and promised that many ratings would go up when I had time to make more thorough classroom visits, the Satisfactory ratings were taken as an insult by many teachers and stirred up quite a fuss.

Some of the school's brashest teachers, sensing my weakness and lack of street smarts, "went off" on me within earshot of others. When I failed to set limits on what could only be described as outrageous and insubordinate behavior, I lost face with the rest of the staff. The "silent majority" secretly wanted me to change the negative culture that had dragged down the school for years, but were so intimidated by the negative teachers that they remained on the sidelines, which greatly discouraged me. To friends outside the school, I took to quoting Yeats: "The best lack all conviction, while the worst are full of passionate intensity."

Over the next few years, the most negative teachers gradually transferred out—but they had understudies. Every year I battled (not always very skillfully) for the hearts and minds of the silent majority, and only very gradually did the school develop a more positive culture. How much better things would have been if we had been unified in a quest for higher student achievement and had ways of measuring our progress each year!

Teacher Isolation

In my first months as principal, I was struck by how cut-off Mather teachers were from each other and from a common schoolwide purpose. I understood teachers' urge to close their classroom doors and do their own thing—after all, that's what I had done as a teacher. But the effective-schools research and my experience in the central office convinced me that if Mather teachers worked in isolation, there might be pockets of excellence but schoolwide performance would continue to be disappointing.

So I struggled to get the faculty working as a team. I wrote the *Mather Memo* every day and tried to focus staff meetings on curriculum and best practices. I encouraged staff to share their successes, publicly praised good teaching, and successfully advocated for a number of prestigious "Golden Apple" awards for Mather teachers. I recruited a corporate partner whose generosity made it possible, among other things, to fund occasional staff luncheons and an annual Christmas party. And I orchestrated a major celebration of the school's 350th anniversary in the fall of 1989 (the Mather is the oldest public elementary school in the nation), fostering real pride within the school and community.

But morale never got out of the sub-basement for long. Staff meetings were often dominated by arguments about discipline problems, and as a young principal who was seen as being "too nice" to students, I was often on the defensive. We spent very little time talking about teaching and learning, and teachers continued to work as private artisans, sometimes masterfully, sometimes with painful mediocrity—and overall student achievement didn't improve.

Lack of Teamwork

Unable to muster the charisma to unite the whole staff around a common purpose, I decided that grade-level teams were a more manageable arena in which to build collegiality. I figured out how to schedule common planning periods for grade-level teams, and they began to meet at least once a week and occasionally convene for after-school or weekend retreats (for which teachers and paraprofessionals were paid). A few years later, a scheduling consultant showed us how to create ninety-minute team meetings once a week by scheduling art, computer, library, music, and physical education classes back-to-back with lunch. This gave teams enough time during the school day to really sink their teeth into instructional matters.

After much debate, we introduced "looping," with all the fourth-grade teachers moving up to fifth grade with the same students and fifth-grade teachers moving back to fourth to start a two-year loop with new groups of students. Teachers found that spending a second year with the same class strengthened relationships with students and parents—and within the grade-level team—and a few years later the kindergarten and first-grade teams decided to begin looping, followed a few years later by the second- and third-grade teams.

But despite the amount of time that teams spent together, there was a strong tendency for the agendas to be dominated by ain't-it-awful stories about troubled students, dealing with discipline and management issues, and planning field trips. I urged teams to use their meetings to take a hard look at student results and plan ways to improve outcomes, and I tried to bring in training and effective coaches to work with the teams, but I had limited success shifting the agendas of these meetings. In retrospect, I probably would have been more successful if I had attended team meetings and played more of a guiding role, but I was almost always downstairs managing the cafeteria at this point in the day, and told myself that teachers needed to be empowered to run their own meetings.

Curriculum Anarchy

During my early years as principal, I was struck by the fact that most teachers resisted aligning instruction with a common set of grade-level standards. During my years in Boston's central office, I had worked on nailing down citywide curriculum goals, and I was saddened by the degree to which these official Boston Public Schools expectations were ignored at the other end of the pipeline. While

Mather teachers (like many of their counterparts around the country) enjoyed their unofficial academic freedom, it caused lots of problems as students moved from grade to grade. While teachers at one grade emphasized multiculturalism, teachers at the next judged students on their knowledge of state capitals. While one team focused on grammar and spelling, another cared more about style and voice. While one encouraged students to use calculators, the next wanted students to be proficient at long multiplication and division.

These ragged hand-offs from one grade to the next were a constant source of unhappiness. But teachers almost never shared their feelings with colleagues in the grade just below who had passed along students without important skills and knowledge. Why not? Well, that would have risked getting into some serious pedagogical disagreements that would jeopardize staff "morale" (that is, congeniality). But *not* having those honest discussions doomed the Mather to a deeper morale problem (lack of *collegiality*) stemming from suppressed anger at what many teachers saw as students' uneven preparation for their grade—and lousy test scores that became increasingly important and public as the years passed.

The lack of clear grade-by-grade curriculum expectations was also a serious impediment to my supervision of teachers. When a principal visits a classroom, one of the most important questions is whether the teacher is on target with the curriculum—which is hard to define when no one is sure exactly what the curriculum is! If principals don't have a clear sense of what (for example) second graders are supposed to learn in math and what proficient writing looks like by the end of fifth grade, it's awfully hard to supervise effectively. And it's very hard for a principal to address this kind of curriculum anarchy one teacher at a time. Supervision can't be efficient and effective until curriculum expectations are clear and widely accepted within the school.

I saw this do-your-own-thing curriculum ethos as a major leadership challenge, and tried repeatedly to get teachers to buy into a coherent K–5 sequence with specific objectives for the end of each grade. At one all-day staff retreat in a chilly meeting room at the Kennedy Library overlooking Boston Harbor, I asked teachers at each grade to meet with those at the grade just below and then with those just above and agree on a manageable set of curriculum hand-offs. People listened politely to each other, but back in their classrooms, they made very few changes. Undaunted, I brought in newly written Massachusetts curriculum frameworks and national curriculum documents, but these didn't match the norm-referenced tests our students were required to take and could therefore be ignored with impunity. When the Boston central office produced a cumbersome new curriculum in 1996, I "translated" it into teacher-friendly packets for each grade level—but once again, these had little impact on what teachers taught. Visiting classrooms, I didn't have detailed, agreed-upon guidelines on what was supposed to be covered, which put me at a serious disadvantage. I could comment on the process of teaching but had great difficulty commenting on content and results.

The lack of coherent learning standards resulted in far too many of our students moving from grade to grade with uneven preparation. At fifth-grade graduation every June, I knew that the students whose hands I was shaking as they walked across the stage to get their diplomas were better prepared than most Boston elementary students, but were entering middle school with big gaps in their knowledge and skills. It was not a pretty picture, and I was intensely frustrated that I could not find a way to change it.

Weak Alignment Between Teaching and Assessment

As I struggled to rationalize the K–5 curriculum, it occurred to me I might be able to leverage the standardized tests that most Boston students took to get teachers on the same page (*what gets tested gets taught*, I'd been told more than once). The citywide test at that time was the Metropolitan Achievement Test, given in reading and math at every grade level except kindergarten, with school-by-school results helpfully published in Boston newspapers. I spent hours doing a careful analysis of the Metropolitan and, without quoting specific test items, presented teachers at each grade level with detailed packets telling what the test covered in reading and math.

Did teachers use my pages and pages of learning goals? They did not. The problem was that the tests teachers gave every Friday (covering a variety of curriculum topics with differing expectations and criteria for excellence) had a life of their own, and I wasn't providing a strong enough incentive to give them up. As hard as it was for me to admit, teachers were not being irrational. The Metropolitan, a norm-referenced test, was designed to spread students out on a bell-shaped curve and was not aligned to a specific set of curriculum goals (Boston's or any other school district's) or sensitive to good teaching (Popham, 2004a). In other words, it was possible for teachers to work hard and teach well and not have their efforts show up in improved Metropolitan scores. Teachers sensed this, and the result was cynicism about the standardized testing and the kind of curriculum anarchy I found at the Mather.

Although my foray into test-based curriculum alignment was unsuccessful, I had stumbled upon an important insight. The key to getting our students well prepared by the time they graduated from fifth grade was finding high-quality K–5 learning expectations and tests that measured them. The problem was that we had neither, and without clear expectations and credible tests, I couldn't coax teachers out of their classroom isolation. For ten years I searched for the right curriculum-referenced tests and tried to clarify and align the curriculum—but until the late 1990s, I wasn't successful. This, in turn, stymied meaningful grade-level collaboration and meant that when I made supervisory visits to classrooms, I was largely flying blind.

Mystery Grading Criteria

Another aspect of the Mather's balkanized curriculum was the lack of agreement among teachers on the criteria for assessing student writing. As is the case in many U.S. schools, the same essay could receive a different grade depending on which teacher read it. The absence of clear, public scoring guides meant that students got very uneven feedback and teachers lacked the data they need to improve their classroom methods.

In 1996, the Mather staff made a bold attempt to solve this problem. Inspired by a summer workshop I attended with Grant Wiggins, an assessment expert based in New Jersey, we created grade-by-grade scoring rubrics that described the specific characteristics of student writing at the 4, 3, 2, and 1 level in three domains of writing:

- Mechanics/Usage
- Content/Organization
- Style/Voice

Now our standards were clear and demanding, and we could say with some certainty that the same piece of student writing would get the same scores no matter who graded it. We began to give students quarterly "cold prompt" writing assessments (they wrote on a topic with no help from their teacher or peers) in September, November, March, and June. Teachers scored the papers together and then discussed the results.

This process had great potential. We were scoring student writing objectively; we shared the criteria with students and parents in advance (no surprises, no excuses); we were seeing students' progress several times each year; and teacher teams at each grade were analyzing students' work, giving students feedback, and thinking about best practices for teaching writing.

But for several reasons, this initiative sputtered. Scoring and analyzing tests took too long (often several weeks passed from the time students wrote their compositions to the time we scored and discussed them); our graphic display of the data from each assessment didn't show clearly where students were improving and where they needed help; team meetings fell victim to the "culture of nice" (most teachers weren't frank and honest and didn't push each other to more effective methods); and we didn't involve students in the process of looking at each piece of writing and setting goals for improvement. Without these key elements, our writing initiative didn't bring about major improvements in classroom practice or significantly boost students' performance.

Not Focusing on Learning

As the years went by, I became increasingly convinced that the most important reason student achievement wasn't meeting my ambitious expectations was that we spent so little time actually looking at what students were learning. The teachers' contract allowed me to supervise classroom teaching and inspect teachers' lesson plans, but woe betide a Boston principal who tried to evaluate teachers based on student learning outcomes. This resistance was well-founded at one level: unsophisticated administrators might be tempted to use norm-referenced standardized tests to unfairly criticize teachers for failing to reach grade-level standards with students who had been poorly taught in previous years.

But not looking at results cuts teachers and administrators off from some of the most useful information for improving teaching and learning. Mather teachers, like their counterparts in other schools, fell into the pattern of teach, test, and move on. The headlong rush through each year's curriculum was rarely interrupted by a thoughtful look at how students were doing and what needed to be fixed or changed to improve results.

At one point I asked teachers to give me copies of the unit tests they were giving—not the results, mind you, just the tests. Almost everyone ignored my request, which baffled and upset me. But when I checked in with a few teachers individually, I realized it wasn't an act of defiance as much as puzzlement at why the principal would be making such a request. Teachers seemed to see their tests as private artifacts that were none of my business. Perhaps they were also self-conscious about the quality of their tests. *(Was he going to look for typos?)*

Unwilling to push the point and distracted by other issues, I didn't follow up. In retrospect, collecting tests and talking about them with teacher teams might have led to some really productive conversations. If I had taken it a step further and orchestrated conversations about how students *performed* on the tests, then we really would have been cooking. But I almost never got teachers to relax about the accountability bugaboo and talk about best practices in light of the work students actually produced.

THE AH-HA! MOMENT: STATE STANDARDS AND TESTS

Looking over the challenges I wrestled with in my first decade at the Mather, it's easy to see why we weren't more successful at reaching higher levels of student achievement. I was haunted by the knowledge that with each passing year, the achievement gap between our students and those in more effective schools was widening. But how could we combat the hydra-headed challenges and get higher expectations, create a more positive culture, and convince teachers to work in teams on clearly defined learning outcomes? How could we avoid the Matthew Effect, the Biblical prophecy that hangs over all educators: "To those who have, more will be given, and they will have abundance; but from those who have nothing, even what they have will be taken away" (Matthew 13:12).

Like other struggling schools, we needed outside help—and it finally arrived when Massachusetts introduced rigorous external standards and high-stakes testing (the Massachusetts Comprehensive Assessment System, or MCAS) in 1998. What really got people's attention was the clear message that in a few years, students who didn't pass the tenth-grade MCAS tests in reading and math wouldn't get a high school diploma. As soon as message sank in, things changed quite quickly.

As our fourth graders took the first round of MCAS tests, one highly respected fourth-grade teacher burst into tears at a staff meeting. "No more Lone Ranger!" she exclaimed and pleaded with her colleagues in kindergarten through third grade to prepare students better so that she would never again have to watch her students being crushed by a test for which they were so unready. On that spring afternoon in the school's library, you could hear a pin drop. The teacher's emotional plea shone a bright spotlight on the very problems that had been festering for so many years.

At first, there was resistance to the idea of preparing students for an external test. This wasn't surprising, given the years of working in isolation with idiosyncratic, personal curriculum expectations and contending with standardized tests that didn't measure what was being taught. But when Mather teachers sat down and looked carefully at sample MCAS test items, they were impressed, and gradually reached the following conclusions:

- Although the tests were hard, they measured the kinds of skills and knowledge students needed to be successful in the twenty-first century.
- We could and should align our curriculum to the tests, and this was possible because MCAS items and Massachusetts standards were available online.
- Most of our current students were not prepared to do well on the MCAS tests at that point.
- Nonetheless, our kids *could* reach the proficient level if the whole school taught a well-aligned K–5 curriculum effectively over a period of years.

This was just where the staff needed to be in order to take the next steps.

It's worth noting that since 1998, Massachusetts has had exemplary curriculum standards and assessments; a recent study by the Thomas B. Fordham Institute rated the Massachusetts materials the best in the nation. Many other states are not as fortunate, which raises questions about how schools in these states should proceed. The best approach would seem to be for principals to adopt a standards-plus approach, preparing students to do well on their state's tests and using national standards (for example, the National Assessment of Educational Progress, or NAEP) and college-ready tests to supplement and enrich the offerings their students receive.

SLIM CURRICULUM BOOKLETS AND ACHIEVEMENT TARGETS

The problem with the 1998 Massachusetts frameworks and tests was that they covered only Grades 4, 8, and 10. As Boston curriculum officials mulled over how to fill in the gaps, the Mather staff decided we could do the job more quickly on our own. The state had published "bridge" documents to accompany the Grade 4 MCAS tests, and we set up committees that worked with consultants over the summer to tease back the Grade 4 standards to Grades 3, 2, 1, and kindergarten and up to Grade 5. That fall, we used the "tease-back" documents to create slim booklets for each grade (about twelve pages long for each level) containing clear learning expectations accompanied by rubrics and exemplars of good student work. Parent leaders helped us scrub the documents of jargon, and our corporate partner printed copies of the booklets for all teachers and parents. The curriculum summaries quickly became drivers for learning in every classroom—and were widely circulated in other Boston schools in what the superintendent at the time referred to as a "curriculum black market." (See Appendix A for a modern example of such a booklet.)

Embracing the new Massachusetts standards was enormously helpful in each of the areas we'd struggled with for so long. Grade-by-grade MCAS-aligned targets put an end to curriculum anarchy and focused teacher teams on methods and materials that would maximize student learning, bringing more substance to grade-level team meetings. Although teachers gave up some academic freedom in the process, their isolation from each other was greatly reduced and teams had a common mission. External standards also helped our staff confront the issue of expectations; having agreed that the new Massachusetts standards were appropriate and attainable (with effective, aligned teaching across the school), we could unite around a relentless push for *proficiency*—a term that acquired special potency when it was attached to the robust third level on the 4-3-2-1 MCAS achievement scale.

External standards also gave us a more focused mission statement and school improvement plan. Our purpose, we now saw, was to prepare students with the specific knowledge and skills to be proficient at the next grade level, so that fifth-grade graduates would be prepared to achieve at a proficient-or-above level in any middle school. Such a simple and measurable purpose was unimaginable before the arrival of MCAS.

At around the same time we took these steps, Jeff Howard made a successful return visit and helped us agree on a schoolwide achievement target for reading, writing, math, and social competency four years down the road. Grade-level teams then spelled out their own SMART goals (Specific, Measurable, Attainable, Results-oriented, and Time-bound) for that year to act as stepping-stones toward the long-range target (see Chapter Four for more details and samples of both of these). Each year, we updated the SMART goals with higher and higher expectations.

NECESSARY BUT NOT SUFFICIENT

Ronald Edmonds often said that the existence of even one successful urban school proved that there was no excuse for any school to be ineffective. With this message, Edmonds laid a guilt trip on educators who weren't getting good results, and his stinging rebuke may have jolted some educators into thinking more seriously about improving their schools. But was Edmonds right that we knew in the late 1970s exactly how to turn around failing schools? Did the correlates of highly successful schools provide enough guidance? Was he fair to thoughtful, hard-working school leaders who were struggling with barriers like those I've described? Was he perhaps a little glib about what it would take to close the gap?

There's no question that Edmonds and his generation of researchers gave us an inspiring vision by showcasing the schools that succeeded against the odds and highlighting the factors that seemed to make them work. It's a tribute to Edmonds and others that the "effective schools" lists they produced have held up so well over the years. But the early literature did not provide a detailed road map to help a failing school get out of the wilderness, and something else was missing: credible external standards and assessments. Without those ingredients, success depended too much on extraordinary talent, great personal charisma, a heroic work ethic, a strong staff already in place—and luck. This allowed cynics to dismiss isolated urban success stories as idiosyncratic and claim that the urban school challenge was fundamentally unsolvable.

That said, Edmonds's extraordinarily important contribution was getting three key messages into the heads of people who care about urban schools:

- Demographics are not destiny: inner-city children can achieve at high levels.
- Specific school characteristics are linked to beating the demographic odds.
- We therefore need to stop making excuses, get to work, and learn as we proceed.

Coupled with standards and good assessments, these insights have started us on the way to closing the achievement gap. Recent research on the "90/90/90" schools (90 percent children of poverty, 90 percent children of color, and 90 percent achieving at high levels) by Douglas Reeves, Karin Chenoweth, and others has updated the early research with exemplars of highly effective practice. Visiting these schools is one of the most transformational experiences an urban educator can have.

But turning around failing schools and closing the achievement gap is still extraordinarily difficult. Principals and teachers can have the right beliefs and embrace standards and still run schools with mediocre student outcomes. In my years at the Mather and in my work coaching principals and reading extensively since I left the school in 2002, I have become convinced that belief and standards are not enough. To be successful, schools need to radically improve the way they handle four key areas: teacher supervision, curriculum planning, interim assessments, and teacher evaluation—all of which can interact synergistically if they are handled well. The following chapters make the case for a new approach that promises to drive significant improvements in teaching and learning.

Supervision and Evaluation

Why We Need a New Approach

*Evaluation has become a polite, if near-meaningless matter
between a beleaguered principal and a nervous teacher.
Research has finally told us what many of us suspected all along:
that conventional evaluation, the kind the overwhelming
majority of American teachers undergo, does not have any
measurable impact on the quality of student learning. In most
cases, it is a waste of time.*

—Mike Schmoker

In most other occupations, it goes without saying that supervision and evaluation are key levers for improving job performance. The boss inspects and the workers shape up—or ship out. In education, that's been the conventional wisdom as well, with principals' classroom visits and year-end evaluations serving as the main vehicles for monitoring and improving teachers' performance. But does this model work in schools? Consider the following real-life scenarios:

• A principal boasts that he spends two hours a day in classrooms—and it's true: he really does visit his school's seventeen teachers daily, chatting with students and occasionally chiming in during a lesson. But when teachers are asked what kind of feedback they get, they say the principal rarely talks to them about what he sees when he strolls through.

• A principal receives several parent complaints about discipline problems in a history teacher's classroom but is so overwhelmed that she rarely observes his teaching. When it's time for the annual formal observation, the teacher stages a carefully planned lesson featuring an elaborate PowerPoint presentation and well-behaved students. The principal feels she has no choice but to do a positive write-up of this lesson and give the teacher a satisfactory rating.

• A principal spends four entire weekends in April and May laboring over teacher evaluations. He puts them in teachers' mailboxes just before the deadline with a cover note: "Please let me know if you have any concerns and would like to talk. Otherwise, sign and return by tomorrow." All the teachers sign, nobody requests a meeting, and there is no further discussion.

• A well-regarded veteran teacher says she hasn't been evaluated in five years and the principal is almost never in her classroom. She takes this as a compliment—her teaching must be "okay"—and yet she feels lonely and isolated with her students and wishes the principal would pay an occasional visit and tell her what he thinks.

• A sixth-grade teacher has good classroom management and is well-liked by students and parents, but his students do surprisingly poorly on standardized tests. The new principal mentions the scores and the teacher launches into a litany of complaints about how he always gets the "bad class," most of his students come from dysfunctional, single-parent families, and he's tired of being asked to "teach to the test." Later that day, the union representative officiously reminds the principal that it's not permissible to mention test results in a teacher's evaluation.

• A principal observes an elaborate hands-on math lesson in a veteran teacher's classroom and notices that the teacher is confusing mean, median, and mode. The principal notes this error in his mostly positive write-up, and in the post-observation conference, the teacher suddenly begins to cry. Ten years later, at the principal's retirement party, he reminds the teacher of this incident (she remembers it vividly) and asks what lessons she took away from it. "Never to take a risk," she says.

Stories like these raise troubling questions about whether conventional *supervision* (defined as observation and coaching of teachers during the year) and *evaluation* (summative judgments, usually toward the end of the school year, for teachers' personnel files) are effective ways to improve teaching and learning. I have serious doubts, which leads me to believe that we need to drastically rethink the existing model and link it to a broader and more robust strategy for carrying out the core mission of schools—one that enlists teachers and students in a common effort to reach high levels of achievement.

THE WAY IT SHOULD BE—AND THE WAY IT IS

A helpful way to analyze the failure of conventional supervision and evaluation is to spell out the "logic model"—the way things should work under ideal conditions—and compare it with everyday reality. As you read this list, ask yourself where you have seen gaps between the ideal and the real:

1. Principals and teachers have a shared understanding of what good teaching looks like.
2. Principals get into classrooms and see typical teaching in action.
3. Principals capture and remember key points from their classroom visits.
4. Principals give teachers feedback on what's effective and what needs to be improved.
5. Teachers understand and accept the feedback.
6. Teachers use the feedback to improve their classroom practice.
7. As a result, student achievement improves.

It makes sense that if all these steps were implemented skillfully, supervision and evaluation would be a significant force for improvement. But human failings, bureaucracy, interpersonal dynamics, and politics all conspire to prevent things from working the way they should. Here are twelve ways that supervision and evaluation breaks down in many schools:

- The principal sees only a tiny fraction of teaching time.
- Teachers often put on a dog-and-pony show.
- The principal's presence changes classroom dynamics.
- Doing good lesson write-ups requires lots of skill and training.
- Even high-quality lesson write-ups can miss the bigger picture.

- Many evaluation instruments are cumbersome and legalistic, making it difficult to give helpful feedback.
- Checklists and numerical ratings lack bite and don't guide improvement.
- Critical evaluations can shut down adult learning or be shrugged off.
- The whole process can feed isolation and jealousy.
- Some principals don't confront bad or mediocre teaching.
- Many principals are too harried to do effective evaluations.
- The focus of evaluation is on pleasing the principal, not student learning.

Limited Point of View

The principal sees only a tiny fraction of teaching time. In a typical school year, a teacher has about nine hundred classes (five a day for 180 days). On average, busy principals thoroughly evaluate only about one lesson per teacher per year. Figure 2.1 puts this in perspective—one box out of nine hundred, or about 0.1 percent. The remaining 99.9 percent of the time, the teacher is essentially alone with students.

Of course some teachers get more intensive evaluation, including rookies and teachers on improvement plans, and some administrators make lots of brief, informal visits to classrooms for other purposes—getting things signed,

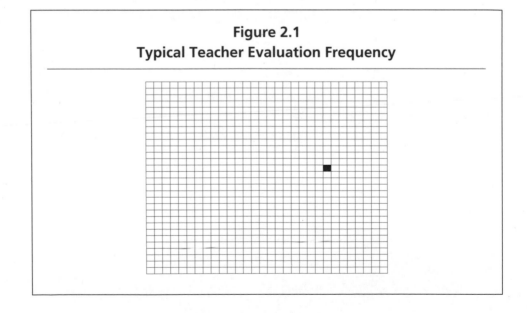

Figure 2.1
Typical Teacher Evaluation Frequency

delivering supplies, wishing students or teachers a happy birthday, and so forth. But the reality is that serious evaluation visits are few and far between. "Hey, no problem!" is the reaction from some teachers. Fewer evaluation visits mean less to be nervous about. But there's a downside. Being judged on the basis of one lesson out of nine hundred can be terrifying. What if you're having a bad day? What if you mess up?

The fact that administrators are in classrooms less than half a percent of the time should foster a little humility. Only principals with a very strong sense of their own power and persuasiveness would imagine changing a teacher's performance and students' achievement after peering through such a narrow window. For evaluations to be credible with teachers, school leaders must somehow capture what's going on the other 99.9 percent of the time, or at least have ways of being sure that teachers are doing the right thing. But how is that possible?

Stage Dressing

Teachers often put on a dog-and-pony show. "Oh, Corinne, I see you're being observed today!" a teacher might say when seeing a colleague dressed in a power suit and wearing her best earrings. In many schools, evaluation visits are routinely announced in advance (sometimes because that's required by the collective bargaining agreement), and teachers want to put their best foot forward and showcase an especially well-planned lesson. If the principal conducts a pre-observation conference, the teacher has an additional opportunity to sharpen the lesson plan so things go well for the boss.

Jazzed-up lessons do give a sense of what teachers are capable of under the best conditions. They're even a little flattering to some school leaders: *Gee, you put this on for me!* But principals aren't stupid; they know that many of the lessons they're evaluating aren't the kind of instruction students are experiencing on a day-to-day basis—not a typical "day in the life" glimpse of the teacher's overall performance. Here's a true story (told to me in July 2008 by a Massachusetts teacher who understandably prefers to remain anonymous) that illustrates the point. In preparation for an evaluation visit, a teacher had distributed a special student handout to her class. When she heard over the intercom that the principal had to postpone his observation, she collected the worksheet from students and proceeded with the "normal" lesson. Incidents like this are part of the folklore of schools, and they bespeak a fundamental flaw in the process.

If the purpose of evaluation is for the principal to give meaningful feedback that affirms and improves teaching and then deposit an accurate assessment in each teacher's personnel file, these pre-announced evaluation visits are inherently bogus. When a principal accepts a glamorized lesson, writes it up, and makes it the most important comment on a teacher's work for the year, it tells the teacher, *You can put on a special show for me and that's what counts.* The unspoken corollary is that it's okay to do something *less* special the other 99.9 percent of the time, when only students are the audience.

Restaurants get regular visits from Board of Health inspectors, and a restaurant critic might also drop in any time and write a make-or-break review. What if restaurant owners knew when these high-stakes visitors were going to arrive? Might they make a special effort to clean up the kitchen and serve a really spectacular meal? Only a foolish manager wouldn't. But then the Board of Health report and the food critic's review would be highly suspect. True, the kitchen might always be spotless and the food unfailingly delicious, but the public would have no way of knowing for sure. From the restaurant patron's point of view, unannounced visits are essential to quality assurance. For a school's customers—students, parents, and taxpayers—the same logic applies to principals' classrooms evaluations.

Some principals are confident they can see through a dog-and-pony show and scope out a teacher's everyday performance even when an evaluation visit is announced in advance. I think they're deluding themselves. Principals who use announced visits to make summative judgments on teachers don't have a true sense of the quality of instruction day after day, week after week, month after month. If the goal is to boost achievement for all students, that's what counts. Principals who rely on one or two announced visits are basically saying a prayer and trusting that teachers are delivering the same quality of instruction all the time. Most teachers act responsibly most of the time, but as they say in the U.S. Army, hope is not a strategy.

Observer Effects

The principal's presence changes classroom dynamics. The moment an administrator steps into a classroom, teacher-student and student-student interactions are altered to some degree. This is especially true for announced evaluation visits, when the level of tension may be high, but it's true at other times as well, especially if the principal doesn't visit that often. Students often sit up a little straighter and show their best behavior, giving a false impression of the level of respect and decorum that exists when the principal isn't there.

Most of the time, the principal's presence works to teachers' benefit by creating a more orderly, cooperative class. But it can also have a negative effect; teachers who feel that their job is on the line or are intimidated by the principal can be thrown off stride. Every teacher's nightmare is to botch one lesson and have the rest of the year painted with the same evaluative brush.

Yes, principals have other sources of information to correct egregiously off-target observations—informal drop-ins, quick impressions of teachers interacting with students, parent comments, colleagues' off-the-record reports, and of course, gossip. But these time-honored sources of information, even when they're accurate, aren't usually admissible in official evaluations. Principals have little choice but to go by the book and use the information from formal evaluation visits, even when they know they're not representative of everyday reality.

Communication Difficulties

Doing good lesson write-ups requires lots of skill and training. Good teaching is extremely complex and challenging, and there is more than one right way to be successful with students (Marzano, 2007; Saphier, Haley-Speca, & Gower, 2008). It takes experience and savvy for a principal to grasp the subtleties of a classroom; it's even more challenging for a principal to capture them in writing; and it's *really* hard to be critical of a teacher's performance in a way that's heard. Some principals have had the benefit of excellent training in observing classrooms and writing up what they see, and some, even without training, are gifted "naturalists" (Howard Gardner's eighth intelligence) and fluent writers who can capture classroom nuances on paper. Teachers fortunate enough to be evaluated by these principals can learn a lot.

But many principals aren't gifted or well-trained. Clueless, clumsily written classroom evaluations reflect poorly on school leaders and become fodder for faculty-room gossip. Word processing is a godsend to busy principals, but it can also get them in trouble. When two Boston-area teachers recently compared their evaluations, they found that the principal had pasted in exactly the same paragraphs, changing only the names. As other teachers in this school compared their write-ups, one of the group told me, they found that the principal had done the same for several of them, but had forgotten to change the teacher's name on one evaluation, which provoked great hilarity.

This is a worst-case scenario; most principals are more conscientious and competent. But the unevenness of training and the temptation to cut corners are built-in disadvantages to a system of evaluation that depends for its effectiveness on high levels of training and skill in writing up classroom observations.

The Forest and the Trees

Even high-quality lesson write-ups can miss the bigger picture. Some principals are required by their districts to produce detailed narratives of each lesson they observe, with an emphasis on scripting what's happening in the classroom minute by minute and capturing actual quotes. This is an important skill, especially when principals need to make the case for dismissing an ineffective teacher. But if the default setting for supervision and evaluation is principals going into classrooms and writing furiously throughout the lesson, they are going to miss a lot. To get a true picture of a lesson, an observer needs to walk around, see what students are being asked to do, look at their work, perhaps chat with a student or two, and carefully observe the subtle interpersonal teacher-student and student-student dynamics. It's impossible to see, hear, and feel all this while sitting at a desk and writing or typing on a laptop.

A second problem with detailed write-ups is that one lesson, however carefully scrutinized, is just a glimpse of the overall quality of a teacher's work. Although a lesson is the fundamental building block of instruction, it's only a part of a teacher's effort to inspire students and convey knowledge and skills. To get the bigger picture, a principal needs to know more: *What curriculum unit is this lesson part of? What are the unit's big ideas and essential questions? How does this unit align with state standards? How will students be assessed?* Principals may try to ferret out these missing pieces by asking for lesson plans and conducting pre- and post-conferences, but evaluations are often overly focused on the lesson that was observed.

This is a problem, because it's impossible to teach most state standards in a single lesson; it's a huge leap from big-picture goals like "understanding number sense" to planning a single lesson. *Unit* plans, which describe a teacher's game plan for teaching skills and concepts over a three- to five-week period, tell far more about whether instruction is coherent and aligned with standards, and broader curriculum plans help put each lesson in perspective. The problem is that principals rarely see unit plans—or the tests that teachers give, or how well students do on them.

A final problem with detailed write-ups is that they often fudge the big-picture question on every teacher's mind after an observation: *How am I doing?* When I was a principal, I wrote hundreds of narrative evaluations, giving detailed descriptions of the dialogue and dynamics of a class. But I rarely stepped back and gave a clear, overall judgment of each teacher's performance. In a narrative-focused evaluation process, the verbiage often obscures the message.

The Tyranny of Forms

Many evaluation instruments are cumbersome and legalistic, making it difficult to give helpful feedback. Teaching is a "complex and uncertain endeavor" (Sato & Lensmire, 2009), and the forms that public-school principals are required to fill out when they evaluate teachers rarely allow them to capture its subtleties. Some forms have highly detailed checklists of the criteria, suggesting that there is "one right way" to produce learning. Some have criteria skewed to fit an ideologically driven view of teaching (for example, teacher-centered instruction). Some are overly simplistic, missing important aspects of instruction. Some list the district's philosophy of teaching in separate documents that get lost in the shuffle so that teachers and administrators don't have access to them when evaluation time rolls around. And although principals are required to share evaluation criteria with teachers at the beginning of every school year, there is usually so much on the agenda at that point that sharing and signing off on the evaluation process is a pro forma exercise. The result is that teachers and administrators rarely have a shared understanding of the district's definition of good teaching.

Evaluation forms are not created in a vacuum. They must pass muster with district management and the teachers' union, and these two parties have quite different goals. The district's bottom-line purpose (aspirational goals aside) is that the evaluation instrument will hold up in an arbitration hearing on the dismissal of an ineffective teacher. This tends to produce boilerplate language and legally safe provisions. The union's core objective is protecting teachers from less-than-competent administrators, so they work hard to negotiate "principal-proof" evaluation formats and often try to require pre-announced evaluation visits. What emerges from this dialectic is rarely a thing of beauty (see Exhibit 2.1); most districts' formats don't foster an honest, open, and pedagogically sophisticated dialogue between principals and teachers. Many forms put principals at a serious disadvantage as they try to work within their required evaluation process to improve teaching and learning.

Exhibit 2.1
New York City Teacher Evaluation Form as of 2009

NEW YORK CITY DEPARTMENT OF EDUCATION
DIVISION OF HUMAN RESOURCES
OFFICE OF APPEALS AND REVIEWS
65 Court Street, Brooklyn, New York 11201
BE/DOP 9955B (5/87) pers d1 (Replaces OP 11B)

**ANNUAL PROFESSIONAL PERFORMANCE
REVIEW AND REPORT ON PROBATIONARY
SERVICE OF PEDAGOGICAL EMPLOYEE**
(OTHER THAN SUPERVISOR, GUIDANCE COUNSELOR, SCHOOL SOCIAL
WORKER, PSYCHOLOGIST, EDUCATIONAL EVALUATOR, SCHOOL SECRETARY)

EMPLOYEE'S FULL NAME	LICENSE	FILE NUMBER

EMPLOYEE'S COMPLETE HOME ADDRESS (Number and Street) | APT. NO | SOCIAL SECURITY NUMBER

CITY	STATE	ZIP CODE	TENURED	PROBATIONER	SUBSTITUTE

CURRENT SALARY RATE $ | FOR PROBATIONERS: Date of Appointment | Jarema Credit | N.Y.S. Tenure Credit (Max. 1 year) | Date of Completion of Probation

SCHOOL | BOROUGH | DISTRICT

	FIRST YEAR				SECOND YEAR				THIRD YEAR				DAYS IN C.A.R.	OR BOR-ROWED DAYS	SUBSTI-TUTE SERVICE NO. OF DAYS
	TIMES NO.	TIME LOST			TIMES NO.	TIME LOST			TIMES NO.	TIME LOST					
		DAYS	HRS.	MIN.		DAYS	HRS.	MIN.		DAYS	HRS.	MIN.			
LATENESS*															
ABSENCE* Exclude Non-Attendance															

* NOTE: For reports on probationers complete 1 to 3 years as applicable. For all other personnel use "First Year" to denote current year.

SECTION 1 - REPORT BY PRINCIPAL OR OTHER APPROPRIATE SUPERVISOR:

COMMENTS (as checked. "NA" indicates "Not Applicable.")	SATIS-FACTORY	UNSATIS-FACTORY	ADDITIONAL COMMENTS
A. PERSONAL AND PROFESSIONAL QUALITIES			
1. Attendance and punctuality			
2. Personal appearance			
3. Voice, speech and use of English			
4. Professional attitude and professional growth			
5. Resourcefulness and initiative			
B. PUPIL GUIDANCE AND INSTRUCTION			
1. Effect on character and personality growth of pupils			
2. Control of class			
3. Maintenance of wholesome classroom atmosphere			
4. Planning and preparation of work			
5. Skill in adapting instruction to individual needs and capacities			
6. Effective use of appropriate methods and techniques			
7. Skill in making class lessons interesting to pupils			
8. Extent of pupil participation in the class and school program			
9. Evidence of pupil growth in knowledge, skills, appreciations and attitude			
10. Attention to pupil health, safety and general welfare			
C. CLASSROOM OR SHOP MANAGEMENT			
1. Attention to physical conditions			
2. Housekeeping and appearance of room			
3. Care of equipment by teacher and children			
4. Attention to records and reports			
5. Attention to routine matters			
D. PARTICIPATION IN SCHOOL AND COMMUNITY ACTIVITIES			
1. Maintenance of good relations with other teachers and with supervisors			
2. Effort to establish and maintain good relationships with parents			
3. Willingness to accept special assignments in connection with the school program			

E. ADDITIONAL REMARKS (additional sheets, signed and acknowledged may be attached):

SECTION 2 - PERFORMANCE EVALUATION

OVERALL EVALUATION S, U, or D (D for first year probation only) For the period: From to	SIGNATURE OF PRINCIPAL (If other - give title) DATE	ACKNOWLEDGMENT BY EMPLOYEE I have received this report on: DATE SIGNATURE OF EMPLOYEE

(Complete Reverse Side for Probationary Personnel Only)

Exhibit 2.1
(Continued)

SECTION 3. - TO BE COMPLETED ONLY FOR PROBATIONARY PERSONNEL

A. RECOMMENDATION BY PRINCIPAL OR OTHER APPROPRIATE SUPERVISOR: To be completed and forwarded to the Community Superintendent or, for Department of Education employees, to the responsible Superintendent.

1. ☐ I recommend approval for continued probationary service.

☐ I recommend certification of completion of probation.

2. ☐ I recommend discontinuance of probationary service.

☐ I recommend denial of certification of completion of probation.

SIGNATURE OF PRINCIPAL (If other, give title)   DATE

B. SUPERINTENDENT'S RECOMMENDATION: To be completed by Community or responsible Superintendent and returned to originating unit for employee's acknowledgement.

I recommend _____

Date _____ Signature of Superintendent _____
                              (If other, give title)

C. ACKNOWLEDGEMENT BY PROBATIONARY EMPLOYEE

I have received this report on:

Date: Signature of Employee

SECTION 4. - DOCUMENTATION

All recommendations for discontinuance or denial of certification must be accompanied by copies of substantiating documentation attached hereto, including, but not limited to, observation reports, letters, time cards or time sheets, or other relevant material.

Item No.	Date	Description or Identification	Key

NOTE: If space is insufficient to list all documentation, listing on additional sheets may be attached. If there are such continuation sheets, check here ☐.   Number of additional sheets: _____

RULES AND INSTRUCTIONS

1. For "Satisfactory" evaluations, prepare two copies: Copy 1 for the employee, copy 2 for the school file.

2. For adverse evaluations (U or D), prepare four copies for distribution as follows: Copy 1 for employee, copy 2 for school file, copy 3 to the appropriate superintendent and copy 4 to the Bureau of Teacher Records, 65 Court St., Brooklyn, N.Y. 11201.

3. For recommendations for continued service or completion of probation for probationers, prepare three copies of report for distribution as follows: Copy 1 for superintendent, copy 2 for originating school and copy 3 for the employee.

4. For recommendations for discontinuance or denial for probationers, prepare *eight copies* of report and *seven complete sets* of documentation as listed in 'Section 4' of this form for distribution as follows: Copies 1, 2 and 3 (with documentation attached) as listed in Rule 3; Copy 4 (without documentation) to the Bureau of Teacher Records; Copies 5, 6, 7 and 8 (with documentation attached to the Office of Appeals and Reviews, 65 Court Street - Room 717, Brooklyn, N. Y. 11201.

5. Appeals: An appeal from adverse evaluation (U or D) must be made in writing by the employee and forwarded to the Executive Director of the Division of Human Resources for the attention of the Director, Office of Appeals and Reviews within three weeks after receipt of such adverse evaluation (exclusive of the summer vacation).

6. All personnel are hereby advised of their right to submit written comments concerning:
   a) each observation report on their performance
   b) evaluation reports

25-3200.05.9 (5000 pkgs) 3/89

Unhelpful Ratings

Checklists and numerical ratings lack bite and don't guide improvement. Many districts use checklists accompanied by a rating scale with two, three, four, or five levels, each with a label (for example, Distinguished, Proficient, Basic, and Unsatisfactory). Scales like these have an aura of precision, but ratings by themselves aren't very helpful to administrators or teachers. In fact, they can become fodder for faculty room comparisons—*Whadjaget? He gave you an Excellent!?*

Perhaps the most unhelpful scales are those with only two ratings: Satisfactory and Unsatisfactory. The rationale for binary scales is to prevent divisive comparisons and get teachers to read their principals' detailed write-ups. But because virtually all teachers are rated Satisfactory, a two-level scale doesn't really *judge* teachers' performance. This seems like an odd statement, since all evaluations are judgmental. But a Satisfactory/Unsatisfactory system throws virtually all teachers into the same level and allows principals to obscure teachers' overall performance status with a lot of words. The combination of a two-level scale and lesson write-ups means that teachers don't find out where they stand with respect to clearly articulated performance standards and don't get helpful direction on the ways in which they can improve their performance. This kind of evaluation is unlikely to motivate a mediocre teacher to improve and spur a good teacher to strive for excellence. As assessment expert Charlotte Danielson told me, 98 percent of teachers are "good enough"—they don't need to be fired. But how can we make them better?

Grade inflation is another problem when rating scales don't include specific descriptions of performance at each level. A study by the New Teacher Project reported outlandish distributions of teacher performance in districts with different rating scales (Weisberg, Sexton, Mulhern, & Keeling, 2009). A few examples:

Denver (2005/06–2007/08)

- Satisfactory: 2374
- Unsatisfactory: 32

Rockford (2003/04–2007/08)

- Excellent: 1583
- Satisfactory: 374
- Unsatisfactory: 18

Chicago (2003/04–2007/08)

- Superior: 25,332
- Excellent: 9,176
- Satisfactory: 2232
- Unsatisfactory: 149

Akron (2005/06–2007/08)

- Outstanding: 638
- Very Good: 332
- Satisfactory: 85
- Improvement Needed: 7
- Unsatisfactory: 0

Statistics like these cry out for more rigorous and thoughtful teacher evaluation criteria tools.

About halfway through my time as a Boston principal, I was invited to be part of a committee charged with revising the district's performance evaluation instrument, and our final product was accepted almost in toto by the superintendent, union, and School Committee. The form spelled out several domains of teaching (Planning and Preparation, Classroom Management, and so on), listed ten to fifteen criteria for excellence in each one, and required principals to write narrative comments on strengths and areas for improvement on every page, concluding with an overall Satisfactory/Unsatisfactory rating and general comments at the end of the evaluation. This seemed like a big step forward from the previous checklist, but in retrospect, it didn't give teachers a clear idea of where they stood, and made possible a lot of rhetoric that didn't get to the heart of the matter. What this experience taught me was that coming up with the perfect evaluation instrument is not a simple task!

Natural Resistance

Critical evaluations can shut down adult learning or be shrugged off. The basic challenge in supervision and evaluation is to activate (or amplify) a supervisory voice inside each teacher's head that guides them as they work with students. *(Ask more higher-order thinking questions. Work on calling on girls as often as boys. Check for understanding!)* One-on-one feedback from an administrator based on actual classroom performance is a golden opportunity for this kind of deep professional development, helping teachers take ownership for a process of continuous improvement. But conventional supervision and evaluation rarely work this way. In fact, the exact opposite is often true, with teachers waiting nervously for their principal to judge them and reacting defensively if there's criticism.

Why does this happen? Although most teachers don't have much respect for the evaluation process, but it still makes them nervous. Collective bargaining agreements provide job protection, but even the best teachers harbor irrational fears of being fired for a botched lesson. This makes it difficult for teachers to listen, admit errors, and talk openly about things that need to improve. In all too many evaluative interactions, teachers put on their game face and get through it with as little authentic interaction as possible. The principal owns the feedback, not them.

Some common interpersonal dynamics can also prevent teachers from learning from critical feedback. A young teacher might see an older administrator as a parent figure, triggering latent adolescent rebellion. A veteran teacher might resent criticism from a twentysomething administrator. *(I was teaching before this kid was born!)* To some teachers, any criticism feels like a power trip on the boss's part, and there's almost always a reason to push back: *You haven't taught in years. You only taught sixth graders. You don't have children of your own. Okay, you do have children, but they're in preschool.* It all comes down to this: *Why should I listen to you? You don't understand my world.*

Teachers, like workers in other occupations, often feel demeaned by the paternalistic, distrustful dynamic at work in conventional evaluation, as contrasted to an approach that aims to foster employee involvement in improving results. In a classic work published in 1960, MIT professor Douglas McGregor called the top-down approach Theory X and the worker-empowering approach Theory Y. In the business world, research has found that Theory X management doesn't improve performance beyond reluctant minimal compliance. Given that the frontline workers in schools are on their own 99.9 percent of the time, it's especially important that they be deeply invested in the mission and constantly working to improve their craft. Nobody has the time to stand over them and make them do it.

Another reason for defensiveness is that evaluations are often a one-way street from administrator to teacher, with the boss doing almost all of the work: observing, writing up, presenting feedback, and submitting the final evaluation. Charlotte Danielson tells me that this goes against everything we know about how adults learn. For teachers to get anything out of the process, they must be active, reflective participants—but in most evaluations, teachers are passive recipients.

The result of these unfortunate dynamics is that teachers reject or ignore a lot of thoughtful feedback from principals. There's a certain emptiness in the professional relationship between school leaders and teachers, with very few professional conversations about teaching and learning. And if principals aren't setting the tone, it's less likely that assistant principals, team leaders, department heads, and colleagues will engage in rich discourse with teachers.

Fostering Tension

The whole process can feed isolation and jealousy. Although evaluations are supposed to be confidential, teachers often compare notes with colleagues. This can lead to bad feelings when one person feels the boss was more generous to someone considered to be less competent—and nothing is more poisonous in a school than the perception of favoritism. At the Mather, teachers were so sensitive to the slightest whiff of extra attention to others that I became convinced that half of them had grown up in families where the parents played favorites among the children.

In all too many schools, same-grade and same-subject teachers don't work together. The evaluation process tends to reinforce this isolation and is rarely a vehicle for getting teachers to talk about curriculum or pedagogy, which detracts from teachers' sense of responsibility to their grade-level or department team, fails to exploit the potential synergy of collaboration, and means that teachers are wasting precious time reinventing the wheel. In schools like this, teacher conversations are dominated by non-school topics, gossip, funny stories about kids—and not-so-funny stories about kids. This is not the way to get high student achievement.

Reluctance to Make the Tough Calls

Some principals don't confront bad or mediocre teaching. I often ask audiences of educators if they have ever worked in a school where there was an ineffective teacher who wasn't dealt with by the administrator in charge. Usually 80–95 percent say yes. What's striking about this is that people believe they can identify bad teachers, even if they haven't observed their classrooms, and know full well that their administrators are not stepping up to the plate.

Dismissing a teacher is a gut-wrenching process that often provokes a sympathetic circling of the wagons by other teachers, even if they know that the teacher in question is incompetent (a product of the us-versus-them dynamic fostered by Theory X management). Knowing the unpleasantness and morale problems that an aggressive stance can cause, a principal might rationalize that the teacher is going to retire in a couple of years, so why jeopardize other initiatives that depend on the cooperation and good will of the rest of the faculty? Some school leaders have an inordinate need to be liked—or maybe they just want to keep the peace. Some have the bad luck to be saddled with staff members who are not only incompetent but downright scary. There's also the problem of not saying exactly what we mean. A recent *Harvard Business Review* cartoon by Randy Glasbergen shows a boss saying to a hapless subordinate: "I'm trying to be less critical. If I say 'Good work,' what I really mean is, 'You're an idiot.'"

Running Fast and Getting Nowhere

Many principals are too harried to do effective evaluations. It's very easy for school leaders to fall into HSPS—Hyperactive Superficial Principal Syndrome—and run around in a reactive, frantic mode a good deal of the time (Marshall, 1996). Student discipline and operational duties are so demanding that the time-consuming and emotionally draining chore of writing up teacher observations tends to become a victim of procrastination and often disappears from principals' calendars until action-forcing contractual deadlines loom.

When evaluation crunch time arrives, principals fall into three types: Saints, Cynics, and Sinners. The Saints go by the book and evaluations consume their lives for weeks at a time. I know a Boston principal who routinely spends eight to ten hours on each teacher: pre-observation conference, lesson observation, write-up (like a little term paper every Saturday, she says), and post-observation conference. Principals who choose to commit this amount of time (or are required to do so by their superiors) have no choice but to shut themselves in their offices for days at a time—or spend evenings, weekends, and vacations at their computers at home. Ironically, this reduces the amount of time these principals spend observing coaching, encouraging, and gently correcting teachers.

The Cynics heave a sigh, sit down at the computer, and bang out the required evaluations as quickly as possible, sometimes with a stiff drink at hand. Administrators in this category have lost faith in the evaluation process and don't believe their write-ups will produce better teaching and learning—but they think they have no choice but to do them.

The Sinners are the most daring; they simply *don't do* most evaluations, writing up only the most egregiously ineffective teachers. The proof that there are Sinners among the ranks of principals lies in the number of teachers who say openly that they haven't been evaluated in years. Sinners are audacious scofflaws, thumbing their noses at contractual requirements and daring the system to catch them. Few teachers complain, since evaluation is as appealing as a root canal. And principals' superiors are often none the wiser or choose to wink at these omissions.

When I present the Saint/Cynic/Sinner model to audiences of principals and ask them to tell me via anonymous clickers which of the three categories best describes them, a few confess to being Sinners, and there are usually significantly more Cynics than Saints. I then ask the "money question": Are the Saints more effective at improving teaching and learning in their schools than the Cynics and the Sinners? Principals are quick to say that the answer is no. This segment of my workshop produces a sinking feeling in many principals' stomachs that they may not have been spending their time in the most effective manner.

I return to this question in Chapter Eight, but three things are clear so far. Teacher evaluation is a major time-management hurdle for principals. The more wedded a principal is to the conventional model (pre-conference, observation, write-up, and post-conference), the more challenging it is to get into all classrooms on a regular basis. And many principals have begun to doubt that spending serious time on conventional evaluation has an instructional payoff, so they cut corners in favor of more urgent tasks and do very little teacher evaluation between September and April. There are simply too many other things on the table, and without deadlines and a clear sense that it makes a difference, evaluation visits get pushed off.

Jon Saphier has suggested a strategy for reducing principals' evaluation workload: a four-year evaluation cycle in which each teacher rotates through four kinds of assessment: peer evaluation, a study group, self-assessment, and a formal evaluation (1993). This approach sounds like it should work: the principal evaluates only a quarter of the staff each year and can spend more time visiting classrooms, doing thorough write-ups, and giving feedback to teachers whose year it is. But there are problems with this approach: the high rate of teacher turnover these days (and the presence of lots of nontenured teachers, who must be evaluated every year) means that principals end up evaluating significantly more than 25 percent of their teachers every year; the focus is still on micro-evaluation of lessons, which isn't the best way to improve teaching and learning; and a four-year cycle gives most teachers a "pass" three-quarters of the time, which could result in the principal losing the pulse of a significant portion of the school and not tuning in on mediocrity or more serious teaching problems.

The Bottom Line Isn't Part of the Conversation

The focus of evaluation is on pleasing the principal, not student learning. When evaluation time rolls around, most teachers' goal is getting a good—or at least a satisfactory—grade from the boss. It's all about pleasing, impressing, charming, satisfying, or "getting over on" the evaluator. Whether students are learning is rarely discussed. Evaluation focuses on the *process* of teaching, not the result. This is true because in virtually all school districts, teacher unions have been successful in preventing teachers from being evaluated on their students' test scores. (More on the merits of this position shortly.)

Does this mean that principals have no way of evaluating teachers on whether their students are learning? Surely a principal can find this out by visiting classrooms, looking over students' shoulders, and asking them questions. But there are three problems with this approach. Many principals are too busy scripting the lesson to get up and check out learning. Even if principals manage to chat with a few students during classroom visits, it's hard to tell whether the whole class understands what's being taught—let alone whether any of the students will remember it a few weeks later. Finally, even if principals look at interim assessment results to check on downstream learning, they are contractually forbidden from using the data to evaluate teachers.

So principals have little choice but to focus on teaching inputs instead of learning outcomes, on chalkboard razzle-dazzle instead of deep understanding, on pretty bulletin boards instead of student proficiency. Squeezed by the supervision and evaluation process, principals appear to be stuck with overmanaging lessons and undermanaging the bigger picture of whether teachers are truly making a difference.

And because evaluation doesn't focus on student learning, principals are rarely able to help teachers emerge from their classroom isolation and reflect with colleagues on what needs to change so more students succeed. Without a push in this direction, all too many teachers gravitate toward an unfortunate but common default setting: assuming that if something is taught (that is, explained or demonstrated), it is automatically learned (Nuthall, 2004).

IS THERE ANOTHER WAY?

These are the twelve reasons that the logic model of teacher supervision and evaluation breaks down. They explain why the conventional model is inefficient and rarely improves teaching (except when it results in the dismissal of an ineffective teacher).

But teacher evaluation is a core part of the principal's job. School leaders are accountable for quality assurance, and it's their moral and legal duty to monitor instruction, get the best possible teaching for every student, and improve or remove teachers who are ineffective. How can they overcome these formidable problems? As school leaders and policymakers have searched for silver bullets, two ideas have attracted a lot of attention: using standardized test scores to evaluate teachers, and supervising and evaluating more aggressively. Could these approaches be helpful?

Using Test Scores

Since student learning is the "bottom line" of schools, this idea sounds eminently reasonable. Advocates contend that "incentivizing" teachers around achievement should be a major force for improving what happens in classrooms. A number of charter schools and districts are either thinking about or implementing plans that award merit pay to individual teachers or whole faculties for improved test scores. Among the most visible have been Denver, with its ProComp plan; Washington, D.C., where Chancellor Michelle Rhee is pushing the teachers' union to accept a plan for higher pay in exchange for greater accountability; and New York City, where Chancellor Joel Klein and Mayor Michael Bloomberg have begun to include test-score gains in schools' "grades" and, in some cases, teachers' compensation.

Teacher unions have stoutly resisted the use of test scores to evaluate teachers, and almost all collective bargaining agreements limit administrators to evaluating teaching inputs. To most non-educators, especially people in the business world, this makes no sense. Surely teachers should be judged on their work product—student learning. *It's the test scores, stupid!*

But while this sounds logical, I believe there are multiple reasons why using students' test scores to evaluate teachers is impractical, counterproductive, and just wrong. For starters, there's a serious problem of timing. Standardized test scores are usually not published until the very end of the school year or the summer, but teacher evaluations typically need to be completed in May. This by itself would seem to make it impossible to make test scores part of teacher evaluation.

Equity is another issue. More than half of all teachers don't give standardized tests (art, music, physical education, health, computer, kindergarten, and first- and second-grade teachers). Similarly, pull-out and push-in instruction by special education, Title I, and ESL staff mean that many students have more than one reading and math teacher, making it tricky to decide who should take credit for students' progress—or be accountable for their lack of progress.

Then there's the fact that standardized tests are designed to measure the learning of groups of students at one moment in time, not the productivity of individual teachers over a school year. Unions are correct when they say that using these tests for teacher evaluation is inappropriate. What about value-added analysis? Doesn't that solve the problem by measuring the learning gains on each teacher's watch—from September to May? Not so. William Sanders, the Tennessee statistician who put value-added on the map, says that at least three years of data are needed before it's fair to draw conclusions about a teacher's performance (Sanders and Rivers, 1996).

Furthermore, making standardized tests a major factor in evaluation can easily backfire by dumbing down the curriculum. Many critics of standardized tests have observed that when teachers focus too much on test preparation and spend their time drilling simpler, easy-to-test skills, students don't get the full college-aligned curriculum to which they're entitled. This is especially true in states where standards and definitions of proficiency are less rigorous, and it's most harmful for students who need to accelerate their learning beyond the basics.

Including student test scores in the teacher evaluation process also increases the possibility that some teachers will cut corners. When students take state tests, they are usually proctored by their own teachers. Most teachers act pro-fessionally, of course, but when the heat is turned up, it's inevitable that some (especially those who have the least confidence in their ability to raise achievement through legitimate means) will give inappropriate help to students or even falsify results, invalidating the assessments and producing deceptively rosy information on students that prevents them from getting vitally needed services down the road.

Finally, using test scores to evaluate teachers can prevent professional learning communities from functioning properly. Same-grade and same-subject teamwork has the potential to be an engine of improvement in schools, but when individual teachers' evaluations depend on their students' achievement, they tend to focus on boosting their own stats and are less likely to share effective practices with their colleagues.

For these reasons, I believe that using test scores for teacher evaluation will produce lower student achievement and demoralize teachers—hardly the outcomes that proponents want.

Intensifying Supervision and Evaluation

The second approach in the limelight recently is increasing the intensity of supervision and evaluation, using criteria that research says are correlated with higher student achievement. In *Rush to Judgment*, a 2008 report released by Education Sector, Thomas Toch and Robert Rothman criticized current practices—"drivebys" is how they describe principals' evaluations—and proposed (among other things) that each teacher should be observed more than once a year by several different evaluators from outside the school. The Teacher Advancement Program (TAP) uses these ideas, bringing "enhanced" supervision and evaluation, along with supportive coaching, to a number of schools around the country. The model is expensive, but Toch and Rothman argue that it's better than what schools are doing now and could be funded by reallocating resources from professional development workshops, which are widely regarded as unproductive.

But the question that hasn't been answered is whether intensive supervision and evaluation actually improve teaching. Toch and Rothman say that expert observations of teaching can *describe* the classroom practices linked to high test scores. But does the process of observing and evaluating teachers *improve* teachers who are not already effective? As earlier chapters have argued, there's little evidence that it does. My hunch is that the coaching in TAP schools is helpful but that supervising the heck out of teachers is having very little effect.

REAL SOLUTIONS

Enough criticism. The next five chapters present what I believe is a much better approach for improving teaching and learning. It includes a strategy for getting principals into classrooms, a way of thinking through curriculum planning with the end in sight, a low-stakes approach to putting student learning at the center of the instructional conversation, and a way of evaluating teachers that helps them improve. First up: mini-observations.

chapter
THREE

Mini-Observations 1

A System Is Born

Frequent high-quality conversations with a skillful observer who has evidence about what went on and how it is impacting students can be immensely valuable to teachers. We should focus on that.

—Jon Saphier, 2007

Within a couple of weeks of starting as principal at the Mather in the fall of 1987, I plunged into what I considered the most important part of my job: sitting in on lessons and popping a page and a half to two pages of write-up into teachers' mailboxes, usually the next day. I was careful to keep my comments almost entirely positive, and many teachers appreciated the richly detailed feedback. Some wondered how I could capture so many direct quotes. *(Was he wearing a wire?)* But a few were horrified by what they saw as intrusive "snoopervision."

41

SUPERVISION HITS A BRICK WALL

It wasn't long before the school's union representative filed a grievance, alleging that my write-ups were evaluative and violated the contract. We had a preliminary hearing and I denied the grievance, arguing that what I was doing was *supervision*—ongoing feedback to affirm good teaching and help teachers improve—not end-of-year evaluation. How could teachers object to this? The union rep was not impressed and took the grievance to the next level, and to my horror my boss, the area superintendent, upheld it. The contract language, he said, spelled out that every time I did a write-up, it had to be accompanied by the entire seven-page Boston Public Schools evaluation checklist and go into the teacher's personnel file.

Losing a grievance is about the worst thing that can happen to a new principal, and it really took the wind out of my sails. My concept of informal, appreciative write-ups and helpful feedback had been forcefully and publicly repudiated, and I didn't know what to do. In the months that followed, I visited classrooms less and less frequently. By my second year, I had retreated to the minimum requirement—one evaluation a year, which later became one every other year for teachers who earned an overall Excellent rating.

Deprived of during-the-year supervisory write-ups, I was determined to make the end-of-year evaluations as meaningful and helpful as possible. I asked teachers to let me know when they were doing a lesson they felt especially good about so I could see them at their best. But my invitation was greeted with deafening silence from almost all teachers, and I had to invite myself into classrooms for the required observations. I procrastinated with my formal evaluation visits, and usually found myself doing a flurry of observations in the last week before the mid-May deadline, staying up late trying to do a good job on the write-ups, and cutting corners on follow-up conferences (I usually put evaluations in an envelope in teachers' mailboxes with a note asking them to sign and return them). Teachers rarely had anything to say; I got the required signature and nothing more.

I became increasingly doubtful about the whole process. Evaluation should be the tip of the iceberg, I believed, with supervision making up the much larger submerged portion where detailed information is gathered and there is a less formal atmosphere in which feedback can be given and problems can be corrected without final sanctions. Wasn't it absurd and unfair, I thought, for a teacher's official "grade" to turn on one lesson?

It also wasn't surprising that many teachers prepared a glamorized lesson for the prearranged evaluation visit and played it safe by not showcasing their more adventurous, risk-taking classroom activities. This is why, again and again, I came away from my formal evaluation visits with the uneasy feeling that I hadn't seen what was really going on in classrooms on a day-to-day basis—which was either better or worse than what I saw as an evaluator.

And when teachers got compliments or criticisms from me, it wasn't surprising that they didn't trust them or take them to heart. *What does he really think of my teaching?* I could almost hear them asking.

A good question, since a great deal was left unsaid. I had major concerns about the very conventional teaching I glimpsed in my visits to classrooms, but didn't have enough information to put together a believable critique for individual teachers. The contractual provisions, combined with a long history of distrust of administrators, conspired to keep teachers and me from talking with real honesty and authenticity about the heart of the matter—teaching and learning. There was just the sigh of relief at the summative grade *(Whew, I got an overall Excellent)*, and the papers were filed away without any real learning or improvement.

All this frustrated me no end. I believed that my failure to give teachers meaningful supervision and evaluation meant that I was not a real instructional leader and had little hope of turning around student achievement. I aspired to be the kind of principal who was always in and out of classrooms and who had useful insights that would help teachers make even more of a difference to kids. Good supervision and evaluation, I thought, were at the center of being a good principal, and I was blocked from doing that part of my job.

MANAGING BY RUSHING AROUND

So I tried a different approach. I made a checklist of all thirty-nine classrooms and resolved to drop in on every teacher every day, either for an errand, to give a student or teacher a birthday greeting (this had become one of my trademarks), or just "show the flag." I felt that this way I would at least get a quick impression of how teachers were doing and how engaged and responsive students were. And since I wasn't writing anything down, I'd be flying below the contractual radar.

But it quickly became apparent that these drive-by visits were utterly superficial. All eyes were on me when I walked in (some teachers insisted on having their students rise to their feet and chorus, "Good morning, Mr. Marshall!"), and regular instruction came to a grinding halt. I wasn't hearing student-teacher interactions in classrooms and was in and out so quickly that I couldn't focus on the curriculum that was being taught or peek at students' work. For all my visibility, I didn't know much more what was going on in classrooms than before. I certainly didn't know enough to say or write anything intelligent to teachers at the end of the day or add items with any validity or specificity to my evaluations at the end of the year.

There was another problem. My flying visits raised the anxiety level among teachers by making them wonder what conclusions I was drawing as I walked through their classroom every day without comment. *What was Kim Marshall thinking, and what was he going to do with the information he gathered?* I actually saw and remembered very little beyond the most general impression (teacher up and teaching, students quite attentive, lots of student work on the walls), but teachers thought I was filing away everything in my field of vision and feared the worst about all the real or imagined inadequacies in their classrooms. The fact that I wasn't *saying* anything to them created a tense communication gap that was not about to be closed: it was simply impossible for me to catch up with thirty-nine teachers before the end of the day; and even if I could talk to them all, what I had to say about their classrooms would have been meaningless.

So my quixotic attempt to see every teacher every day fizzled out. With so little emotional and substantive payoff, I lost motivation and I soon fell into a pattern of six or seven desultory visits a day, driven by specific errands I needed to run. I was back to seeing virtually no classroom instruction and cobbling together perfunctory, ill-informed evaluations at the end of each year.

That's when I began to get addicted to HSPS—Hyperactive Superficial Principal Syndrome. An administrative intern who shadowed me at one point documented a staggering two hundred interactions in a typical day—and that didn't count saying "Hi there!" to students I encountered around the school. Constantly in demand, juggling people and activities, racing around the building doing this and that, I became an intensity junkie, hooked on a frenetic pace that became increasingly enjoyable and ego-boosting.

The never-ending challenges fed my addiction: a weeping girl with a splinter under her fingernail; a fight in the cafeteria; a teacher mourning over a dying relative; a dog sneaking into the school; a pigeon flapping around in an upstairs corridor; a parent cussing out the office staff about her child being bullied on the bus; a jammed photocopier (I became an expert at pulling out little bits of paper and getting the machine working again); a discipline crisis in a rookie teacher's classroom; the laminating machine grabbing the end of my favorite tie; a paraprofessional having a seizure and requiring emergency medical care; a call from the central office in support of the angry parent; a teacher sending a misbehaving boy to the office for the umpteenth time; a delivery from a trucker who didn't do stairs; and on and on. All this made me feel important, kept me very busy, and was sometimes fun. But I knew that I wasn't dealing with the heart of the matter—teaching and learning.

Chatting with other principals and dipping into the professional literature, I found that I wasn't alone. It appeared that few principals were successful at getting into classrooms on a regular basis, and powerful, almost inexorable forces conspired to keep most of us from a meaningful instructional role. Here is how I analyzed HSPS:

- The principal is trapped in the office dealing with one crisis after another.
- Each day is so chopped up by interruptions that it's very hard to focus on deeper stuff.
- If the principal escapes, he or she wanders around without a systematic agenda and misses a lot.
- Evaluation visits happen only when they are absolutely required and aren't representative of teachers' everyday practice.
- Teachers rarely get feedback, and teachers and principals have few authentic conversations about teaching and learning.
- Teachers are mostly on their own and get used to working in isolation, which means that mediocrity flourishes in many classrooms.

In my more morose moments, I concluded that this pattern had major consequences for the equitable education of all students. Those who entered school with disadvantages fell further and further behind. The gap between the haves and the have-nots got wider each year. A *real* instructional leader would be able to strategically push back against these forces, go beyond superficial management (while still meeting students' and colleagues' needs), and run a school that closed the achievement gap. I clearly wasn't doing this—which made me a walking, talking gap-widener.

But was it possible to be an instructional leader, given the wall between me and real classroom observation and the flurry of other distracting activities?

I began to think that the structural reality of the modern principalship precluded meaningful supervision and evaluation. I wondered if, as some suggestion, it was hopelessly idealistic for the principal to be more than a disciplinarian and crisis manager.

AN IDEA IS BORN

These questions gnawed away at me for another year. Then at a staff meeting in June 1993, our gym teacher blurted out that Mather teachers didn't feel appreciated. I wasn't telling people often enough that they were doing a great job, he said. Lots of heads nodded. He went on to say that with the college soccer team he coached after hours, he constantly told the players that they were terrific, even when they weren't, and Mather teachers needed to have their work praised in the same way.

My silent reaction was that this kind of fluffy praise would be meaningless and teachers would end up just as unsatisfied. But the exchange set a new train of thought in motion. The official teacher evaluation process would probably remain captive to announced observations, checklists, comments, and ratings. But I began to formulate a new strategy for giving more frequent, less formal feedback to teachers in a way that was substantive and helpful—a way that would make supervision more meaningful and might even improve teaching and learning.

The new scheme was based on three beliefs: First, all teachers, even very good teachers, need reassurance that they are doing a good job, but praise from the principal must be based on specific examples of actual events in their classrooms, not just a glib, uninformed "Great job!" Second, teachers are well aware that they're not perfect, so if all they get are positive comments, they'll know that the principal is not leveling with them. And third, teachers need candid criticism, specific and constructive, to improve their craft and do the best possible job with students, but it has to be delivered with tact and skill. I figured that to put these beliefs into action, my supervision would have to look something like this:

- Classroom visits would have to be brief (to fit into my hectic day) but not so brief that I wouldn't be able to focus on what was happening.

- Each teacher would need frequent visits; otherwise there wouldn't be enough of them to balance specific praise with specific criticism. (It's tricky to criticize a good teacher if your critical comment is the only one you've made all semester.)

- Visits would have to be unannounced; otherwise I wouldn't be seeing everyday reality as students were experiencing it.

- I would need to give feedback after each visit, as promptly as possible; otherwise teachers would be left guessing what I thought.

- Feedback would need to be delivered in a low-key, nonevaluative, and non-threatening way to increase the chance of openness and two-way communication. This pointed to staying away from written comments, which would lead me to be more cautious about giving criticism, and would be more threatening to the teacher (and would be considered formal evaluation under our contract).

I dubbed this scheme "mini-observations," and as I started my seventh year as principal, I briefed teachers on it in my *Mather Memo* newsletter and prepared to swing into action. I had forty-two professionals to supervise (thirty-nine teachers, the nurse, our special education team leader, and our student services coordinator), and figured that if I saw an average of four people a day, I could make a complete cycle of the staff every two weeks with room to spare. If I kept up that pace for the whole year, I would have visited each staff member a total of nineteen times. That was the goal. Here's what actually happened.

In September, even though I was absolutely determined to break out of HSPS and launch my mini-observations, I had great difficulty getting started. Every day there was a new list of reasons for not getting into classrooms. Our music teacher unexpectedly took early retirement and I had to find someone new— immediately! There were some glitches in the schedule that urgently needed to be fixed. Two new teachers were demanding their share of classroom supplies as well as carpets for their reading corners. We had to get our School-Site Council up and running to comply with the Massachusetts Education Reform Act. I had to work closely with our new assistant principal to get her acclimated to the school. One legitimate reason after another kept me from starting my mini-observations.

But as the days passed with no classroom visits, I realized that the biggest barrier was in my own head. I was actually *nervous* about taking more than a superficial look at what teachers were doing. It was as if a force field surrounded each room, and even if I was already in someone's classroom on an errand, the invisible shield kept me from slowing down, turning it into a mini-observation, and seeing what was going on instructionally.

I knew what I wanted to do. I knew how to do it. And I knew how important it was. I just couldn't get started! What was going on?

Part of the problem was my addiction to HSPS. I had grown to love the fast-paced, superficial way I had been operating for years, never stopping in any one place or any one conversation for very long, constantly zooming around the school. Another problem was the ambivalence of many teachers at having me in their rooms. They craved feedback and affirmation, but they also wanted to be left alone, fearing that I might take them out of context, hurt their feelings, or come up with some fundamental criticism that would pose a threat to the way they had been teaching.

And I had my own fears and insecurities. I would be walking in with no evaluation checklist or procedural script to hide behind. Would I be able to see what was really going on in each class? What if I missed something important and looked foolish? What if I didn't have anything intelligent to say? I had been writing lengthy end-of-year evaluations for years, but these were almost always delivered in an envelope and were rarely accompanied by a face-to-face conversation. Doing a mini-observation and having a conversation afterward seemed quite a bit more challenging.

MINI-OBSERVATIONS TAKE OFF

Enough! On the evening of September 29th, I jotted a note in my diary and *shamed* myself into getting started. To make it easier, I told myself I would begin with the teachers I thought would be the least threatened by my visits. I decided that on the first cycle, I would concentrate on finding something positive to say—catch teachers doing good stuff. The next morning, I pushed through the force field and visited four classrooms for five minutes each.

It felt great! I was able to really *see* things when I slowed down and became an observer. And when I caught up with each teacher later on, I was able to share what struck me in a way that they appreciated. I complimented one of our Reading Recovery teachers on her patience working with a beginning student who had virtually no reading skills, noting her gentle tenacity hanging in there with him minute by minute. I reinforced a second-grade teacher for her restraint in pulling back from directing the whole class and allowing the kids to start working on their own (her tendency to overdirect instruction was something I had touched on in her evaluation the year before). I raved to our newly hired music teacher about the way he led a class singing "Fly Like an Eagle." And I praised a third-grade Vietnamese bilingual teacher for having her students do mental math while they read *Ping*. It felt good to give specific commendations; for once, I knew what I was talking about when I gave a compliment, and each teacher walked away with something specific from the boss—which they doubtless shared with their significant other when they got home. The principal taking the time to observe instruction and give personal feedback—that was something new!

Encouraged by this first day, I forged ahead, trying to do four quick observations a day. Some days I couldn't squeeze them in, but I completed my first full cycle of the staff in four weeks. Slow, but not bad for a beginner. I began my second round, and completed it in only three weeks. I had now racked up more than eighty observations with feedback. My confidence grew, and by December I had completed a cycle in two weeks. I was on a roll!

What proved most challenging was catching teachers later in the day and having an informal yet meaningful conversation about what I had seen. In a few cases, I was able to give the teacher some feedback while I was in the classroom (if students were busy working in groups). But most of the time, my feedback occurred when I caught up with the teacher during a break later that day or early the next. If my comment was positive, I sometimes shared it with the teacher while other colleagues were within earshot; if I had something critical to share, I needed to talk to the teacher alone, which sometimes took some doing. My instinct was to have stand-up feedback conversations in a classroom, corridor, or parking lot; I didn't want to raise the threat level by summoning the teacher to my office.

On a few occasions, I picked a bad moment—a teacher was rushing off to the bathroom between classes or preoccupied with something else. Sometimes several days passed before I found the right time and place to share critical feedback with a teacher. One teacher told me of her tension and annoyance when I kept her waiting over a long weekend.

At first, teachers had their doubts about the mini-observation idea. I had introduced it at the beginning of the year, but teachers were still uncertain about what to expect. Several were visibly relieved when I gave them positive feedback after their first mini-observation. One primary teacher practically hugged me when I said how impressed I was with her children's Thanksgiving turkey masks. But others were thrown off stride when I came into their rooms, and I had to signal them to continue what they were doing. I hoped that as my visits became more routine, these teachers would relax and be able to ignore my presence. And that's what happened in almost all cases.

From the beginning, five minutes felt like the right amount of time. That's how long it took me to get the feel of what was going on and decide on my "teaching point." I found that if I moved around the room, looked at students' work, and listened carefully, I was always able to find something that could serve as a beachhead in my conversation with the teacher later on. On each visit, I asked myself, *What strikes me in here? What's interesting, different, or problematic? What is worth sharing with the teacher? What will give this teacher a new insight?* It could be anything in the room—the teacher's interactions with students, the lesson, the materials, or students' questions and insights.

DEVELOPING A STYLE

I quickly learned to enter the room looking casual, upbeat, and non-officious, giving a quick nod if the teacher caught my eye to signal that I didn't need to speak to the whole class. I never wrote down anything while I was there, even if I needed to remember something unrelated to the lesson (say, to pick up milk on the way home). I allowed the style of the lesson to shape the way I handled myself in the class. If it was teacher-directed, I would perch on a windowsill or a desk at the back of the room and watch the kids while listening intently to the teacher. If students were actively working on something, I would circulate and look at what they were writing, sometimes chatting with students about what they were thinking as they did their work. Sometimes I worked for a few minutes with one student, getting a sense of what made the task easy or difficult. And sometimes I was able to chat with teachers about what they were trying to do—although usually I tried to maintain the fiction that I was invisible in the room so that the lesson could go on as normally as possible even though the principal was in there wandering around thinking goodness knows what.

As I got into a groove, I found that four or five teachers a day was a manageable number to cover. The brevity of mini-observations made it much easier to fit them into even the most hectic day. Many times, I was called to the office while I was in the middle of an observation, but I was almost always able to find something worth commenting on before I left. On one occasion, a visitor showed up early for an appointment. I gave him the school fact sheet, excused myself, and ran upstairs and fitted in one more observation before we met. Nooks and crannies of the day became much more productive. On one occasion, I visited a primary teacher last period on a Friday afternoon before a vacation. The class was going full steam, and I joked with her later that she had passed the ultimate test—first-rate instruction at the tail end of the last period before a vacation! But if the class had been in transition, I wouldn't have counted that as a mini-observation. It was great to have that flexibility.

On the rare days when I managed to visit six or seven teachers (usually to try to finish a cycle by the end of a week—an artificial deadline that I nonetheless felt driven by), I found that the feedback started to suffer. It was impossible to catch up with that number of people and give meaningful individual comments within twenty-four hours—and my memory was stretched recalling the details to share with teachers. So five mini-observations a day became my maximum.

After I completed my second cycle of observations—I'd done almost ninety visits with feedback so far—I began to feel more comfortable offering criticisms. In the third round, I told one teacher that a particular student seemed lost in an activity and wasn't getting help. I told another teacher that she needed to use a firmer tone to make sure all students were paying attention when she gave directions. And I commented on another lesson where there were three different activities going on—a tape playing, a worksheet, and an explanation by the teacher on another topic—and some students appeared to be confused.

I wasn't always at my best. Visiting a first-grade classroom one afternoon, my eyelids began to droop. Chronically sleep-deprived, I was infamous among my fellow Boston principals for dozing off in boring administrative meetings. I didn't think this would happen during such short, active supervision visits, but in this class it did. When I talked with the teacher later in the day, she hissed, "Mr. Marshall, you fell asleep in my math class!" I apologized profusely, but as we talked, she acknowledged that it hadn't been her best lesson; she felt pressured by the upcoming standardized test and was teaching a low-interaction, drill-and-practice lesson. The truth was that she was a little bored with the lesson too.

I made the decision early on to count brief observations only if active teaching was going on. If I came into a classroom and the kids were in transition, eating a mid-morning snack, or taking a test, I usually left and came back later. (In retrospect, I should have paid more attention to the tests students were taking.) I also decided not to focus on the nonclassroom areas of teaching—parent interactions, working with colleagues, professional development, and routine duties. If necessary, I would comment separately on those areas, or take them up in the formal evaluation every year or two in the required Boston checklist.

KEEPING TRACK OF VISITS

Early on, I realized that I needed a way to record which teachers I had visited and what I saw. This was partly because I didn't trust my memory and wanted to be sure I didn't miss anyone, and partly to keep track of which subject I observed each time around. I composed a one-page list of all forty-two staff members with a line after every name, made fifteen copies (that's the number of cycles I thought I could complete in the year), and stapled them together at the top. Each evening, I jotted down a brief description of the day's visits, for example, "Wed. Jan. 26—Kids writing autobiography sheets in cooperative pairs. Quite engaged." After each follow-up conversation, I added a check mark to the left of the teacher's name. As it turned out, I was pleasantly surprised with my ability to remember what struck me in each classroom, even if a day or two passed, and I seldom needed to refer to any notes when I gave teachers feedback.

In the first couple of rounds, I visited teachers in random order, dropping into classrooms when I happened to be in that part of the building or if another errand took me into the room and it seemed like a good moment. After the first two cycles, I began to try to map out certain classrooms to visit in certain periods (working from a master schedule of the school that told me when math, science, reading, and other subjects were being taught). But I found that teachers had often changed their schedules and that my own plans were usually thrown off by unexpected visitors or events. I did try to rotate the subjects I observed with each teacher, so if I arrived for an observation and found the same subject being taught as in my last observation, I left and came back later to see a different subject. I tried observing teams of teachers on the same day (for example, all the fourth-grade teachers one period, all the specialty teachers one day), but it almost never worked out because of interruptions that called me back to the office.

Toward the end of December, as I neared the end of my fifth cycle, I noticed something interesting: even though I wasn't planning the sequence of visits, the same four or five teachers always wound up being at the end of the line. These were classrooms, I realized, in which I felt unwelcome and awkward or dreaded the negative feedback I knew I would have to give, and had been subconsciously avoiding them. My checklist made me aware of which classrooms I was putting off visiting and made me think about why. If it hadn't been for the self-discipline imposed by my rotation, I would have gone for months without visiting them.

The biggest challenge with classroom visits was depth. What I found hardest was slowing down, getting other worries out of my head, and smelling the roses in each classroom. This meant being sharp and fresh (yet another reason for getting enough sleep, exercise, and downtime). When I was "in the zone," I could see a huge amount in a few minutes. When I was tired, stressed, and distracted, I could observe for a while—that is, sit there and look around—and pick up very little.

With each cycle, I got better at seeing what was really going on in each classroom and sharing one interesting insight with the teacher when we talked later on. Some of the follow-up conversations were short and awkward. On a few occasions, I was rushed and gave the impression that I was talking to teachers to check them off my list rather than to impart an interesting insight on their teaching or hear what they had to say. This happened most often when I got behind and was rushing to do too many teachers a day. I found that the key to quality was slowing down and doing just four or five teachers a day on a consistent basis—and, like a good politician, focusing on the person I was with and getting other thoughts and to-dos out of my head. When I did this, conversations were more likely to go into depth about a particular teaching moment, the goal of the lesson, how their kids were doing, and teachers' fears and dreams.

After a few months, teachers and students got so accustomed to seeing me in classrooms that they barely looked up when I entered and made no effort to behave differently. Most students never completely understood the concept of mini-observations. When I sat down in one second-grade classroom, a boy turned to me and asked, "Mr. Marshall, so when you don't have anything to do, you come and visit classrooms?"

KEEPING IT UP

Even on relatively calm days, getting into four or five classrooms a day was a struggle. Like a recovering alcoholic tempted to have a drink, I felt the tug of HSPS and it took a lot of discipline to stick with the program. At several points that year, crises struck or deadlines loomed and I went for one or two days without doing a single mini-observation. When this happened, I found it quite difficult to get back into the groove. So deeply ingrained were my old habits that I quickly slid back into rushing around madly, and the force field around classrooms sprang up again. Each time, I had to self-consciously rally my willpower to get back into the routine. This made me realize just how important it was to have a target number of classrooms to see each day. Visiting forty-two people felt like an impossible challenge, but visiting four or five a day was doable, and I knew that if I kept up the pace steadily, I would get to everyone in about two weeks.

It terms of time management, it was most efficient to fit in my brief visits between other errands and expeditions around the school. *(I'm up on the third floor, so let me see Joyce, and maybe I'll have time to see Alan too before the fifth-grade team meeting.)* Sometimes I was successful in blocking out a whole period for classroom visits, but that amount of time rarely went by without something else coming up. Mostly I squeezed my visits into the nooks and crannies of each day.

No one was pushing me to keep up this crazy plan. There was zero external pressure. The Boston evaluation process didn't demand it. My superiors never bought into it. Teachers, despite the fact that they appreciated the substantive conversations we were having, were not clamoring for it. The union was basically indifferent, as long as I wasn't using the visits inappropriately. The only thing pushing me to keep it up was my own belief that this would make a difference in teachers' morale and effectiveness with students. Lacking any external motivation, I had some very shaky moments during the winter and spring, times when I was sorely tempted to return to my old ways. But I dug in.

One important source of support in this formative period was reading Stephen Covey's book, *The Seven Habits of Highly Effective People,* in which he describes "Quadrant II" activities: those that are important but not urgent, and tend to get pushed aside by activities that are urgent and important, and also by those that are urgent and not important. The concept works for schools, too, as shown in Figure 3.1.

It struck me that my five-minute visits were a perfect example of a Quadrant II activity. There is no immediate consequence for letting it slide, but in the long run, I theorized, not doing mini-observations would seriously undermine my instructional leadership.

I was also encouraged that teachers were responding well to my comments. In most cases, I was the only person giving them professional feedback, and as it became clear that most of what I said was going to be positive and specific, my comments were often greeted with smiles and animated conversation about other things that were going on with students.

There were other rewards as well. After a solid day with four or five visits and follow-ups, I felt like a real principal: I was talking to teachers about teaching and learning. I was helping them see things about their teaching that could help them

Figure 3.1
Stephen Covey's Quadrants, Modified for Schools

	Must do right now	Don't have to do right now
Important to student achievement	I	II
Not important to student achievement	III	IV

improve. I was deepening and enriching collegial relationships. I was creating an opportunity for them to talk to me about what they were trying to do in their classrooms—opportunities that had been virtually absent before. I was also seeing students in a positive setting (which wasn't always the case when I was dealing with discipline referrals, stopping students from running in the halls, and supervising the cafeteria). Conversely, on days when I made no visits, I felt superficial and insubstantial and knew I wasn't really earning my pay. On those days, I was very busy. I was working very hard. I was coming in contact with a large number of people and solving a lot of problems. But I wasn't dealing with the heart of the matter.

The insights I gained from mini-observations also made me a much more knowledgeable participant when I met with grade-level teams, the parent group, and the School-Site Council. I felt increasingly authoritative about what was going on in classrooms; I was the only person in the school who had this broad perspective and detailed knowledge.

All this fueled my willpower and kept me on task, and I was able to maintain the pace, sometimes slower, sometimes faster, through the difficult middle portion of the year.

CLOSING THE LOOP WITH TEACHERS

Feedback was an essential complement to the mini-observation. I found that it usually fell into one or two of these general categories:

Praise, for example, commenting on some amazing writing in third-grade students' weekly picture books, or on the way a bilingual class was combining with a monolingual class for a lesson, or on the way a teacher called on and drew out a shy student in the middle of a forest of eager hands. I tried to curb the tendency to preface my positive comments with "I liked . . . ," talking instead about the impact an effective practice seemed to be having on students. I didn't want to reinforce the typical supervisor-teacher dynamic in which the goal is pleasing the boss rather than thinking together about what's working for kids.

Reinforcement, for example, commenting on a teacher's animated modeling of a textbook passage (as contrasted to the halting round-robin reading I'd criticized earlier).

Suggestions, for example, sharing ideas about how to convey specific concepts. On one occasion, after watching fourth graders struggling with how to remember the < (smaller than) and > (greater than) signs, I recommended that the teacher ask students to visualize a dwarf standing beside the small end and a giant standing beside the larger end. With a teacher who was covering the four traditional food groups, I suggested she use the new food pyramid that was just beginning to appear on cereal boxes.

Criticism, for example, pointing out problems I'd noted in class. I came down on a teacher for correcting papers while her students watched a movie that most had seen at home, and expressed strong concern about the way another teacher "dissed" a student in front of classmates. It was difficult to give critical feedback, even in brief, informal conversations. On several occasions I pulled my punches out of fear that teachers wouldn't be able to handle the criticism and put it to constructive use. Each situation was a judgment call, and I tended to err on the side of caution. On several occasions, I asked myself if I had been cowardly—or done the smart thing by avoiding a defensive and angry reaction. When I did give critical feedback, I found it was a winning strategy to confess that I had made the same mistake when I was a teacher; this made it more likely that the teacher would accept my comments. I always tried to offer a suggestion that the teacher could easily put into practice.

On a few occasions, especially when I was unclear about what I'd observed, I used the time-honored supervisory ploy of leading off the feedback conversation by asking, "Well, how did you feel the lesson was going?" Some teachers showed real annoyance at this approach, not quite putting into words what they were thinking: *You get paid the big bucks to tell me how things are going!* I also realized that leading off with an open-ended question was a trap for teachers: if they said that everything was hunky-dory and I didn't agree, I was in the awkward position of telling them they were wrong and here's what I thought. I therefore tried to lead off every follow-up conversation with a declarative statement about what I'd seen and what struck me, trying to be as concrete and descriptive as possible. Then the teacher could react, disagree, or ponder the point.

What happened with increasing frequency was that after I shared my observations, the teacher and I would get into a longer discussion. Teachers often gave me some background on what had been going on before I came in or what happened after I left. In so doing, they also gave me a sense of where this lesson fit into the overall curriculum and their classroom goals for the year. There was also an increasing amount of give-and-take in these follow-up conversations. What started as a criticism might become a compliment when I understood more of what the teacher was trying to do, and what started as a compliment might evolve into a suggestion on how to handle the situation differently next time.

On a number of occasions, teachers and I debated the value of a particular approach. An example of this was round-robin reading. Whenever I saw teachers having students read one at a time in an all-class setting, I criticized what I believed to be an inefficient and ineffective approach to teaching reading. One teacher responded that her students enjoyed reading out loud, but she also said, a little defensively, that she rarely used that approach. With another teacher who was using round-robin reading, I shared a copy of an *Elementary School Journal* article describing a different approach. The teacher read the piece and proceeded to put it into action, and said it made a big difference. She had each student rehearse a page of a high-interest book with her or her paraprofessional and then read their pages into a tape recorder. At the end of the lesson, the whole class could listen triumphantly to their well-read, coherent cooperative chapter.

Interchanges like these were strikingly different from the stilted, wary interactions that had previously taken place around evaluation time. What made the difference was that comments after a mini-observation didn't carry a judgmental, boss-employee, superior-subordinate tone and instead became part of an ongoing dialogue about teaching and learning. These were conversations between professional colleagues, and I was convinced that teachers and I were both able to learn a great deal more in this low-stakes climate.

How did all this relate to the formal evaluation process I was required to go through at the end of the school year? Although the mini-observations were supervision, not evaluation, they helped me form an overall impression of each teacher and provided background for my formal evaluations. They also helped my assistant principal and me zero in on teachers who needed support. In several cases, mini-observations identified teachers who had not been on our radar screens before, leading to more detailed evaluation and suggestions. The assistant principal and I decided to target four teachers for additional help, and spent more time with them in the formal process.

ASSESSING THE FIRST YEAR

Despite some slow patches, I was able to keep the mini-observations going for the whole year. By the end of June, I had completed eleven cycles of the staff. The time for each cycle ranged from two weeks to six weeks, averaging about three weeks. This means that I made only eleven visits per staff member, not fifteen, as I had hoped.

But "only" eleven visits per teacher added up to 460 mini-observations for the year, and that was 460 more than I had ever made before. Most important, almost all were high-quality observations followed up by good feedback conversations. This was a quantum leap for me and I was elated.

Most important, my frequent unannounced visits gave me an excellent grasp of what was going on in classrooms. Comparing the system to what I had used before—one formal observation a year (see Figure 2.1), mini-observations provided a systematic sampling that gave me a far more representative sampling of each teacher's performance. Figure 3.2 shows what it looks like graphically.

How did teachers respond to the feedback they received? In our end-of-year questionnaire (which most staff members filled out anonymously), I asked teachers to circle any adjectives that applied to my comments after five-minute visits. The most frequent comments were Perceptive, Gave me insights, Honest, Affirmed my teaching, Sparked discussion, and Helped me improve. Only a small minority of teachers had negative comments (one from a teacher who apparently missed the September explanation of mini-observations and distrusted the whole

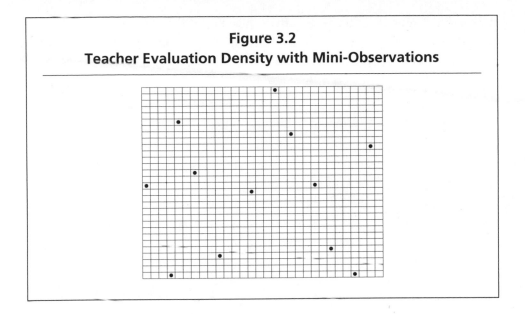

Figure 3.2
Teacher Evaluation Density with Mini-Observations

process). A strong majority said they liked the prompt feedback and wanted me to get around more frequently.

What about teachers' morale and the sense that I appreciated their work? These, after all, were the concerns that sparked the idea of mini-observations in the first place. I believe that my detailed, specific feedback contributed to a sense that I was saying what I really believed about people's classrooms. The frequent compliments and occasional criticisms struck teachers as authentic and helpful. All this built trust and improved morale. The staff questionnaire recorded the biggest improvement in morale in years.

But we were still not a truly happy school. To reach that exalted state, we needed to bring about major improvements in our students' achievement, and that hadn't happened. Were mini-observations moving us toward that goal? I believe they were, but at this point, the links between curriculum and tests were still so tenuous that teaching-learning gains were hard to pin down. All that lay in the future.

MINI-OBSERVATIONS: NECESSARY BUT NOT SUFFICIENT

For the next eight years, I kept up a steady pace of short classroom visits, averaging three or four a day, totaling about five hundred each year. In my best year, I completed fourteen cycles, totaling 630 mini-observations with follow-up talks. In my worst year, because of the challenges of breaking in a new assistant principal and being required to attend a lot of out-of-school meetings, I did only seven cycles.

After a few years, the staff became so comfortable with mini-observations that almost everyone allowed me to use my brief observations to write their official performance evaluations (the union reps organized a formal sign-off process). Dog-and-pony shows—contrived, unrepresentative, nervous-making lessons solely for my benefit—were largely a thing of the past. I simply stopped doing formal, announced observations except in a rare instance where a teacher specifically requested one or a teacher was in danger of being rated Unsatisfactory.

As the years passed, mini-observations became the core of my identity as a principal. I began to give workshops to graduate-school classes and groups of principals and published two articles in *Phi Delta Kappan* ("How I Confronted HSPS (Hyperactive Superficial Principal Syndrome) and Began to Deal with the Heart of the Matter" in January 1996, and "Recovering from HSPS (Hyperactive Superficial Principal Syndrome): A Progress Report" in May 2003). Speaking and writing about the system helped me think through the pitfalls and details of mini-observations, and I more clearly formulated the most essential elements:

- Being organized and systematic about getting into all classrooms on a regular basis
- Not announcing visits in order to get a representative sampling of teachers' work
- Keeping visits to five to ten minutes in order to boost frequency and observe each teacher at least every two or three weeks
- Giving prompt, thoughtful, face-to-face feedback to the teacher after every observation
- Making visits and follow-ups informal and low-stakes to maximize adult learning

I also became clearer about the potential benefits of mini-observations. Done right, I believe they are the best way for the principal to accomplish a number of valuable tasks:

- Get an accurate sense of the quality of instruction students are experiencing on a daily basis.

- See students in an instructional setting and get to know their strengths and needs.

- Get to know teachers better, both as instructors and as people.

- Develop "situational awareness"—having a finger on the pulse of the school's culture and climate.

- Build trust, the lubricant of effective schools.

- Identify teachers who are having difficulty so they can get additional support.

- Develop a de-bureaucratized, informal style that facilitates collegial learning.

- Be well-informed for meetings with the leadership team, teacher teams, and parents.

- Gather lots of data for end-of-year teacher evaluations.

These are all powerful drivers of school improvement, and I urge school leaders to embrace them.

But the coaching, school visits, and research I've done since leaving the principalship in 2002 have convinced me that when it comes to getting all students to high levels of achievement, mini-observations are *necessary but not sufficient*. To bring about dramatic improvements in teaching and learning, I believe, schools need to implement three complementary initiatives—team curriculum unit design, use of interim assessments, and teacher evaluation rubrics—all of which increase the power of mini-observations and are in turn enhanced by them. Chapters Five, Six, and Seven explore these strategies and the synergy that can develop among them.

But before we get to these essential components, Chapter Four presents a set of best practices for implementing mini-observations.

 A Note on Terms

You may be wondering why I chose *mini-observation* rather than *walk-through,* a term that is often used to describe short classroom observations. For example, Carolyn Downey and her colleagues titled their 2004 book *The Three-Minute Classroom Walk-Through,* and a number of recent articles have used the term in the same way. What's the distinction and why do I prefer *mini-observation?*

First, walk-throughs are often confused with *learning walks*—a very different strategy for observing classrooms. Learning walks were first conceived by Lauren Resnick and her colleagues at the University of Pittsburgh and become one of Anthony Alvarado's signature innovations when he was superintendent of District 2 in New York City in the 1990s (Mooney & Mausbach, 2008). Alvarado encouraged a small team of administrators, teachers, and sometimes outside observers to periodically do a complete tour of the entire school, usually focusing on particular aspects of classroom instruction (for example, student work on the walls). Learning-walk teams usually spent two or three hours scrutinizing a school, then met to share their impressions and give a general report, either verbally or in writing, to the principal and staff. Learning walks are still used in some schools, districts, and charter organizations, and they are an excellent way to get an overall picture of how a school is doing—provided the observers are perceptive and well-trained (and providing that the whole school doesn't engage in a dog-and-pony show; I recently heard from a colleague who visited a school the day after it received a glowing report from a learning-walk team and saw the exact opposite of what the outside visitors had seen: most teachers were sitting at their desks doing paperwork and students sat silently filling out worksheets).

Clearly, learning walks are not the same as mini-observations. In fact, the two strategies are complementary and it makes sense to do both. But because they are so different, it's important to use different terms. *Learning walk* aptly describes the process of moving through an entire school, while *mini-observation* captures the idea of doing short, focused classroom visits to get a feel for what is happening.

Second, *walk-through* has the unfortunate connotation of the principal *walking through* classrooms, rather than *pausing* to conduct a thoughtful observation. The term draws attention to how little time the administrator spends in each classroom (a point often seized on by those who are skeptical about this approach) and has the ring of a superficial, bureaucratic drive-by. This is not the way we want teachers to see this innovative and helpful strategy for observing classrooms and providing feedback.

Third, although learning walks are helpful and informative, mini-observations are a much more time-intensive and powerful strategy for improving teaching and learning. They involve significantly more frequent visits to all classrooms (around twelve each per year, compared with two or three for learning walks), individual feedback to each teacher, and individualized, ongoing communication about teaching and learning based on the observations.

For these reasons, I believe we should call short, unannounced classroom visits *mini-observations,* clearly distinguish them from *learning walks,* and avoid the term *walk-through* to prevent confusion.

Mini-Observations 2

Suggested Best Practices

> *People change less because they are given analysis that shifts their thinking than because they are shown a truth that influences their feelings.*
>
> —John Kotter and Dan Cohen

The basic idea of mini-observations is simple: the principal makes frequent unannounced classroom visits and gives prompt feedback to teachers, and as a result, teaching and learning improve. But from doing countless mini-observations myself, coaching novice principals, talking to seasoned practitioners, hearing reactions to my presentations, and reading the literature, it's clear that this system can be implemented in ways that don't improve anything. This is likely to happen if the principal

- Doesn't stay long enough in each classroom to gather helpful information
- Makes too few visits to foster a productive dialogue with teachers
- Lacks a clear sense of what to look for

- Doesn't have a system for capturing key insights from visits
- Fails to give teachers feedback, or gives it in ways that don't foster learning
- Fails to link mini-observations to the school's strategy for improving achievement
- Doesn't arrange for occasional full-lesson observations of teachers
- Mishandles the link to summative teacher evaluation

This chapter presents solutions to each of these potential pitfalls.

HOW LONG TO STAY

The amount of time a principal needs to spend in a classroom depends entirely on the purpose of the visit. If it's to show the flag (*Good morning, boys and girls*), five seconds is plenty—a quick in-and-out. If it's to check on a substitute teacher, six seconds will do (*Thank God, the kids seem to be working quietly*). If the purpose is in-depth professional development, the principal needs to stay for the whole period. And if the principal aims to dismiss an ineffective teacher, there will have to be multiple full-period visits, each followed up with a specific improvement plan and a chance for improvement.

But if the principal's goal is to get a regular sense of whether the curriculum is being taught well, I believe that five to ten minutes is enough (provided, of course, that visits are unannounced). At first blush, this strikes many educators as too little time. *What can you possibly see in five minutes?* is a common reaction. But a lot happens in most classrooms in five minutes, and short visits can be highly informative. The best way to convince skeptics of this is to play a five-minute videotape of a classroom in action. I've done this scores of times with groups of teachers and administrators, and invariably, people's reaction is that it seemed like *much* more than five minutes and there would be no shortage of "teaching points" to discuss with the teacher afterward.

Here's why. The second an observer walks into a classroom, there is a flood of new information on student climate, the physical characteristics of the room, and what students and the teacher are doing, and the visitor's learning curve is steep. After five or ten minutes, the amount of new information levels off and then gradually declines for the remainder of the period. Figure 4.1 is a rough graph of what this looks like:

If the graph were different—if new information kept increasing with each additional minute spent in the classroom, sloping steadily upward, as in Figure 4.2, then clearly, principals should stay the whole period.

But I believe that in most cases, the graph in Figure 4.1 is more accurate. This suggests that for a very busy principal (and what principal isn't?), staying beyond a certain point has diminishing returns and is a relatively inefficient use of time

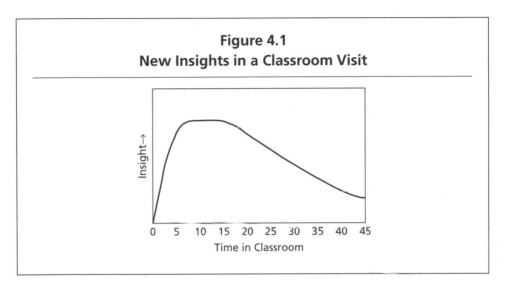

Figure 4.1
New Insights in a Classroom Visit

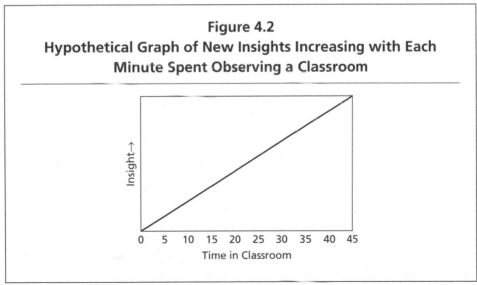

Figure 4.2
Hypothetical Graph of New Insights Increasing with Each Minute Spent Observing a Classroom

(in business jargon, it has a high opportunity cost). For administrators who want to be in classrooms a lot, short observations get the maximum amount of information in the least amount of time. Mini-observations are also much easier to squeeze into the nooks and crannies of a busy day, and are therefore much easier to orchestrate than longer classroom visits.

What is the shortest visit that still yields a decent amount of information? As a principal supervising a staff of forty-odd, I found that if I stayed less than five minutes, my impressions were superficial and I was unable to give teachers feedback that was credible or helpful. If I stayed longer than five minutes, I couldn't see teachers as often and the insights I picked up in the incremental minutes didn't compensate for the loss of frequency. Five minutes worked for me, yielding surprisingly rich and plentiful information on each classroom.

Not all principals agree with this. Paul Bambrick-Santoyo, executive director of the North Star Academy charter schools in Newark, New Jersey, feels strongly that principals need to stay fifteen to twenty minutes to process the initial flood of information and then focus on the lesson's objectives, the teacher's pedagogy, and how much students are learning. Jon Saphier, a veteran staff developer and expert on the skills of teaching, makes the same point. I hear what they're saying, and recognize that it may reflect a higher standard for supervision than I became accustomed to in the pre-standards era in which I developed mini-observations at the Mather. In small schools, or in schools with several administrators doing mini-observations, this length of visit makes perfect sense. But in a large school with thirty to forty teachers to supervise on a regular basis, longer visits mean seeing teachers less frequently, and this poses a tough trade-off for the principal: which is more important, depth or frequency? Short term, I lean toward frequency. It's amazing how much a perceptive observer can see in just five minutes. Long term, the principal should try to build up the administrative team and spread the work of doing mini-observations among several colleagues so everyone can stay a little longer.

The key point is that there's an inverse relationship between the length of each visit and the number of classrooms administrators will be able to visit on a regular basis. The shorter each visit, the more visits can be fitted into each day; the longer each visit, the fewer classrooms will be seen. Figure 4.3 shows the dramatic difference that visit length makes to the number of visits a principal can make in a year.

Each principal should do the math. Count how many teachers are being supervised, how many administrators are doing mini-observations, and the other

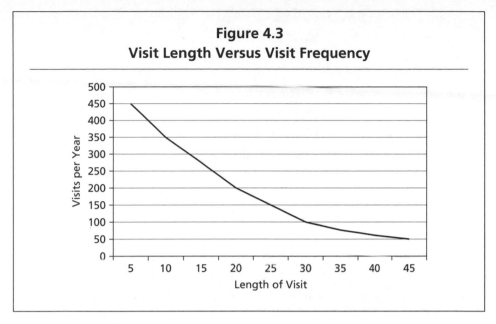

Figure 4.3
Visit Length Versus Visit Frequency

demands on time, and calculate a visit length that makes sense. Explain the rationale to teachers, and then start observing—always reserving the right to stay longer in a classroom if there's a good reason for doing so.

HOW OFTEN TO DO MINI-OBSERVATIONS—AND HOW TO KEEP UP THE PACE

Short classroom visits will benefit teaching and learning only if they are frequent and substantive, and that means deciding on a "Goldilocks" number of mini-observations per day. If the number is too low, teachers won't get feedback often enough; if too many visits are crammed into a day, the quality of feedback will suffer. What's the happy medium?

When I was a principal, I was responsible for about forty teachers and my assistant principal wasn't doing mini-observations (bless her, she was dealing with many of the things that would have kept me out of classrooms). When I launched mini-observations, I jotted down how many I might do each day and figured out the number of visits each would produce by the end of the year:

- 5 mini-observations a day = 19 visits for each teacher for the year
- 4 mini-observations a day = 15 per teacher
- 3 mini-observations a day = 12 per teacher

- 2 mini-observations a day = 8 per teacher
- 1 mini-observation a day = 4 per teacher

I was ambitious about the number of classroom visits I wanted to do, so in my first couple of years, I shot for four or five a day. But there was always slippage—crazy days when I got into only one or two classrooms, and days when I was out of the building for meetings and made no visits at all. Those days pulled down my average to about three mini-observations a day, or about twelve per teacher per year, totaling not quite five hundred. That was a lot, but I wanted to do even better, and figured that to raise my frequency closer to nineteen per teacher per year, I needed to push myself to do more than five mini-observations on good days.

But every time I did more than five, I found that my memory of what happened in classrooms was taxed and the quality of feedback was not as good. This pointed to reducing my target to a more realistic figure like three visits a day—after all, that's what I was actually doing, on average. But I knew that if I shot for three, I would end up averaging considerably less than that and seeing teachers only seven or eight times during the year—and that didn't seem like enough. So I decided to set my goal at five visits a day and try hard to do that many, knowing that there would be bad days and accepting a somewhat lower average because that still yielded a pretty impressive number of high-quality visits per teacher per year. Going forward, my mantra was 5 x 5: five mini-observations a day of five minutes each, with thoughtful feedback for each one.

A numerical target is *very* important to maintaining the pace amid all the distractions and crises of the principalship. Fuzzy goals *(I'm going to get into more classrooms this month)* don't work because they can't be measured and don't provide the data to assess progress. It's like exercise: without a specific goal (three vigorous twenty-minute workouts a week is what most doctors recommend), you won't keep it up. As noted, I recommend that principals do the math on the number of teachers and how many other administrators are visiting classrooms and then decide on a personal "stretch" goal that will result in seeing each teacher at least eleven or twelve times a year. Deciding on a target number of daily mini-observations and pushing relentlessly to meet it is the key to frequency. So is tracking the data. I was very conscious of how long each cycle was taking, and that helped get me out of my office and into a classroom when I didn't particularly feel like it.

In addition to a numerical target, four other elements are helpful to keeping mini-observations going through thick and thin: a strong conviction that this strategy makes sense, self-discipline, positive interactions with teachers after each visit to reinforce the practice, and support from your boss. I had the first three, but never had the fourth. Principals whose immediate supervisor understands and agrees with the idea of mini-observations have a big advantage. Imagine the impact of a boss who regularly asks questions like these:

- How are your classroom visits going?
- How long do you stay?
- How many are you managing to do each day, on average?
- When you can't get to mini-observations, what are usually the reasons?
- What do you look for?
- How do you know if the lesson is aligned with the curriculum?
- How much are students *learning* and how do you know?
- How do you give teachers feedback? How are they reacting?
- What are you noticing these days? Any trends in the building?
- How are you keeping track of your visits? Can I take a look at your notes?
- Are there any teachers you're particularly concerned about?
- Who are the teachers you're thrilled about?
- How long is it taking you to complete a cycle of the whole staff?
- How many cycles do you think you'll complete this year?

It's even more helpful if the district has a thoughtful policy on mini-observations, has negotiated certain key elements with the teachers' union (including what good instruction looks like), and provides training and collegial problem-solving and support. That is truly a formula for success.

WHAT TO LOOK FOR IN MINI-OBSERVATIONS

During a classroom visit, the principal needs to slow down, breathe, walk around, observe the kids, maybe chat with a couple of them (*What are you working on right now? How does this fit in with what you've been learning up to now? Why is it important for you to learn this?*), look at what they are being asked to do, listen carefully to the teacher, and "smell the roses"—in other words, really get "into the moment." Robert Marzano believes that trying to use long checklists during classroom visits is inappropriate (2007), and I heartily agree. Trying to keep track of items on a lengthy summative instrument or rubric makes it much more difficult to be a thoughtful and perceptive observer.

A short mental checklist of the essentials of good teaching is much more helpful to sizing up a classroom and zeroing in on the most important points for follow-up. A number of lists have been developed, and most of them are too long to keep in mind. The best one I've seen was developed by Achievement First, a network of charter schools in Connecticut and New York (reprinted with permission, with minor adaptations):

- *Great aims:* Rigorous, bite-sized, measurable, standards-based goals are on the board and drive the lesson.

- *Assessment of student mastery:* Learning of the aims is systematically and diagnostically assessed at the end of the lesson.

- *Content-specific knowledge and strategy:* The teacher knows the content cold and uses a highly effective and efficient strategy to guide students to mastery.

- *Modeling and guided practice:* The lesson includes a clear "think-aloud," explicit modeling, and a heavily guided mini-lesson that's captured in a display available to students.

- *Sustained, successful independent practice:* Students have plenty of high-success "at bats" to practice, with the teacher moving around to support them.

- *Classroom culture:* Behavior expectations are crystal clear (for example, being attentive, no calling out, no laughing at classmates' mistakes) and there is a positive, energetic, joyful tone with a high ratio of positive to corrective comments.

- *Academic rigor:* Students do most of the heavy lifting, the teacher uses a good mix of higher-order questions and content, and the teacher refuses to accept low-quality student responses (instead requiring acceptable grammar, complete sentences, appropriate vocabulary and understanding) or to let students opt out.

- *Student engagement:* High-involvement strategies keep all students on task and accountable (no desk potatoes!), and there is an accountability mechanism to get all students to complete top-quality work.

- *Cumulative review:* In the lesson and homework, students get fast, fun opportunities to systematically review and practice skills already mastered.
- *Differentiation:* The teacher sees that all students' needs are met by providing extra support (especially during independent practice) and varying the volume, rate, and complexity of work.

Succinct and excellent though it is, I believe this list is still too long to be used for mini-observations (it's better suited for longer observations and follow-up conferences). So is it possible to boil down the essential ingredients of good teaching into a really short list?

In a graduate course I teach for aspiring school leaders every summer, I challenge participants to come up with a list of the five irreducible elements of effective instruction—what they would want to see in their own children's classrooms, kindergarten through twelfth grade. The goal is to reduce teaching to its essence and come up with an acronym that principals can keep in their heads. I've gone through this exercise a number of times, and the best product so far is SOTEL:

Safety: The class is running smoothly and students can focus on learning.

Objectives: It's clear where the lesson is going.

Teaching: Learning experiences are being skillfully orchestrated.

Engagement: Students are paying attention and are involved in the lesson.

Learning: What's being taught is being learned.

SOTEL can be teased out into two levels: Proficient, representing solid professional practice, and Expert, a truly exemplary level of performance:

	Proficient	Expert
Safety	The classroom is physically safe for students—there is no violence, name-calling, bullying, or the like.	In addition to physical safety, the class is psychologically safe—students feel able to take intellectual risks.

(Continued)

	Proficient	**Expert**
Objectives	The lesson is aligned with state standards in terms of rigor and content, and its purpose is clear to students.	In addition, students see how the lesson fits into the unit and the year's curriculum; "essential questions" are on the wall and the class frequently refers to them (see Chapter Five).
Teaching	The teacher is using a repertoire of well-chosen instructional strategies to teach the material.	In addition, the lesson is skillfully differentiated to reach student subgroups, and students are operating at all of Bloom's levels see page 116.
Engagement	Students are attentive and involved in the lesson.	There's "minds-on" involvement and students are taking responsibility for their own learning.
Learning	The teacher regularly uses on-the-spot assessments to check for understanding, and follows up when learning problems appear.	In addition to on-the-spot assessments, the teacher uses interim assessment results to ensure that all students are learning (see Chapter Six).

SOTEL is a work in progress. If you have ideas on the most important things that observers should look for in classrooms, please e-mail me at kim.marshall 8@verizon.net. Remember the criteria: the irreducible elements of good teaching, no more than five, and presented in an acronym that's easy to remember.

 ## On-the-Spot Assessments

During mini-observations, one of the best ways to get a sense of the L in SOTEL (Learning) is to watch the teacher's effective use of formative or on-the-spot assessments. In their influential 1998 study, "Inside the Black Box," British researchers Paul Black and Dylan Wiliam presented voluminous evidence of the powerful impact that in-class assessments can have on learning—especially with struggling students. Here are some examples of on-the-spot assessments:

- After initial instruction, having students turn and talk to a classmate about a follow-up question while the teacher circulates and listens to see how well they understand

- Randomizing which students are called on to get a better sense of the whole class's level of understanding; one method is writing students' names on popsicle sticks, putting them all in a container, and pulling one out to see which student will answer the next question

- "Quick-writes" and journal-writing sessions that allow the teacher to look over students' shoulders and get an immediate sense of how well they grasp what's being taught

- Having students write answers to questions (for example, what's a fraction between 1/6 and 1/7?) on small individual whiteboards and then asking students to simultaneously hold up their answers so the teacher can assess how many are on track

- Using electronic audience response devices ("clickers") that gather instant data on in-class questions and graphically display the number of students choosing each multiple-choice answer; questions can be followed up with a "convince your neighbor" segment in which students, still not knowing the correct answer, try to persuade their seatmates of the answer they believe is correct (Mazur, 1997)

- Exit cards to gauge student understanding of one or two key points at the end of a lesson and allow immediate follow-up the next day

Dylan Wiliam is a leading proponent of this kind of in-classroom checking for understanding, and he stresses the urgency of putting the assessment information to immediate use to fix learning problems (2007, p. 191):

> If students have left the classroom before teachers have made adjustments to their teaching on the basis of what they have learned about the students' achievement, then they are already playing catch-up. If teachers do not make adjustments before students come back the next day, it is probably too late.

Why do on-the-spot assessments have such a good research track record for improving student achievement? Because, used well, they set up a continuous feedback loop between teaching and learning, producing much better levels of student proficiency (see Figure 4.4).

Here is the "logic model"—how on-the-spot assessments work under ideal conditions:

- When students know that they may be called on at any moment to show whether they understand, they stay on their toes and are more engaged and active learners.

- On-the-spot assessments give teachers immediate insights into students' misconceptions and confusions and allow them to clarify and re-teach before learning problems compound and widen the achievement gap. As Fisher and Frey put it in their 2007 book, these quick assessments "provide a window into the minds of learners by answering the teacher's perpetual question: What is the next instructional move?" (p. 134).

- If teachers understand why students aren't learning, they can fine-tune future teaching so learning is more efficient next time.

- Recent research at the University of Washington/St. Louis has shown that quick assessment of learning (within twenty-four hours of initial teaching) makes students retrieve and review what they have learned, which forges better brain connections and significantly improves long-term memory (Glenn, 2007).

Highly effective teachers have used on-the-spot assessments through the ages (perhaps because they have a deep conviction that they are responsible

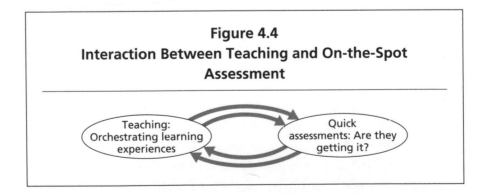

Figure 4.4
Interaction Between Teaching and On-the-Spot Assessment

Teaching: Orchestrating learning experiences

Quick assessments: Are they getting it?

for reaching all students), but many teachers don't check for understanding as they teach, or if they do, they often mishandle the classroom dynamic. During mini-observations, principals should watch for failures to check for understanding, for example:

- Lecturing with very few opportunities for questions (a common pattern in college classrooms).

- Ineffectively checking for understanding, including "Is everyone with me?" and "Thumbs-up, thumbs down."

- Falling into the COPWAKTA syndrome: Calling on People Who Already Know the Answer. This is very common in classrooms, resulting in only confident, high-performing students participating actively, and the teacher getting the misleading impression that the rest of the class understands (whereas in fact they are engaging in school prayer: *Please, God, don't let this teacher call on me!*).

- Giving quizzes without prompt feedback, or treating the grades as summative and not giving students a chance to correct their errors and have another chance at mastery.

Another way for principals to see if students remember and understand what's being taught is looking at data from unit or interim assessments. Chapter Six explores ways of making student learning part of the supervisory conversation.

HOW TO CAPTURE AND REMEMBER INFORMATION FROM VISITS

Principals often worry that they'll forget what they saw during a mini-observation, so there's an urge to jot notes. But the minute a principal takes out a pen or flips open a laptop, the visit becomes more official and bureaucratic. Many teachers, however irrationally, believe that when the boss writes things down, their jobs are on the line. This makes visits more stressful and less authentic than they should be. Mini-observations work better—and adult learning is more likely to take place—when visits are informal and low-stakes and teachers don't feel under pressure.

As described in Chapter Three, my approach as principal was to resist the urge to write anything down during mini-observations; instead, later in the day,

I'd jot brief notes in a one-page format, adding a check mark when I had given feedback to the teacher. Exhibit 4.1 shows a fictitious checklist about a quarter of the way through a cycle of visits. I've never had a great short-term memory, but I was pleasantly surprised at how readily I remembered the important details of what happened during each mini-observation when I wrote my notes that

---

Exhibit 4.1
Mini-Observation Notes

MINI-OBSERVATIONS 2009-2010   FROM: _November 10th_   TO: _November_

	Teacher	Notes
	Elizabeth Abidi	
✓	Sylvia Alcock	Tues. Nov. N - Going over worksheet, low participation, doing too much for them.
	Kwame Amoah	
	Sonia Astrid	
	Monica Avila	
✓	Angela Bailey	Mon. Nov. 10 - Worksheet on African climate and natural resources. Rigor level?
	Constance Bartlett	
	Mark Bonner	
	Alice Buchner	
	Natalie Chan	
	Denise Colombo	Tues. Nov. 11 - Cooperative groups doing science exp. on levers, clear roles. Great!
	Henry Cueva	
	Frank Cupido	
	Raymond Garcia	
	Jeff Gold	
	Brian Gottlieb	
✓	Sartreina Harvey	Mon. Nov. 10 - Spelling words copied from board, dictionary. More individualization?
	Kathleen Hennessy	
	Lada Jaworski	
	Kelly Jones	
	Andrew Kelsey	
	Adrienne Kinsey	
	Joshua Koren	
	Marc Leopoldo	
✓	Lynn Liu	Mon. Nov. 10 - Circle discussion of HBJ story. Lots of eagerness, participation, pizzazz
	Tyson Matsumoto	Tues. Nov. 11 - Read aloud of strega Nona - animated. Kids too passive. Method?
	Katherine May	
	Jacqueline Maynard	
	Matthew Ong	
	Agnes O'nias	
	Jo Phan	
	Michael Priest	
	Sebastien Renard	
	Glea Riss	
	Misha Roth	Tues. Nov. 11 - Social studies big book on weather, lots of participation, good questions
✓	Deepak Shah	Tues. Nov. 11 - Hands-on money lesson - bills, coins, making change - real-world!
	Naomi Simon	
	Ginger Sims	
	Robert Singleton	
	Katarina Smirnova	
	Jessica Wolk	
✓	Kathy Zimmer	Mon. Nov. 10 - Round-robin reading, very hum-drum. Gotta develop alternatives!

afternoon or evening. There's something about being able to recall a specific scene—Room 12 just before lunch—that helps even the most cluttered mind recapture what happened.

After completing a cycle of all the teachers, I moved on to a new sheet. This collection of very brief notes (which were only for my reference) was helpful when I forgot what I had seen in a particular classroom.

There are plenty of other possible formats—paper and electronic—to capture information after mini-observations. The simplest is a note card for each visit with the teacher's name, the day and date, the period visited, the content, and quick thoughts on one or more of the SOTEL criteria. Paul Bambrick-Santoyo of North Star Academy says it has been very helpful for his administrators to write down one change they'd like to see after each classroom visit—and also to track whether teachers are improving or continuing to have the same problem (they write these notes on a single sheet for each teacher). More elaborate forms can also be designed, and some principals give a copy to each teacher. (Some teachers like getting a paper record, others prefer to keep things at a verbal level, and others don't care one way or the other.) The downside of a written feedback sheet for each teacher is more paperwork and more time—which can make mini-observations more cumbersome and cut down on the number of classrooms visited each day. Anything that undermines frequency is a problem, so the key questions are: What is gained from note-taking and sharing written feedback with teachers? Is it worth the time it takes? And is there a simple way of keeping track of which classrooms have been visited in each cycle?

Some enterprising companies are marketing software for handheld electronic devices so that principals can record classroom impressions on their Palm Pilots, BlackBerrys, Treos, and iPhones. While this technology has undeniable appeal for busy principals—"Point, Click, Done" boasts one advertisement—I believe this approach has serious disadvantages. First, the principal is tied to a simple checklist that can't possibly capture the subtleties of a classroom. Second, entering data consumes attention better spent on being a careful observer. And third, to a teacher, having someone tap-tapping on an electronic device at the back of your classroom is pretty darned disconcerting.

Whatever method is used, the most important thing is to maintain a nonbureaucratic, informal atmosphere *during* each mini-observation, retaining the most important information, recording it afterward in a format that works for you, and having the information in your head when you close the loop with the teacher.

HOW TO DELIVER FEEDBACK

After virtually every mini-observation, principals will have several follow-up thoughts for the teacher. These might include praise, reinforcement, questions, suggestions, criticism, or blunt redirection. It's important for the principal to decide on no more than one or two items; too much information will be overwhelming and greatly reduce the teacher's chances taking it in and following up.

What's the best way to share the feedback? Some principals leave a Post-it note on the teacher's desk on the way out with quick jottings. *(Great lesson! Where did you find that amazing map?)* Others prefer to fill out a checklist and put it in the teacher's mailbox. Others devise their own formats for written notes (a box for "Wow" and a box for "I wonder . . ."). And others e-mail their comments. All of these methods convey feedback, and all are better than no feedback at all. (That drives teachers crazy: *What did he think?!*)

But putting mini-observation feedback in writing has several disadvantages. It raises the anxiety level on both sides, especially when there is criticism. Written communication also limits the amount and subtlety of what's communicated and makes administrators that much more leery about lowering the boom. It's time-consuming, which can make the whole mini-observation process more daunting and cut down on frequency. And finally, written feedback almost always ends up being a one-way street from principal to teacher (few teachers take the time to respond to written notes or checklists). Without dialogue and active reflection on the teacher's part, it's much less likely that adult learning will take place. In the words of Steven Levy, writing in *Newsweek* (2007),

> In conversations, I can talk with [people], and a casual remark can lead to a level of discussion that neither party anticipated from the beginning. I am more likely to learn from someone in a conversation than an e-mail exchange, which simply does not allow for the serendipity, intensity and give-and-take of real-time interaction.

For these reasons, my strong preference is for face-to-face feedback after each mini-observation. Informal, low-stakes conversations (mine were almost always stand-up chats in classrooms, hallways, the copy room, or the parking lot after school) have these important advantages:

- It's possible to communicate a lot of information quite quickly.

- Teachers are less nervous and more likely to be open to feedback.

- The principal can get a sense of whether the teacher is ready to receive critical feedback; if the teacher seems to be in a fragile or hostile frame of mind, it's smart to hold off.

- The teacher can quickly give the principal additional information about the lesson or unit, filling in the bigger picture of what happened before and the visit.

- The principal can get quick answers to questions about the curriculum or materials.

- The teacher can correct a possible misunderstanding of something that happened during the mini-observation.

- The conversation can segue into a more general assessment of how the year is going and ideas for the future.

- Finally, there's no paperwork and the process is much less time-consuming.

These are compelling reasons for always giving feedback in person and engaging each teacher in a genuinely two-way conversation about the substance of what was observed. Ideally, teachers leave feedback conversations with specific ideas for improving their practice—or a warm feeling that their work is appreciated by an intelligent and thoughtful colleague.

Quick service is important after mini-observations. It's best if follow-up talks happen within twenty-four hours, and that's easier to pull off if they are kept quick and informal. Brevity is easier to achieve if the principal thinks through the opening thirty seconds of the feedback conversation in advance. I tried to plan and mentally rehearse my opening thoughts so we could quickly cut to the chase. There's a lot to be said for beginning with a declarative statement: "I was really struck by how well those math manipulatives were working to teach the part-whole principle," or "I'm concerned that boys were dominating that discussion on the causes of World War I." When a principal leads off with an open-ended question, teachers can become wary, sensing that a point is being made indirectly and that there's a "right" answer they should be giving. But if the principal is genuinely puzzled, leading off with a question is the right thing to do.

Face-to-face talks can be richly informative for teachers (and principals too), but principals sometimes pull their punches. School leaders who are overly concerned with maintaining harmonious relationships with the staff (or being *liked*) may hold off on criticizing teachers who need it. Intestinal fortitude and a willingness to accept a certain amount of anger and stomach-churn are obviously vital to overcoming this barrier. Frequent classroom visits and informal, low-stakes feedback chats are also very helpful. Teachers are much more likely to accept criticism from a principal who gives them lots of feedback, most of it positive and appreciative.

Okay, face-to-face feedback has strong advantages—but is it possible for a principal to catch up with every teacher after every mini-observation? And what about superstar teachers? Do they really need feedback when they're already performing at a very high level?

I believe that all teachers, including superstars, are hungry for feedback. They spend most of their working days with students and are intensely curious about what other adults think—especially their boss. When I was a principal, I kept a small laminated copy of the school's master schedule in my shirt pocket to help me target teachers' free periods, and I made it my business to track down every teacher I'd observed and give in-person feedback within twenty-four hours. Sometimes I missed my self-imposed deadline, but I kept pushing myself until I'd closed the loop. It's a question of priorities. If you believe something is important, you make the time. One thing is very clear: talking to teachers about teaching and learning in their classrooms is a much better use of a principal's time than doing e-mail.

Large schools are more of a challenge, but principals don't have to do this work all alone. Assistant principals, department heads, deans, and others can share the job of doing mini-observations. In one Massachusetts high school, the principal and assistant principal split the staff in two. Other administrators prefer doing mini-observations in tandem, comparing notes after they leave each classroom (people often see quite different things in the same visit). Others prefer having all administrators see all classrooms, comparing notes in weekly meetings on what they're seeing and which teachers need follow-up. Some principals do mini-observations with an instructional coach; since coaches have deeper pedagogical content knowledge than principals, they can "tutor" the boss on the finer points of lessons in their area after each visit.

LINKING MINI-OBSERVATIONS TO PROFESSIONAL DEVELOPMENT AND SCHOOL IMPROVEMENT

If mini-observations are followed only by private conversations with teachers, a good deal of their potential is lost. Smart principals get a multiplier effect from classroom visits and follow-up chats by using what they learn to bolster the school's overall plan for improving student achievement—especially the "Big Rock" projects that are the special focus for each academic year (see Chapter Eight for more on this). Principals who are in classrooms every day have a unique schoolwide perspective and are constantly getting ideas for improving teaching and learning. They are ideally situated to be *cross-pollinators,* suggesting best practices to individual teachers or teams and getting people to observe colleagues in other parts of the school. Principals can also pass along insights to instructional coaches to provide clear direction for their work, and also arrange for training in specific areas of need, drawing on expertise from within the building or from outside consultants.

Here's an example. Boston principal Emily Cox noticed that a number of teachers weren't launching their math lessons effectively; specifically, they weren't communicating their goals so students understood the overarching purpose, weren't using effective "hooks" to grab students' attention up front, and weren't checking for understanding as they proceeded. Cox decided to devote a complete cycle of classroom visits to looking at "lesson launches" and made a point of being in classrooms for the first five to ten minutes of each lesson. The insights she gained led to a series of grade-level discussions, peer visits, and an all-staff professional development session—all of which improved the way many teachers used the opening minutes of each lesson.

Mini-observations can also be an entry point for talking about student learning. Chapter Six makes the case for using interim assessment data to spark low-key discussions about results, but several other strategies can also be used as part of the mini-observation process. First, principals can watch to see how well teachers are tracking student learning (see sidebar titled "On-the-Spot Assessments" on page 74). Second, principals can use follow-up chats to ask questions: "How is the Egypt unit coming along?" "What Fountas-Pinnell levels have your lowest reading groups reached?" "How did the algebra test go?" If the principal has established a trusting climate, a teacher might feel comfortable saying, "My team just spent two weeks teaching quadratic equations and my kids bombed in the quiz. Can you help me figure out what happened?" Teachers need to know that their boss is keenly interested in how well students are learning (not just on high-stakes state tests, but on their assignments, projects, and classrooms tests) and feel able to reach out for support. The essence of these conversations should be an ongoing, collegial exploration of what's working in each classrooms and what's required to take teaching to the next level and reach all students.

A third way to shift the conversation to results is taking a mid-year break from mini-observations, setting up several short appointments with teachers every day, and asking them to bring their grade book, copies of a recent assignment or test, and a few samples of student work. When Mike Schmoker was a young middle-school English teacher in the 1970s, he worked for a principal who used this approach (in addition to making frequent classroom visits). During her conversations with teachers, Mike's principal asked questions like these:

- How did this assignment go?
- What elements of the rubric are kids struggling with?
- How do you intend to improve in those areas?
- Do you need any help or support?

"You can't imagine how powerfully these simple, time-efficient rituals influenced the quality of our teaching and ensured a guaranteed and viable curriculum," says Schmoker.

The ultimate goal of supervisory feedback, whether it's the principal's mini-observations, one-on-one conferences, or a more extensive visit by a coach or peer, is to install a supervisory voice in teachers' heads and foster an acute consciousness of whether students are learning what's being taught. Achievement will really soar when individual teachers and teacher teams are constantly puzzling and theorizing and debating about how students are responding and how teaching can be improved.

ORCHESTRATING FULL-LESSON OBSERVATIONS

In schools implementing mini-observations, teachers often ask why the principal doesn't stay longer. *Hey, stick around!* is a common response. *I want you to watch my amazing lesson from beginning to end!* In Chapter Two, I argued that pre-announced dog-and-pony-show evaluations are rarely helpful to teachers and aren't a good use of a principal's time. But under different conditions, a thoughtful analysis of an entire lesson can be a powerful form of professional development, especially if it gives the teacher insights that become part of the instructional repertoire.

This means that someone should observe teachers for a whole lesson once or twice a year, providing detailed feedback on how instruction unfolds and how students are responding minute by minute. But how can this happen if the principal is doing mini-observations? Except in very small schools, there just isn't enough time for both. Fortunately, there's a workable compromise: the principal keeps up a regular rhythm of mini-observations and does full-class observations only for teachers who are unsatisfactory and need a detailed diagnosis and prescription from the boss. This prioritizes one of the most important pieces of business in any school—dealing with ineffective teachers—while still allowing the principal to get into all classrooms on a regular basis.

What about full-lesson feedback for all the other teachers? Principals can make this happen at least once a year by using one or more of these alternative strategies: instructional coaches, peer observations, videotaping, and Lesson Study:

• Instructional coaches are becoming increasingly common in schools, and with their pedagogical content knowledge, they are ideal observers of lessons in their areas of expertise. Feedback from a coach or teacher leader is less threatening and more palatable to teachers because they are usually in the same bargaining unit and are not acting as evaluators. Coaches also have more time than harried principals for focused observations and conversation.

• Peer observations can be very helpful, and some districts—notably Toledo, Ohio—have developed thoughtful protocols for experienced teacher leaders to observe their colleagues. There is one problem with peer observations: the "culture of nice." It's hard for teachers to give critical comments to people they eat lunch with every day. Colleagues may say they want honest feedback but turn chilly when they get it, which hurts relationships that are important to a congenial workplace. Training and clear protocols are needed to make peer observations effective.

• The video camera takes an unsparing look at what happens in a classroom and allows the teacher to examine every detail, including doing instant replays. Watching a videotape of one's own lesson with a critical friend is powerful way to see teaching flaws and appreciate strengths. Videotaping requires much less skill than writing up a lesson observation, and the interpersonal challenges of giving critical feedback are virtually eliminated; the tape speaks for itself, holding up a mirror to the teacher's practice. Watching a videotape of one's own teaching can feel narcissistic; teachers learn most when they watch with a critical friend who can help them see past little quirks and really analyze the lesson.

• Lesson Study is the most sophisticated and demanding format for observing and giving feedback on whole lessons. Japanese schools have developed this protocol to a high level in recent decades (see *The Teaching Gap* by James Stigler and James Hiebert, 1999). In Lesson Study, teacher teams develop, pilot, observe, and perfect individual lessons to address specific student needs. Stigler has suggested that American schools adapt Lesson Study by using videotaped lessons as discussion tools. In schools where teachers craft effective lessons and evaluate their impact, the quality of instruction can improve by leaps and bounds. In addition, teachers' sense of efficacy and professionalism—the deepest kind of morale—will benefit from this kind of nitty-gritty, solution-oriented focus on lessons. Principals can be members of Lesson Study teams, or drop in occasionally, getting insights on the curriculum and the best teaching practices.

USING MINI-OBSERVATIONS FOR TEACHER EVALUATION

When I first implemented mini-observations at the Mather School, the idea was that they were low-key supervision with a firewall between them and summative evaluation. But as teachers became comfortable with my short visits and personal feedback, they became more and more disenchanted with formal evaluations and began to wonder if we could allow data from mini-observations to be used in the year-end review. Within a few years, virtually all teachers agreed (via individual sign-offs, with the assent of the union representative) to allow me to skip formal observation visits entirely and use my twelve or so short classroom visits-with-feedback to write their final evaluations. (For teachers who were in danger of getting overall Unsatisfactory ratings, I followed the district's regular procedures.) This was remarkable, since the Mather had tough, no-nonsense union leadership: mini-observations helped us get to the point where teachers trusted my informal feedback enough to waive business as usual.

This agreement was an enormous gift of time to me, saving scores of unproductive lesson observations and write-ups and allowing me to focus even more intently on frequent mini-observations and high-quality follow-up talks with teachers. The fact that we were able to arrive at such an arrangement at the Mather makes me optimistic that it could happen in other schools and districts. The key is a clear agreement up front, honest feedback during the year, and, most important, *trust* (which has been defined by Aneil Mishra as "one's willingness to be vulnerable to another based on the confidence that the other is benevolent, honest, open, reliable, and competent").

Clearly, including mini-observation data in final evaluations requires an explicit union agreement, which would also include a different process when a teacher shows signs of being unsatisfactory. When that happens, the principal should shift gears, contact the union representative and central-office HR staff, and embark on a more formal process: clear notice of what needs to change via the summative evaluation instrument, longer visits with a detailed diagnosis and prescription, several opportunities to improve, plenty of support, and, if things don't get better, dismissal.

Since I left the Mather School, I've developed a set of rubrics for end-of-year teacher evaluations. In Chapter Seven, I discuss these in detail, and describe what I believe is the ideal scenario: data from numerous mini-observations during the year feed into the evaluation conversation with teachers, finally taking the form of rubric scores.

TAKING STOCK

Chapter Two presents a list of twelve problems with conventional supervision and evaluation. I believe that a skillful implementation of mini-observations can solve four of them:

- By providing frequent, unannounced samplings of everyday instruction, mini-observations allow principals to see what's really going on in classrooms and give feedback that most teachers will accept as credible.
- Unannounced visits avoid the "dog-and-pony show" dynamic, allowing the principal to see everyday instruction.
- With frequent mini-observations, teachers and students grow so accustomed to the principal's presence that it no longer distorts classroom reality.
- Adult learning is much more likely because teachers are getting specific feedback on real events in their classrooms every two or three weeks in a low-stakes format.

These are significant gains in the supervision and evaluation process, but eight other important problems remain to be solved. The coming chapters tackle them with the goal of giving principals better insights on the curriculum they are observing in classrooms, helping them find a way to make student learning central to the instructional conversation, and improving conventional end-of-the-year evaluations.

Curriculum Design
The Foundation of Good Teaching

*We contend that teachers can best raise test scores over the long
haul by teaching the key ideas and processes contained in
content standards in rich and engaging ways; by collecting
evidence of student understanding of that content through
robust local assessments rather than one-shot standardized
testing; and by using engaging and effective instructional
strategies that help students explore core concepts through
inquiry and problem solving.*

—Jay McTighe, Elliott Seif, and Grant Wiggins

When a principal walks into a classroom for a mini-observation,
one of the most important questions is where the lesson fits
into the curriculum unit and the larger game plan for the year.
This is something children wonder about too, as in the *New Yorker*
cartoon.

"Please, Ms. Sweeney, may I ask where you're going with all this?"

Robert Weber, *New Yorker*, March 26, 2001; reprinted with permission.

How can principals answer this big-picture question for every classroom they visit? How can they be sure the right curriculum content is being taught at the right level of rigor? One way is to hold a pre-observation conference in which the teacher spells out the standards covered and puts the lesson plan in a broader context. This certainly helps the principal get a sense of the purpose of the lesson, but it comes with all the disadvantages of announced classroom visits discussed in Chapter Two. In addition, these conferences occur only when formal observations are scheduled—every year or two—which is certainly not often enough to give the principal a sense of whether the curriculum is appropriate on a week-by-week basis.

Another way to answer the where-are-you-going-with-this question is asking teachers to write lesson objectives on the board. This nudges teachers to clarify the aim of each class, helps students know what they are supposed to be learning, and allows a visitor to see the purpose of the lesson at a glance. But if Ms. Sweeney in the cartoon had a lesson objective on the board, the inquisitive student still wouldn't be satisfied. What the kid wanted to know—and what a thoughtful principal visiting the class also wants to know—is the longer-range purpose of what's being taught. Lesson-specific objectives are too narrow to answer that question.

Speaking of longer-range learning objectives, consider this actual dialogue between a science teacher and Keith, an average fifth grader, at the end of a four-month teaching unit on the solar system:

Teacher: Where is the sun after it sets?

Keith (pausing)*:* I don't know . . .

Teacher (pointing to the student-made colorful globes with attached labels hanging from the classroom ceiling and to students' pictures and drawings on the walls)*:* Is there anything in our classroom exhibit that can help you think about this?

Keith (looking around)*:* No . . . but I know it doesn't go into the ocean.

Teacher: How do you know that?

Keith: Because it would splash the water.

Teacher: Oh. So where does it really go?

Keith (pausing)*:* Maybe to China?

Teacher (relieved)*:* And where is it when it sets in China?

Keith (troubled)*:* I don't know . . .

—Meir Ben-Hur, Phi Delta Kappan, *May 1998*

This is every teacher's nightmare. How could Keith have missed such an important concept after four months of instruction? How could all those hands-on experiences building model planets and moons have failed to teach this central idea? What went wrong? If you were a principal overhearing Keith and the teacher, you'd wince—and you'd wonder about how well your own supervision was working. When you dropped in on the fifth-grade classes during the solar system unit, things probably seemed to be going just fine. Students were engaged, artifacts were being created, and the teaching seemed competent. After your mini-observations, you might have gone out of your way to compliment the teachers. Now you find out that Keith—not a student with major learning problems—is deeply uncertain about a concept that goes to the heart of the unit. How could your mini-observations have missed such important information?

THE CURRICULUM PLANNING GAP

My hunch is that this happened because of superficial curriculum planning. The unit had lots of engaging, hands-on activities, but teachers probably hadn't thought through and articulated a few "Big Ideas" and anticipated likely misconceptions—that the sun orbits the earth, for example. When the learning objectives of a unit aren't clear, it's much harder to pick up on problems with student learning along the way—and assess how much they've learned at the end. And without knowing the unit plan, it's difficult for a principal doing mini-observations to know what to look for; even the most sharp-eyed observer will be guessing about the bigger curriculum picture. This means that comments to teachers afterward will be limited to the *process* of teaching, which is interesting and important, rather than the content, alignment, and rigor, which are key to student achievement.

In my experience, effective curriculum planning is rare. Why? Because few teacher-education programs do an effective job on unit planning and many principals and district leaders engage in fuzzy thinking when it comes to "curriculum mapping." When I hear this term, I never know whether people are referring to year-end expectations, the scope and sequence, unit plans, lesson plans—or some combination of the above. Teachers rarely have clear direction on exactly what their students need to know and be able to do by the end of the year or support for working with their colleagues to think through unit objectives and assessments.

The result is that most teachers, under intense time pressure (all those papers to correct!), do their lesson planning the night before, aiming toward vaguely defined unit goals, and write tests shortly before students take them. Principals unwittingly reinforce this by inspecting lesson plans rather than unit plans, rarely looking at teacher-made tests, and supervising and evaluating teachers based on how well they perform in one or two lessons, not on how curriculum units and assessments are planned and executed over time.

All this produces a worst-case scenario in classrooms: teachers, students, and principals working hard, but a big discrepancy between the *intended* curriculum, the *taught* curriculum, and the *learned* curriculum, as shown in Figure 5.1. Many important understandings don't end up in students' heads.

The inescapable conclusion is that principals need to pay as much attention to *what* is taught as they do to *how* it's taught. When I was at the Mather, I was a slow

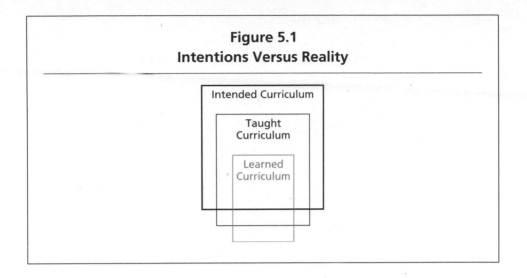

Figure 5.1
Intentions Versus Reality

Intended Curriculum

Taught
Curriculum

Learned
Curriculum

learner in this area (despite having been Boston's curriculum director for several years) and didn't provide teachers with nearly enough guidance and support. Since leaving the Mather, I've steeped myself in the literature on curriculum and unit planning, especially the work of Grant Wiggins and Jay McTighe (authors of the seminal book *Understanding by Design,* 2005), attended numerous workshops, and begun to coach principals on ways to supervise curriculum content more thoughtfully than I did.

Figure 5.2 shows what I believe to be the essential elements of curriculum planning, all requiring leadership, support, and continuous monitoring from the principal. At the bottom are the grade-level learning expectations—what students need to know and be able to do by the end of the year to be successful at the next grade level. Next is a calendar showing how all curriculum units fit into the school calendar—a road map for getting students to the year-end standards. Next is a "backwards-designed" plan for each of the year's curriculum units, each consisting of fifteen to twenty-five lessons and well-crafted assessments to see how well students are learning. Finally, there are lessons, each playing an important part in the unit's plan for moving students toward year-end learning goals and assessments that are stepping-stones to college success. The remainder of this chapter looks at each of the four components in more detail.

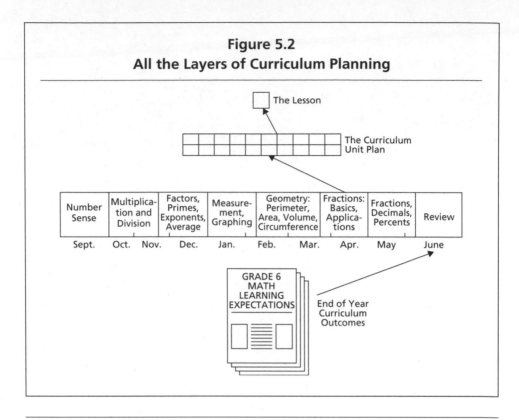

Figure 5.2
All the Layers of Curriculum Planning

The Lesson

The Curriculum Unit Plan

Number Sense	Multiplication and Division	Factors, Primes, Exponents, Average	Measurement, Graphing	Geometry: Perimeter, Area, Volume, Circumference	Fractions: Basics, Applications	Fractions, Decimals, Percents	Review
Sept.	Oct. Nov.	Dec.	Jan.	Feb. Mar.	Apr.	May	June

GRADE 6 MATH LEARNING EXPECTATIONS

End of Year Curriculum Outcomes

 ## Seven Uses for the Word *Curriculum*

When educators and members of the lay public use the word *curriculum,* it's often with totally different meanings in mind. In fact, *curriculum* is used to describe seven quite distinct school documents and processes. This semantic confusion is not life-threatening, but ambiguity can cause problems, especially when we're talking to parents and school boards and debating hot-button issues like a "national curriculum."

In a quixotic attempt to straighten this all out, I've listed all seven meanings here and suggested a distinct name for each one. If we can be more precise about the way we talk about curriculum, it might help us make our way through some interesting educational debates in the years ahead.

• *Curriculum as in state standards.* "We have no choice but to follow the Illinois curriculum." Standards are broad statewide learning goals, usually for certain grades (as in the Massachusetts Frameworks for Grades 4, 8, and 10). Almost all states have now linked their standards to high-stakes tests.

- *Curriculum as in K–12 articulation.* "The curriculum nixed teaching about evolution!" This is a district's kindergarten-through-high-school plan, spelling out which skills and content will be taught at each grade. It answers questions like: When do we cover Africa? When do we do division of fractions? When do we teach about magnetism? When should students master the persuasive essay? Thoughtful K–12 articulation prevents the overlap and duplication that occur when teachers at different grade levels are in love with the same topic (for example, dinosaurs). Articulation ensures that the limited time students have in classrooms will be used efficiently, and that children will move through the grades without major gaps in their education.

- *Curriculum as in grade-level learning expectations.* "The curriculum expects my students to be able to write a five-paragraph persuasive essay by the end of this year." Taking articulation a step further, these documents give teachers their marching orders. They are clear statements of what students should know and be able to do by the end of each year. (Districts sometimes include a "scope and sequence" that maps out the topics for the year, the order in which they should be taught, and how much time should be spent on each one.) Grade-level expectations have often been ignored in the past, but the advent of high-stakes testing has definitely gotten teachers' attention. Curriculum writers have also found that when expectations are accompanied by exemplars of proficient student work and examples of the types of problems students should be able to solve, passages they should be able to read, and writing they should be able to produce—along with the rubrics used to score open-ended student work—they get much better traction in classrooms. If expectations documents do their job, it's crystal clear to teachers, parents, students, and principals what proficient student work looks like at each grade. No surprises, no excuses.

- *Curriculum as in classroom methods.* "We're using a really rockin' science curriculum this year that says we have to do tons of hands-on experiments." These are the pedagogical approaches (cooperative learning, project-based learning, direct instruction, and the like) that teachers use to convey the standards and learning expectations to students.

- *Curriculum as in commercial programs.* "Our district just bought the most fantastic new reading curriculum from Houghton Mifflin." Facing History and Ourselves, Success For All, and Open Court Reading are examples of published packages that include materials, an approach to instruction, assessments, and teacher training.

- *Curriculum as in teaching units.* "My team just wrote a four-week curriculum on the colonial era in Africa." These are carefully crafted chunks of instruction of limited duration (a six-week history unit on World War II, for example, or a three-week English unit on poetry) that often include Big Ideas, Essential Questions, assessments, teaching strategies, and daily lesson plans. Units are most often planned by teams of teachers who share the same grade level or subject area.

- *Curriculum as in classroom materials.* "We're using a new computer curriculum that teaches students how to solve multi-step word problems." Narrower than programs and more focused than units, curriculum materials are usually commercial (but sometimes teacher-created) print or other tools, including textbooks, workbooks, worksheets, software, or other media (Wordly Wise and Mario Teaches Typing, to name two). They are designed to teach or drill a specific part of the overall curriculum.

I hope this is helpful in clarifying some of the widespread confusion around the use of the word *curriculum* and helping us be more precise in this critical area of schooling.

YEAR-END LEARNING EXPECTATIONS

State standards—and how they are assessed by state tests—are the North Star when it comes to school-level curriculum planning. They clarify *what* students should learn in K–12—the skills, knowledge, and understandings (not *how* it will be taught; that's decided by districts, schools, and teachers, informed by research and best practices). The push for state standards in recent years represents a major shift from the previous era, when school-based educators were often without clear guidance on what was expected of them. For independent-minded teachers like my younger self, this provided a heady degree of freedom, but it undoubtedly widened the achievement gap by allowing expectations to be watered down for many students.

State standards, however, have not solved the equity problem. Because of the federalist approach the United States has taken so far, there are huge variations among the fifty states in the quality and rigor of what's expected of students. The National Assessment of Educational Progress (NAEP), often referred to "the nation's report card," is the closest thing we have to a national test. Every time the NAEP is given, it reveals stark differences in what "proficiency" means from state to state. In the next few years, policymakers will decide whether to continue with the federalist approach or not (see the sidebar titled "National Standards" for my view on this hot topic). Meanwhile, educators at the district and school level have work to do. In the words of Mike Schmoker and Robert Marzano (1999, p. 21): "Every teacher deserves a clear, manageable, grade-by-grade set of standards and learning benchmarks that make sense and allow a reasonable measure of autonomy. Anything less is frustrating, inhumane, and counterproductive." What's involved in putting documents like this in all teachers' hands? In states with flaccid standards, it's up to districts and schools to supplement the standards with more rigorous content so that their students will be on track for college success. That means extra work, but it's essential if students are to receive accurate feedback on how they are really doing as they progress through the grades and not be blindsided by low SAT and ACT scores at the end of the line.

Even in states with robust standards, districts often need to identify the "power standards"—those most important to future success—and translate them into a teacher-friendly format that provides clear guidance on what students at each grade level and in each course need to learn by the end of the year. This job is often done poorly, or not at all, by districts, which makes the job of curriculum alignment far more difficult at the school level. As I have visited classrooms in a number of states, I'm dismayed by how few teachers have a succinct learning-outcomes booklet to guide them toward appropriate student outcomes. The teacher's most basic request of the district—*Just tell me what to teach*—often goes unanswered.

What happens when the district fails to provide high-quality year-end learning expectations? Principals and teachers have to do the job themselves. As described in Chapter One, our Mather School team produced just this kind of document when Massachusetts state standards and testing first came over the horizon in 1998. Our slim, grade-by-grade learning expectations booklets, complete with exemplars on-grade-level reading passages and proficient student writing and problem-solving, were extraordinarily helpful to teachers and parents, and helped bring about significant gains in our students' achievement.

The bottom line: however it's done, one of the most important things a principal can do is put crystal-clear learning goals in every teacher's hands at the beginning of the school year. Appendix A provides a sample.

National Standards

When I was a sixth-grade teacher in Boston in the 1970s, I thoroughly enjoyed the freedom I had over what I taught. Pretty much anything that intrigued my students was fair game, and nobody held me accountable for what was learned.

A decade later I became a principal, and it dawned on me that when teachers are allowed to operate as independent artisans, there can be major gaps and redundancies in what students learn (the rain forest three years in a row, perhaps, or no mention of the Holocaust). I concluded that teachers needed to follow a thoughtful K–12 sequence of *what* to teach and have creative control over *how*—as long as their students are learning.

The problem in the late 1980s was that we didn't have authoritative K–12 learning expectations, and I wasn't able to craft good standards with enough clout to convince teachers to give up the autonomy to which they'd become accustomed. I was endlessly frustrated that our students weren't getting a well-thought-out curriculum as they moved through the grades.

Along came the "standards movement" of the 1990s, which was meant to solve that problem. Every state spelled out learning expectations and gave tests to make sure students were on track. Sounds good. But in my travels (I now coach beginning principals in several different states), I'm seeing problems:

- Curriculum goals and tests are different from state to state, district to district, even school to school, making life tough for millions of students whose parents move from place to place.

- There are huge variations in what different states consider "proficient." The same child can score low in a state with rigorous standards and then cross the border and score high in a state with watered-down standards.

- There are far too many standards for teachers to cover in any depth; one estimate is that it would take twenty-two years to do a thorough job teaching the typical K–12 curriculum.

- Many state standards are poorly written and some assessments are low-quality, mostly multiple-choice tests that lead teachers to focus on basic skills and "test prep" rather than teaching students how to write, think, and solve problems.

- To sell their textbooks to a national market, publishers include a super-set of standards from numerous states, resulting in texts so heavy they strain kids' backs.

- Despite state standards, most of the teachers I talk to *still* aren't guided by clear end-of-year learning expectations.

This is bad for teachers and bad for kids. When curriculum goals are murky, overwhelming, and inadequately assessed, talented teachers can work their hearts out and get disappointing test scores. There's also less teacher teamwork and sharing, which disproportionately hurts disadvantaged students. Middle-class kids can draw on their home advantages and muddle through, but those who enter school with learning deficits fall further and further behind.

So why don't we adopt national learning standards? Horrors! Big Brother in Washington dictating lesson plans in Waikiki! Teacher creativity stifled! The wrong people (that is, people with educational views different from our own) controlling the process! When national standards were last proposed, one commentator quipped that Republicans wanted no part of "national" and Democrats wanted no part of "standards."

But attitudes are changing. Reinventing the curriculum wheel in every state has had one positive outcome: some first-rate standards and tests. The American Diploma Project, a fruitful collaboration of three politically diverse groups, has crafted a solid set of high school graduation standards; Department of Defense schools have common standards (and a good track record of closing the achievement gap); and more and more Americans are looking nervously over their shoulders at other countries that have lean, well-thought-out standards and are producing higher student achievement. In early 2009, the governors of forty-six states agreed in principle to craft voluntary national learning standards.

Why not create a bipartisan commission to build on all this, synthesizing the best reading, writing, math, history, geography, and science standards, teasing them out through the grades, and whittling them down to a manageable number, with room for states and districts to supplement with local content? The best assessments could then be tweaked to produce good national tests aligned with the standards.

It wouldn't be easy, but done right, this process could find common ground on hot-button issues like evolution and phonics. Done right, national standards would save a good deal of time and money at the state and local level. Done right, national standards would give K–12 teachers sensible direction on what to teach and allow them devote their full energies to the fun part—how it's taught.

How would I feel returning to teach sixth grade with national standards in place? I'd have to give up some of the "academic freedom" I enjoyed in the 1970s (that cool lesson on the Kennedy assassination would probably have to go). But I'd be much more confident that new students I got each fall had acquired a common body of fifth-grade knowledge and skills, no matter which U.S. school they had attended. My students and I would be crystal clear on the material and tests we needed to master by June (no surprises, no excuses). And my fellow sixth-grade teachers and I would have every reason to share ideas and materials, collaborate in analyzing students' learning during the year, and tap into a trove of Internet resources that would blossom to support the national sixth-grade curriculum. Surely this synergy would make our school more successful, prepare our students better for the global economy, and close the achievement gap that is the shame of our nation.

A CURRICULUM CALENDAR

Almost every school district has "scope and sequence" documents for major subjects, but they often gather dust. That's because they are usually written in the central office and don't reflect classroom realities. Pacing guides get more respect, especially if principals are the enforcers, but are often bitterly resented by teachers, who feel they are on a forced march through the curriculum without discretion to take extra time to solidify learning, re-teach, and help struggling students. Arguments over pacing guides sometimes involve imprecations about who has low expectations of students, who is out of touch with classroom realities, and who needs to pick up the pace and use better teaching methods.

Thinking through the curriculum calendar is important, and teachers need to be involved every step of the way. Here are my recommendations on how principals can make that happen:

- Provide teacher teams (grade-level and subject-area) with at least a half-day of uninterrupted time just before the school year begins and ask them to agree on a common calendar of their curriculum units for the year.

- Provide each team with the "slim booklet" of student learning expectations, state and district assessments, and any other documents and exemplars that spell out what students need to know and be able to do by the end of the year, and how (and when) students will be held accountable.

- Create an elongated Excel grid (see Figure 5.3 for a shrunk-down version) with a column for each week of the school year, with all school vacations, marking periods, report card times, state tests, and other important events clearly noted. Have multiple copies of this document (converted to a PDF) printed on paper thirty-six inches wide (Kinko's and other copying stores can do this at minimal

Figure 5.3
Miniature Version of Curriculum Calendar

CURRICULUM CALENDAR 2009–2010

		Week 1* 9/8–9/11	Week 2 9/14–9/18	Week 3 9/21–9/25			Week 37** 6/7–6/11	Week 38 6/14–6/18	Week 39 6/21–6/25
Mathematics									
ELA									
Science									
Social Studies									

9/7 NO CLASSES LABOR DAY
9/28 NO CLASSES YOM KIPPUR
6/10 NO CLASSES CHANCELLOR'S CONFERENCE DAY

* - Not a full week of classes with the break in the beginning or end of the week
** - Not a full week of classes with the break in the middle of the week

cost, or schools can print their own on regular paper and tape the pieces together to create the elongated format), and give copies to all teams.

- Ask each team to agree on how they will "chunk" the year's curriculum into units, estimate how long each one will take (usually three to six weeks), and rough out how the units will fit onto the calendar strip (being sure that tested material is covered before state tests).

- Look over all calendars for any obvious problems. Then get the information from all units entered into a composite Excel document, make copies, and distribute them to teams with instructions to scope out areas for cooperation and cross-fertilization between teams (and suggestions on curriculum units that might be shifted on the calendar to make collaboration easier).

- At a beginning-of-the-year staff meeting, discuss the composite curriculum calendar with an eye to identifying times and ways that teams might collaborate during the year.

- Finalize the whole-school composite calendar, print multiple (full-size) copies, and post them in the teachers' room, the curriculum center, and all administrators' offices for easy reference.

- Revise the calendar as needed during the year.

This kind of curriculum calendar can be enormously helpful to teachers and administrators, leading to ongoing conversations about pacing, content, cross-fertilization, and more. But it's just the beginning.

CURRICULUM UNIT PLANS

Once the curriculum calendar is figured out, grade-level and subject-area teams can begin to plan their lead-off curriculum units, ideally using the approach developed by Grant Wiggins and Jay McTighe in *Understanding by Design* (UbD). The key feature of UbD is planning each unit "backwards"—that is, starting with the final learning goals and working back through all the steps necessary to get students to master them. Here are the critical components that a team would decide as it produces an first-rate unit plan (the sequence is up to each team):

- The subject of the unit and how long it will last
- The state standards covered by the unit (written out verbatim)

- Three or four Big Ideas or Enduring Understandings (each preceded by "Students will understand that ... ") to guide teachers throughout the unit and keep the bigger picture in mind (*Ms. Sweeney, where are you going with all this?*)

- Three or four Essential Questions, written in provocative, student-friendly language, to be posted on the classroom wall during the unit, leading the class toward "discovery" of the Big Ideas

- The most important factual knowledge students will acquire

- A list of skills to be taught or reinforced (including habits of mind)

- Assessments (quizzes, tests, a performance task) *written in advance* to assess student mastery formatively and summatively, accompanied by exemplars of proficient student work and a scoring guide

- A lesson-by-lesson instructional game plan, showing when some or all of these components will be used: lectures, mini-lessons, readalouds, independent reading, discussions, dialogues, debates, partner or small-group work, student presentations, reports, journals, reflections, films, website exploration, field trips, in-class assessments, written reports, essays, research, and homework

UbD unit planning has huge payoffs in terms of the quality of instruction and student achievement. Who among us wouldn't want our children taught by teachers who use this kind of approach to thinking through each curriculum unit? But backwards design is time-consuming and challenging, and it's not something most teachers will do on their own. The default in most schools is last-minute lesson planning. Fortunately, there are excellent resources to support UbD, including Wiggins and McTighe's books, other ASCD resources, and a low-cost website (www.ubdexchange.org) that makes available thousands of curriculum units developed by teachers around the world.

The principal plays an absolutely critical role in good unit design. The essential first step is getting teachers working in same-grade and same-subject teams to plan *common* units (no more Lone Ranger). UbD planning is intellectually demanding and difficult to do alone, but it becomes manageable when teachers pool their content-area expertise, share ideas and insights, and bring their collective brainpower and resources to the task—textbooks, Web resources, reference books, and all the rest. Unit-planning meetings should be part of the regular cycle of grade-level team meetings, preferably run by teachers or instructional coaches, with the principal making regular visits, partly for quality control—but also for the pleasure of watching substantive, collegial meetings. Here are other key steps for the principal and leadership team:

- Giving teacher teams the mandate, perhaps in the context of a long-range goal of having all major units in the school backwards-planned within two or three years
- Providing the training and the support they need to be successful
- Giving teacher teams enough time to do backwards design, over the summer and during the school year
- Making unit design one element in the regular rotation of meeting agendas (the others might be looking at interim assessment data and student work, discussing effective teaching strategies, and dealing with logistics, discipline, and student culture issues)
- Buying a school subscription to the UbD website so teachers can download units in their area
- Arranging to have each new curriculum unit subjected to peer review (Wiggins and McTighe have developed a helpful protocol for this)
- As part of their unit planning, having teachers develop standard ways for students to store their work (for example, a reading log, a reading response journal, a writing portfolio, a math folder)
- The principal critiquing each unit before it is finalized
- Monitoring the implementation of units by mini-observations, visits to team meetings, and debriefs with team leaders, with feedback at every stage
- Collaboratively analyzing the learning outcomes of each unit: what went right—and what can be improved

The most challenging part of UbD is framing the Big Ideas of a curriculum unit and writing matching Essential Questions. I once watched a group of experienced Brooklyn eighth-grade social studies teachers struggle for almost an hour to come up with the Big Ideas of a unit on the Civil War that they had taught for years; they had never been asked to think at that conceptual level, and became better Civil War teachers for having done so. Teacher teams need time and guidance to do this work well.

As an example, here are Big Ideas and Enduring Understandings for a fifth-grade curriculum unit on the solar system:

BIG IDEAS—students will understand that:

- The sun's gravity has held the planets and other objects in regular orbits for billions of years, which is what makes our solar system a system.
- If the sun were the size of a large beach ball, the Earth would be the size of a pea, but the great distance between them makes the sun appear much smaller.
- The Earth's distance from the sun is just right for life to develop; if we were closer, we'd burn up, and if we were further out, we'd freeze.
- Day and night are caused by the Earth turning on its axis every twenty-four hours; it's daytime on the side facing toward the sun, nighttime on the side facing away.
- A year is the amount of time it takes a planet to orbit around the sun; the length of a year is different on every planet because each planet takes a different amount of time to orbit around the sun.
- Moonlight is actually reflected sunlight, and the moon's phases (waxing from new moon to half moon to full moon and waning back again) are caused by the angle at which the sun's rays strike the moon relative to a human observer.

ESSENTIAL QUESTIONS to evoke the Big Ideas:

- Why are the sun and the planets called the solar system?
- How are most diagrams and models of our solar system inaccurate? Why?
- Why has life flourished on the planet Earth and not on other planets, moons, and asteroids in our solar system?
- What causes night and day on Earth?
- If you lived on Mars, would a year be the same length of time as on Earth? Explain.
- Why does the moon change shape over the course of each month?

The first time a team creates a UbD unit, there should be a half-day of professional time, a common unit-design template to work with, and support from consultants, instructional coaches, or administrators familiar with the process. Wiggins and McTighe recommend that teams start by designing one unit, teaching it, discussing learning outcomes, and making revisions. Once a good unit plan has been created, it's money in the bank; it can be used by the team that created it—and by other teams.

Then teams can focus on the next unit plan—but not every unit has to be written from scratch. Successfully creating one UbD unit makes it much easier to adopt and adapt units from colleagues, other schools, or the website, saving valuable time. It's unrealistic to expect every teacher team to write an entire curriculum in high-quality UbD style—that would take years. But once the pump is primed, teachers can build on and adapt the work of others and spread high-quality curriculum units throughout the school in a fairly short time.

Some educators, feeling under the gun from high-stakes tests, say they can't afford what they call "the luxury" of UbD unit planning; they say they need to focus on test preparation. But as the quote at the beginning of this chapter suggests, there's no either-or between thoughtful planning and higher student achievement. Good backwards curriculum planning supports better teaching, higher test scores, and a trajectory toward successful completion of college. Of course, unit planning has little value if it's not aligned to state (or provincial) standards. When teachers design impressive units and then go looking for standards that plausibly match, that's the wrong way around! Standards should come first, along with a sense of how those standards are assessed by state tests and what is aligned to a college-ready curriculum. The unit's knowledge and skill objectives and essential questions should flow directly from those high standards.

Team unit planning time is one of the best forms of professional development for teachers—and principals. A rigorous backwards-planning process, skillfully facilitated, gets teachers thinking about every aspect of their craft—the intended, the taught, and the learned curriculum and how to bring them into the closest possible alignment. Unit planning improves teacher collaboration, the quality of teaching, and student achievement. In schools that have begun to use systematic unit design, classroom teaching is much more focused and results-oriented and a mini-observing principal can concentrate on the most important thing: how well the material is being taught and how well students are learning. With three or four essential questions on the wall that are frequently referred to by the teacher, any student, if asked, should be able to articulate the big picture of what the class is learning.

Test Preparation: Good or Bad

A fierce debate is raging on the impact of high-stakes testing on the everyday life of American classrooms. Supporters say the tests have raised curriculum expectations and focused much-needed attention on struggling students. Critics say that "teaching to the test" is ruining the quality of instruction and making schools into sweatshops. Who's right?

As an educator and a parent, I'm convinced that when high-stakes tests are handled well (as I believe they have been in Massachusetts, where my own children went through public schools K–12), they are an engine of school improvement, raising standards and bringing order out of curriculum chaos. But what about teaching to the test? Well, it's not always a bad thing. If teachers are using first-rate classroom methods and materials to teach to standards that are measured by the tests, that's great. If students who have fallen behind are getting skilled tutoring that boosts their confidence and performance, excellent. If nervous students are given test-taking tips and familiarized with the test format a couple of weeks before testing time, fine. But if low-quality "test prep" materials and recycled test items are being used to drill and kill the subject matter, that's a problem.

How much teaching-to-the-test is going on? While exact figures aren't available, a national survey by *Quality Counts* in 2001 found that four out of five teachers were devoting "a great deal" or "somewhat" of their time to test-focused teaching. How much of this is at the bad end of the spectrum? Again, I don't have precise data, but one thing is clear: wherever drill-and-kill is happening, it's not good for kids. Bad test prep is like junk food: it can give students a quick burst of energy (short-term test score gains), especially if kids were malnourished (deprived of good teaching and learning), but all too quickly, students get that empty feeling (their achievement sags). Test prep is like junk food if it

- Bores students (tests, tests, tests all the time) and turns them off school

- Demoralizes teachers, making them feel like they're working in a test prep factory

- Promotes lazy pedagogy: just assign and correct

- Uses de-contextualized passages so kids don't read whole stories and books

- Overuses multiple-choice questions in daily classroom teaching
- Drills lower-level skills and skimps on writing and teaching for understanding
- Focuses on memorizing facts rather than expressing ideas in an authentic voice

Why would any self-respecting educator indulge in the junky kind of test prep? Why are some schools wasting precious time and resources that could be devoted to high-quality teaching and materials? Why is it even necessary to have a parallel test-prep curriculum to teach kids what they should cover in their regular classes?

First, most districts' learning expectations contain far more material than it's humanly possible to teach. Researcher Robert Marzano calculated that it would take roughly 15,500 hours to teach the average K–12 curriculum—and there are only about 9,000 hours of classroom learning time available from kindergarten through high school. Teachers can only cover a portion of the total curriculum—and the tests can only assess a portion. For students to do well, the portion that's taught needs to overlap with the portion that's tested. Test prep seems like the easiest way to make this happen.

Second, some school districts have not taken the obvious step of fully aligning their curriculum with test expectations. Even in states where clear curriculum goals and previous tests are posted on websites, there are still alignment problems. Among the reasons: bureaucratic inertia, sentimental attachment to time-honored units, pedagogical disagreements with state curriculum decisions, and resistance to the whole idea of state-imposed standards (some folks don't like being told what to teach). In addition, textbooks written for a national market are not perfectly aligned with the curriculum of individual states, and marching chapter by chapter through the book (which some teachers still do) can leave big gaps. Test prep thrives on this kind of misalignment.

Third, even when school districts have aligned with the standards, some principals and teachers aren't confident that following the curriculum on a day-to-day basis will produce good test scores. They fall prey to the misconception that students will score high only if they are fed a steady diet of worksheets with cloned test questions.

Fourth, there's a lot of talk about how awful the tests are. In states that are using off-the-shelf norm-referenced tests or tests that don't include writing and higher-order thinking, this distaste is understandable. Test prep can be seen as a way to game the system and beat the test.

Finally, educators' anxiety about high-stakes tests can create a kind of group panic attack: if we don't take desperate measures, our kids will fail! Gotta have some test prep—even if it displaces good teaching. Superintendents, principals, and teachers have been known to succumb to this kind of thinking and make unwise curriculum choices.

These are five reasons why junky test prep has found its way into all too many classrooms and after-school programs. Opponents of high-stakes testing pounce on this. They argue that low-level "drill-and-kill" teaching is an inevitable by-product of such tests. They say that when a state spells out what should be taught and holds everyone accountable with tests, it in effect dictates how it should be taught—poorly. Their solution? Get rid of the tests!

But dumping high-stakes tests would slow the positive momentum of education reform. Scary testing may seem like a strange way to help children, but state-level assessments with some consequences attached to them are the only way that has yet been discovered to get schools to focus their curriculum and take responsibility for teaching all students to high standards. True, teachers have less freedom in what they teach, and some have had to give up beloved (sometimes excellent) curriculum units that didn't fit the standards. But something had to be done to forge a more coherent K–12 curriculum sequence, eliminate overlap and fill some gaps, and make the high school diploma a more meaningful document. There is a strong equity dimension to this: the students who suffer most from an individualistic, chaotic curriculum and a lack of clear standards are the least advantaged. If standards are handled well, they can be a powerful lever for closing the achievement gap.

The key point is that teachers don't have to teach badly to raise test scores. Tests dictate the *what,* not the *how-to,* of teaching. The research is clear that what produces well-educated graduates and high test scores is good teaching. Junky test prep is a shortcut that doesn't work. Students need the real thing—challenging subject matter, engaging, hands-on classroom activities, and energized teachers who know their subject and make it exciting and relevant. Having students do a lot of writing is especially important; Doug Reeves, a national expert on standards, has found that writing develops the kind of higher-order thinking and understanding that translates directly into better performance on all kinds of tests—including those with multiple-choice questions.

Anti-testers do have a point: the pressure of high-stakes testing can lead some educators to make unwise curriculum choices. But with a little prodding, these educators will come to their senses and do the right thing. If you are a school administrator with your pen poised to sign a requisition for test prep materials, use the checklist in this sidebar to determine the level of junkiness; if it's high, just say no! If you are a teacher, student, parent, or community leader and you see junky test prep in your school, speak up! It's not good for your school—and it's not going to produce high test scores on the long run.

The path to good teaching and really solid achievement is clear. Schools need to accept the reality of high-stakes tests—and work to improve the quality of those tests where they fall short. They need to align their grade-by-grade curriculum with test expectations, reducing what's required of teachers to a teachable amount. They need to ensure that 99 percent of classroom time is devoted to high-quality, aligned instruction with no cheesy test prep. They need to put a premium on creative, involving, relevant pedagogy and teacher teamwork, trusting that excellent teaching is the best way to get and sustain high scores—even on tests that are not perfect. And they need to provide teachers with the support, training, and materials to do the job.

So let's swear off the junk food of test prep. Let's give our children the kind of education that will prepare them for any kind of test—including the real world. Let's ensure that high test scores mean that students are truly proficient, not just good test-takers. And let's give them a classroom curriculum that will nourish them for years to come. They deserve no less.

LESSONS: WHERE THE RUBBER MEETS THE ROAD

Clearly, supervising and supporting unit planning is a high-value use of the principal's time. Supervising lessons (through frequent mini-observations) is equally important, since lessons are the vehicle that delivers all that curriculum planning, constituting 90 percent or more of instruction. But what about lesson plans? Is inspecting them a valuable exercise?

Lesson plans matter. The principal has every reason to expect that teachers plan thoughtfully for every class they teach, aligning instruction with the unit plan and end-of-year standards. But I have serious doubts about the wisdom of a principal requiring teachers to submit lesson plans in advance and spending lots of time going through them. First of all, a lesson plan can be brilliant on paper and implemented poorly (and vice versa). Second, it's a waste of time critiquing lesson plans based on a unit plan that's poorly thought-through—or nonexistent; better to work with the team to improve the quality of the unit plan so that high-quality lesson plans will flow from it. Third, in the same way that an army battle plan rarely survives contact with the enemy, a teacher's lesson plan rarely survives contact with students. What counts on the battlefield is knowing the "commander's intent"—the overall goal of the operation (Heath & Heath, 2007); what counts in the classroom is knowing the essential learning outcomes in the unit plan; having these clearly in mind leads to inventive, intelligent adaptations as conditions change on the ground—and to successful outcomes.

Then there's the sheer number of lesson plans: in a school with thirty-five teachers, about 700 lessons are taught each week, which means 700 lesson plans, which adds up to 24,500 a year. Inspecting them all would be ridiculous micromanagement, not to mention masochistic. Finally, inspecting lesson plans involves the principal working with one teacher at a time, while nurturing team UbD planning increases collegiality and empowers teachers to take collective responsibility for student learning.

Of course teachers should plan their lessons well, and principals should spot-check lesson plans if they see a pattern of lessons that are not well-planned. There's also real value in helping teachers plan good lessons; this is a high-value activity for instructional coaches and mentor teachers. The principal's time, however, is best spent working with teacher teams on unit plans. In the same school with 24,500 lesson plans mentioned in the preceding paragraph, grade-level teams might teach six common units per subject in the course of the year. That's a total of only about twenty-five unit plans every six weeks. If the principal collaborates with teacher teams on polishing each of those unit plans—and uses mini-observations to look for evidence that unit plans are being skillfully executed—there will be handsome dividends in the quality of teaching and learning.

TAKING STOCK

I believe that the ideas presented in this chapter solve one more of the supervision and evaluation problems listed in Chapter Two—that even skilled write-ups can fail to capture important aspects of a teacher's performance. In schools that have clear end-of-year outcomes, a curriculum calendar, an increasing number of backwards-designed units, and a sharp focus on how all this comes together in each individual lesson, teachers are constantly thinking about the most important questions: alignment with standards, the knowledge, skills, and understandings students must acquire, potential misunderstandings, and how learning will be assessed.

When principals do mini-observations with this broader perspective in mind, they have far greater insight and significantly enhance their supervisory power. Their follow-up conversations (and year-end evaluations) are more efficient and helpful, and they are more effective cross-pollinators as they move from class to class and grade to grade. Figure 5.4 shows how this relates to the four-part scheme of the book. There's a strong synergy between schoolwide curriculum clarity, team unit planning, and mini-observations, each supporting the other and producing better teaching and learning. So far, five of the problems presented in Chapter Two have solutions.

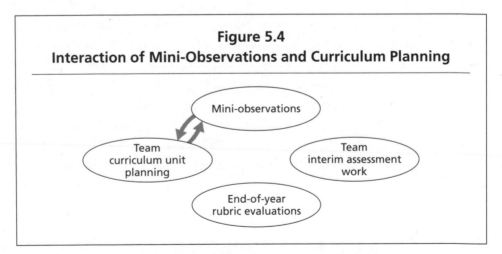

Figure 5.4
Interaction of Mini-Observations and Curriculum Planning

The next chapter tackles the thorniest one of all: the fact that student learning is rarely part of the supervision and evaluation conversation. It proposes a solution: effective use of interim assessments to shift the conversation to what students are actually learning as the year progresses.

Interim Assessments

Using Results to Continuously Improve Instruction

*The more you teach without finding out who understands the
information and who doesn't, the greater the likelihood that
only already-proficient students will succeed.*

—Grant Wiggins

One of the biggest limitations of conventional supervision (and mini-observations as well) is that they are focused on teacher inputs, not student results. A supervisor can talk to a teacher about what went on during a classroom visit, but addressing how much the kids learned is tricky. Contractual provisions (discussed in Chapter Two) are one reason for this, but the inherent limitations of classroom supervision are even more important. A principal can read the posted lesson objective, watch the teacher in action, examine the work students are being asked to do, peruse what's on the walls, chat with a few students, and see how well the teacher checks for understanding. But even the sharpest-eyed observer doesn't have a true sense of the class's level of mastery of the knowledge and skills being taught in the curriculum unit—and can only guess at how much students will retain in two or three months. As long as supervision is limited to classroom visits, there's no way principals can make student learning a meaningful part of follow-up talks with teachers.

This chapter presents a way that principals can supplement mini-observations with another layer of supervision that puts student learning at the center of ongoing conversations with teachers and teacher teams. School leaders can do this by orchestrating and monitoring an effective interim assessment process —ongoing "professional learning community" meetings about real-time student achievement results—while being careful to keep everything low-stakes and non-evaluative.

Before describing this process, it's worth asking why it's so important for student learning to be part of the conversation between principals and teachers. What's wrong with focusing supervision on inputs that can be observed during a classroom visit? If the inputs are the right ones, won't the outcomes take care of themselves? Not necessarily. That's why classroom supervision must be supplemented by a rigorous, ongoing look at evidence of student learning. The best way to dramatize this point is looking at what I call the moment of truth in classrooms.

I TAUGHT IT, THEREFORE THEY LEARNED IT

Imagine this scenario: you've completed a well-taught chunk of curriculum (perhaps a six-week unit of geometry) and given an assessment to see how well students learned. You mark the assessments, record the grades, and then simplify them into a tally graph showing the number of students who scored at the Advanced, Proficient, Needs Improvement, and Failure level (Proficient is mastery, about 80 percent). In Figure 6.1, each tally mark represents one student.

The bottom line: only 52 percent of students scored proficient and above— hardly a smashing success—and yet a bell-shaped pattern of achievement is quite common at this point. What do you do next? This is a defining moment.

Figure 6.1
The Scatter of Achievement Scores

4 – IIII
3 – IIIIIIIII
2 – IIIIIIIII
1 – IIII

We all know what a teacher *should* do, but if your reality matches that of most classrooms, you record the grades and move on to the next unit. Why? Teachers are under lots of pressure to cover the curriculum and get their students ready for high-stakes tests. Most feel they don't have the luxury to slow down and work with the students at Level 2 who haven't fully mastered the material, much less the students at Level 1 who outright failed. And there are other reasons. Some teachers believe this pattern of achievement reflects differences in intelligence that can't be changed by any amount of re-teaching. Some are concerned that high-achieving students will be bored if they have to go over material again, leading their parents to complain to the principal. Some teachers aren't confident they have the skills to help students who didn't get it the first time around. And some believe that if they have done a good job presenting the material, they've fulfilled their obligation. The cartoon below captures the spirit of this belief.

King Syndicate.

These are all powerful reasons, but let's be blunt: every time a teacher moves on with this many students below mastery, the achievement gap widens. That's because the students at Levels 2 and 1 are most often the students who were already having difficulty in this and other subjects, have special needs or language barriers or both, and entered school with learning disadvantages stemming from home and neighborhood factors beyond their control. You could probably have predicted which students were going to fail before the first day of the unit.

Benjamin Bloom addressed this syndrome in his 1970s theory of Mastery Learning. If the teacher moves on, he said, students below mastery (defined as scoring 80 percent or better on a preliminary test) will enter the next segment of the curriculum that much more confused, that much more discouraged, and that much more likely to think they're stupid, adopt a negative attitude, and act out in class. Bloom proposed Mastery Learning as the solution: teachers should stop, re-teach, and bring as many students up to mastery as possible before proceeding. Unfortunately, Mastery Learning never really caught on, and very few teachers take the time to follow up with students who are struggling.

What happens when teachers move on? Paul Black and Dylan Wiliam paint this depressing picture: "The worst scenario is one in which some pupils who get low marks this time also got low marks last time and come to expect to get low marks next time. This cycle of repeated failure becomes part of a shared belief between such students and their teacher" (1998, p. 144).

The students who enter with disadvantages tend to be the ones who are confused after initial teaching, and they are the ones who are harmed the most when teachers proceed with the curriculum without checking for understanding and following up. This is what made Paul Tough conclude in a *New York Times Magazine* article about the achievement gap: "The evidence is now overwhelming that if you take an average low-income child and put him into an average American public school, he will almost certainly come out poorly educated" (2006, p. 77).

All this points to an inescapable conclusion: a powerful gap-widening dynamic is at work in most classrooms. It's not caused by evil people or racism or incompetence. It's caused by a deeply embedded paradigm of teaching—the one most of us experienced in school: teaching, testing, and moving on without fixing learning problems. Most teachers don't have the mandate, the training, or the tools to *pause* when significant numbers of students are below mastery and fix what they don't understand before the gap widens even more.

I believe the principal's most important moral and professional challenge is changing the teach-test-move-on pattern. But where to begin? In an ideal world, all students would be well-behaved and attentive and only need to be told once. But in the real world, a significant number of students walk into classrooms with a variety of distractions, impairments, and learning gaps, and we're lucky if initial teaching produces mastery in half of them. Jayne Boyd-Zaharias and Helen Pate-Bain said it well—and hinted at the implications: "No matter what the instructional format—lecture, small-group activity, or individual assignment—students make their own sense of what they're taught. Ideas don't fly directly from teachers' minds into learners' minds. Effective teaching requires teachers to assess what students are taking away from instruction to meet the differing needs of students" (2008, p. 43).

In other words, salvation lies in giving during-the-year assessments, paying attention to what they reveal, and relentlessly following up with students who don't understand (while providing meaningful enrichment activities for those who do). Most teachers know this, but principals need to empower them to put on the brakes when they see evidence that their teaching hasn't reached some students (which happens virtually all the time, even with highly accomplished teachers and well-prepared students) and fix the problems before they compound.

FINDING THE RIGHT ASSESSMENTS

But what kinds of information on student learning is most helpful to teachers intent on catching problems early? There's plenty of data around: the previous year's test scores, students' report card grades, student work, student projects, and portfolios. Are these helpful? Here's a quick run-down:

- *Year-end test scores:* This method is most authoritatively advocated in the two *Data Wise* books produced by a group of Harvard researchers who worked with Boston Public Schools educators for several years (*Data Wise,* 2005, and *Data Wise in Action,* 2007). The problem is that to most teachers, the previous year's test results are, as Douglas Reeves says, autopsy data. Reeves elaborates:

> For teachers, getting annual test scores several months after taking the test and in most cases long after the students have departed for the summer sends a message: "Here's the data that would have helped you improve your teaching based on the needs of these students if

you would have had it in time, but since it's late and there's nothing you can do about it, we'll just release it to the newspapers so they can editorialize again about how bad our schools are." (Reeves, 2004)

There are plenty of instructional uses for test data from the preceding year—doing a big-picture analysis of areas of strength and weakness in the curriculum, for example—but I believe it's much more productive for teachers to look at evidence of student learning within the *current* school year. The next four meet that criterion.

• *Report card grades:* At one point in my principalship, I carefully recorded and graphed the grades of each homeroom, comparing one marking period to the next. I soon discovered that this was not a helpful exercise. Grades tend to be quite stable over time, and the grades teachers give often mush together achievement, effort, improvement, and behavior. In addition, grades provide very little diagnostic information about students' learning needs. So, like end-of-year tests, grades are not the best kind of data for during-the-year data discussions.

• *Student work:* During the 1990s, a number of school districts, including Boston, became excited about Looking at Student Work (LASW). As an elementary principal, I understood the rationale for teachers having in-depth discussions about samples of their students' writing and problem-solving. But I was always troubled that LASW meetings didn't look at the overall achievement of the class. *What percent of students met the standard? Where did students excel? What were the most common learning problems?* Without whole-class achievement and diagnostic data, I found LASW sessions frustratingly limited and superficial. They were certainly not the most powerful way to get teachers and administrators thinking about how to improve achievement for all students.

• *Student projects:* Several progressive reform initiatives (including the Coalition of Essential Schools and the Big Picture Company) have made projects and performances the core of assessment and professional analysis. But projects and performances tend to be quite topic-specific, and students still need to be assessed on the full body of knowledge and skills they've been taught, giving teachers insights on what's been learned and what needs to be retaught or supplemented. At best, projects are a small part of a good during-the-year assessment system. In addition, to get the full value from projects, well-trained teachers need to align the projects with standards and use well-crafted rubrics for scoring students' work—which is not always the case.

- *Portfolios:* Some educators are enthusiastic about using collections of student work over time, scored with rubrics, to assess learning. Portfolios can be a helpful way to gather and evaluate students' writing, creative work, and other assessments. But all too often they are random collections of work without systematic curriculum coverage or rigorous evaluation. It is also quite cumbersome for teacher teams to use portfolios to get specific diagnostic information at several points in the school year—and by *diagnostic* I mean information they can put to work immediately to improve teaching and learning.

Teachers' professional time during the school year is precious, and if the goal is focusing on what's been learned and catching learning problems immediately, it's important to have the best possible data on the table. I've concluded that the preceding year's test scores, report card grades, student work, projects, and portfolios aren't the best data to use. Team conversations based on these measures and materials are not worthless, but too often they will be general, superficial, and lack the kind of clinical detail necessary to have real impact on teaching and learning.

The research points to two different kinds of assessments that are far more effective at improving teaching and learning: *on-the-spot* assessments (sometimes called *formative* or *classroom* assessments; discussed in Chapter Four, pages 74–77) and *interim* assessments (sometimes called *benchmark* or *periodic* tests), which are the main focus of this chapter. When implemented well, both can be powerful engines of improvement, setting up a continuous feedback loop between teaching and learning, making it possible to correct learning problems before they widen the gap.

In the pages that follow, I discuss how interim tests complement on-the-spot assessments, touch on some operational details, list the ways that interim assessments can be mishandled, describe a set of best practices, and show how they can become an integral part of a principal's supervision of teachers.

INTERIM ASSESSMENTS

Interim assessments are designed to give schools information on student learning every four to nine weeks. They usually mirror state tests, using the conventional pencil-and-paper format, a mix of multiple-choice and open-response questions, and the usual style of administration (students aren't allowed to get help from the teacher or their peers). Some districts write their own interim tests, commissioning committees of teachers and following state standards and tests and using a variety of school-based or central scoring approaches. Some individual schools write their own tests; for example, administrators and teachers at the North Star Academy charter schools in Newark, New Jersey, have created quarterly tests (typically about eight pages long with fifty test items) and hand-score them, entering correct and incorrect student responses into customized Excel spreadsheets.

Many schools purchase interim assessments from test companies, which customize the tests to state standards and district specifications and usually do the scoring and data analysis in a central location, giving teachers and principals a password to retrieve their test data online. Some schools use a hybrid approach, buying commercial tests but scoring them at the school level for faster turnaround.

Another type of interim assessment uses tests taken on computers (Scantron and NWEA are two companies using this approach): if a student answers incorrectly, the computer provides an easier item from the item bank; if the student answers correctly, the computer finds a more challenging item. Adaptive tests produce a detailed profile of skills and knowledge immediately after each student finishes taking the test (but have the disadvantage that students don't take the same test items so teachers can't compare students' responses to specific items).

Interim assessments are hot in American schools and have a number of strong proponents. Richard DuFour, Mike Schmoker, Robert Marzano, Douglas Reeves, Jeffrey Howard, Grant Wiggins, Jay McTighe, and others believe that interim assessments, done right, are a powerful strategy for producing high levels of achievement. Interim assessments also have detractors: James Popham and Dylan Wiliam, among others, say that there is much stronger research evidence for on-the-spot assessments, and have slammed test companies for exploiting confusion over terminology to market unproven benchmark tests. Interim assessment supporters disagree, pointing to research evidence and success stories supporting their case.

This debate will probably go on for years, and it's hard to see who's right, especially since the ambiguous use of the word *formative* makes it unclear which studies favor which camp. There's also the fact that either kind of assessment can be mishandled in the real world of schools. In the meantime, responsible educators need to decide which is the best way to check for student understanding during the year and use the data to improve teaching and learning.

What Interim Assessments Add

But do schools have to choose? It's clear that on-the-spot assessments, done right, are a powerful way to improve achievement. But they have limitations. I believe that interim assessments, done right, provide an ideal complement. Here's how:

- Interim assessments check on whether students remember material several weeks after it was taught.

- Interim tests can be more wide-ranging and rigorous and require students to apply what they have learned in novel situations.

- Interim assessments allow teachers to measure students' progress or lack of progress as the year unfolds.

- The data from interim tests can be made visible to teachers, administrators, and students in spreadsheets and wall charts, which means they can be analyzed more thoughtfully.

- Data displays make it possible for same-grade and same-subject teams of teachers to discuss collaboratively what students misunderstood, why they misunderstood it, what's confusing them, and how the material can be taught more effectively. Team discussions take assessment data out of the privacy of the classroom and make possible a synergistic sharing of best practices across several classrooms. When teachers confront specific data on their students' short-term errors and confusions, admit that certain teaching practices aren't working, and listen to colleagues who have better ideas ("Have you tried this?"), teaching can improve dramatically.

- Interim assessment data help administrators and instructional coaches get involved in the discussion, contributing their wisdom and experience—and their ability to provide materials and professional development.

- Administrators who have taken part in interim assessment discussions are much more perceptive observers in classrooms. (It's like putting on 3-D glasses, says Paul Bambrick-Santoyo, a Newark school leader.)

- Interim assessment data contain the names of struggling students and the specific areas in which they are having difficulty, making it easier to provide small-group tutoring and focused interventions.

- Interim assessments that simulate the content, format, and rigor of state tests can help reduce students' stress level when they take the real thing and boost their confidence when they take any kind of test.

- Because the results of interim assessments are shared within the school, they prod teachers to be on the same page in their curriculum pacing and level of rigor. Common assessments and open discussions of student results implicitly challenge teachers to do the very best they can in the classroom and see if their methods and materials pass the ultimate test: all students learning at high levels.

Problems Implementing Interim Assessments

The factors I've just described explain the popularity of interim assessments and the ways they can complement on-the-spot assessments and fuel productive team and schoolwide conversations about improving student learning. But unfortunately, the concept of interim assessments is frequently misinterpreted and mangled at the district and school level. In my work coaching principals in a number of cities and suburbs, I'm seeing a slew of implementation glitches that produce cynical and discouraged teachers and disappointing student achievement results. Some of these problems are caused by poor communication that affects how teachers and students use interim assessments. Others have to do with the quality of tests, the way they are scored, and how they are followed up.

For example, administrators often don't do a good job explaining the rationale of interim assessments, and as a result teachers see them as "one more thing" from the central office: *All we do is test, test, test. Why don't they just let us teach?* This dynamic prevents teachers from investing their energy in the interim assessment process, and teachers sometimes communicate their negativity to students. Teachers often fear that interim tests will be used to blame them for student failure, especially if the central office collects test data. Nervousness about how the results will be used makes teachers tighten up and not engage in the kind of free-flowing discussions of assessment data that improve teaching and learning.

Some interim tests are poorly aligned with standards, state tests, and pacing calendars. When students are required to take tests on material they haven't been taught, they get discouraged—and their teachers get angry.

And there are other problems with tests. If interims are short and superficial, teachers don't get enough diagnostic information to have useful conversations with their colleagues on ways to improve instruction. If tests are given infrequently—only two or three times a year (September, January, and June in some districts)—too much time passes before teachers have a chance to fix learning problems. January is awfully late to find out about serious gaps in understanding. The opposite—too *many* assessments—is a problem too. Some schools make the mistake of not eliminating other tests that cover the same ground in the same time frame as interim assessments (for example, classroom unit tests, standard Friday tests, or full-blown simulations of state tests). Overtesting leads to underperformance as students become jaded and don't put forth their best effort. I visited one high school in the Bronx where students were so fed up with tests that they deliberately sabotaged an important reading assessment.

A related problem, more common in middle and high schools, is when students figure out that interim assessments don't count on their report cards and GPAs (teachers may have been at pains to say that the tests are "low-stakes") and proceed to blow them off, filling in pretty patterns on their bubble sheets. When this happens, interim assessment data reports have no value and all the instructional time taken for testing is wasted.

If teachers are not involved in the interim assessment process, the whole effort can suffer. When interim tests are scored externally, teachers have less ownership and interest and may slough off the test reports. When they have to go online to get their results and navigate to several different locations, few are likely to persist and pull out the data they need to improve their own teaching, much less share ideas with their colleagues.

The way interim assessment results are reported can also cause problems. When turnaround is slow (two to three weeks in some districts), the results are stale and outdated by the time teachers sit down to discuss them; they've long since moved on. When the "grain size" of test reports is too fine, listing data on countless micro-skills, teachers can get lost in the details and fail to focus on a few doable challenges. When data reports are overly general (aggregated into categories like "number sense" or "comprehension"), follow-up conversations are vague and unhelpful.

Grade-level and subject-area meetings are where interim assessment results can come alive, but union or scheduling issues sometimes prevent teams from meeting to discuss the data, depriving teachers of one of the best forums to figure out learning problems and share best practices. Cross-grade teacher meetings are good for other purposes, but the most powerful data conversations occur when teams of teachers give common assessments to the same level of students—and have enough time to pore over the results.

Even when the right people meet with timely interim assessment data in front of them, teachers sometimes fall victim to the "culture of nice"—chatting amiably about interesting curriculum ideas and not confronting ineffective practices and pushing each other to higher levels of performance. It's not easy to be blunt and exacting with colleagues.

Some schools give interim assessments and then don't block out time to follow up with re-teaching and assistance for struggling students. This leads teachers to move on because of the pressure to cover the curriculum and keep up with the pacing guide. If this happens, the critics of interim assessments are right: they are nothing more than summative tests in sheep's clothing, adding absolutely no value to the instructional process and wasting precious instructional time.

Finally, some schools use interim test results to focus only on the "bubble students"—those who are on the cusp of proficiency and might help the school make AYP (the No Child Left Behind Adequate Yearly Progress target) if they improved their test performance. This amounts to educational triage and does a huge disservice to other students who need help.

Doing Interim Assessments Right

As I've watched well-intentioned, hard-working educators make some or all of these mistakes, I've realized that interim assessments are a lot harder to implement well than a lot of us naively believed. Working with my colleagues in New Leaders for New Schools and educators in a number of schools, I've gradually honed a list of the most important steps to implementing interim assessments in a way that will really make a difference. Principals' leadership is absolutely key; they have to ensure that teachers understand and trust the process and are fully involved from start to finish; that learning outcomes are clear; that the assessments are high-quality (although they don't have to be psychometrically perfect); that there is rapid turnaround; that assessment data are presented in a user-friendly format; that teacher teams have honest discussions of the implications of the data; and that there is immediate, effective follow-up with students. Here's more detail on what school leaders must do in each of these areas:

Build Understanding and Trust   The principal needs to explain interim assessments to the leadership team and staff so that everyone has a good conceptual understanding of the powerful role they can play in closing the achievement gap.

I've found that the "moment of truth" scenario described under "I Taught It, Therefore They Learned It" is an effective way of making this point. In addition, teachers need *repeated* assurances that interim assessments are low-stakes and will not be used as part of the performance evaluation process. It's essential to create what Hector Calderon, a New York City principal, called in a conversation with me a "data without blame" climate in which continuous adult learning can take place. One way of building trust is distributing copies of interim assessments well before students take them and involving teachers in refining and improving the tests; this approach is in marked contrast to the mistrustful, secret way that tests are usually handled.

 ## Response to Intervention and Finland's Approach

In recent years, Response to Intervention (RTI) has been a hot topic in U.S. educational circles. RTI received a boost in the 2004 reauthorization of the federal Individuals with Disabilities Education Improvement Act, which endorsed the approach as a way to bring services more promptly to students experiencing difficulty in regular-education classrooms. RTI is all about using assessments to diagnose learning problems and help students succeed. It conceptualizes teaching in three tiers. Tier 1 is the instruction all students receive, which should be as effective as possible, using proven methods to get the maximum number of students to mastery. On-the-spot and interim assessments monitor all students' achievement and identify those who are not succeeding. Tier 2 promptly addresses the needs of struggling students in small-group instruction, tutoring, and other interventions short of special education. Students who are still having difficulty after Tier 2 assistance get even more specialized and intense interventions, often in special education (Brown-Chidsey, 2007).

Finland's schools, which have successfully narrowed achievement gaps over the last thirty years and climbed to the top in international comparisons, use a similar approach. Teachers intervene immediately with students who are experiencing difficulty, often the same day. The clear mandate is that each classroom teacher is responsible for recognizing when any student is failing to master any particular competency (for example, letter combinations, number facts, or history concepts). Teachers work with struggling students one-on-one or in small groups before school, during class time while the rest of the class is doing small-group or individual work, during lunch, or after school.

RTI and Finland mirror the basic ideas underlying on-the-spot and interim assessments: as instruction proceeds, teachers check frequently for student mastery, fix as many learning problems as possible early on, and use assessment data to inform increasingly intense interventions to students who are still having difficulty.

Source: Grubb, 2007.

Clarify Learning Outcomes As described in Chapter Five, all teachers need clear, manageable, standards-aligned descriptions of what their students should know and be able to do by the end of the year—not on websites or in hulking three-ring binders but in slim booklets right on their desks (see Appendix A for a sample). Teachers need to make these standards visible to students and parents, accompanied by exemplars of proficient student work. No surprises, no excuses.

Set a Multi-Year Target and Annual SMART Goals Boosting student achievement significantly takes three or more years, so it's very helpful for the leadership team and teachers to agree on an ambitious yet attainable long-range goal—for example, 85 percent of graduating fifth graders reading at Fountas-Pinnell level W (instructional level) four years down the road. Grade-level teams can then set annual SMART goals (Specific, Measurable, Attainable, Results-oriented, Time-bound), for example, 85 percent of first graders will be reading at Level I by the end of June. SMART goals should gradually ratchet up each year as high-achieving students progress through the grades.

Get High-Quality Tests Wherever a school gets its interim assessments, there are important criteria to consider. I believe that interim assessments should

- Cover reading, writing, and math (and other subjects at the secondary level).
- Cover the skills and content tested in high-stakes state assessments at the appropriate level of rigor.
- Have open-response as well as multiple-choice questions and writing prompts.

- Incorporate user-friendly scoring rubrics.
- Define on-the-way-to-college-success standards, including higher-order thinking skills (even if state standards don't).
- Be aligned with the sequence of school-based curriculum materials.
- Reassess previous standards, as well as new learning, to provide ongoing, cumulative review and a way of measuring progress.

Finding the right length for interim assessments is another Goldilocks dilemma: they should have enough items so teachers can have substantive conversations about the results, but not be overwhelming for students to take or teachers to administer, score, and analyze. Interim assessments are low-stakes and don't have to meet the same psychometric standards as state tests (for example, having seven items per standard). But interim assessments should be good enough to provide teachers with real insights for classroom follow-up.

It's also important that interim assessments not duplicate unit tests or classroom tests, resulting in overtesting and wasted classroom time. *Less is more* is a good rule of thumb. Better to have a few high-quality interim assessments with good follow-up than a bunch of interim tests that aren't thought through. At the elementary level, this probably means limiting interim assessments to reading, writing, and math. At the secondary level, it suggests using unit tests as interim assessments in science and social studies and staggering the schedule so the tests don't all happen at the same time.

How are commercial interim assessments working out? My sense from talking to scores of principals, teachers, district leaders, and testing experts is that James Popham and Dylan Wiliam are right: the assessments produced by test companies are not going well in most schools because of problems with item quality, slow turnaround, and clunky data display. The result: in many cases, teachers give the interim tests because they're required to and move on. The interim assessment process seems to be working best (and producing some extraordinary gains in student achievement) in small schools, often charters, that create their own tests and do the scoring in-house. But this approach is very labor-intensive and most schools can't replicate it.

So where does that leave a principal whose school district mandates commercial interim assessments that have slow turnaround or low-quality items, or both? I have worked with principals in several major districts who found themselves in this position, and they've taken a variety of approaches: hand scoring district tests to speed up turnaround; duplicating the district's interim assessments with assessments they create in-house (and deemphasizing the district's tests); getting permission from the district to use alternative assessments (New York City allows schools to apply for a Design Your Own option); and "leading up"—attempting to persuade the district to improve its assessments. Unfortunately, some principals become cynical and give up on interim assessments altogether, which is most unfortunate.

We should all work hard to improve the quality of the interim assessment process because of its great potential to improve teaching and learning. Let's hope that, in the years ahead, technology and enlightened district leadership will make it possible for schools to customize interim assessments from high-quality commercial or state item banks and then do all scoring and analysis locally to minimize turnaround time and maximize teacher involvement and ownership.

Schedule Time for the Assessments and Immediate Follow-Up   Principals should block out time in the calendar for interim tests every four to nine weeks and also schedule time for prompt scoring and teacher analysis and data meetings, ideally within twenty-four to forty-eight hours. It's also important to allocate several days for re-teaching after each round of interim assessments. Unless these dates are in everyone's calendars, interim assessments will constantly be pushed aside by other events, and teacher teams won't look at data with any regularity. The Greater Newark Academy, a Grade 5–8 school in Newark, New Jersey, schedules its interim assessments every six weeks following this pattern:

- Wednesday and Thursday: students take interim assessments
- Friday is an early-dismissal day (11:30 AM) and teachers score, analyze, and discuss tests and write their follow-up action plans, leaving at 4:00 PM
- Monday is the first of several days scheduled for re-teaching and enrichment.

When the year's interim assessments are scheduled, principals should be careful to avoid a common trap: overtesting. The leadership team should put all the school's assessments on the calendar—diagnostic tests, interim assessments, unit tests, teachers' classroom tests, state tests, practice tests—and look for duplication. The team should then push hard to eliminate redundancy and consolidate tests to the absolute minimum needed to give teachers timely information on student proficiency as the year progresses. With during-the-year assessments, less is more.

Get Teachers Involved in Making Sense of the Assessments Teacher involvement in the interim assessment process is vital. Some may complain about the work involved in scoring and analyzing interim assessments, but if professional time is blocked out that doesn't take them away from their students, teachers will end up appreciating and learning a great deal from working on their own students' tests. Of course schools should take advantage of scanners and other test-scoring technology to save needless paperwork—but it's essential that teachers score students' written responses and stay close to the item analysis process so they can celebrate their students' successes and form initial hypotheses about why students did poorly on some items. The heart of the interim assessment process is for teachers to be able to make new instructional decisions based on timely information.

Display Data Effectively Succinct spreadsheets and wall charts should make students' current status and progress graphically clear to teachers, administrators, students, and parents, and answer these questions: How did students do on each test item? How did students do on each standard? What's the big picture of achievement at this point (that is, what percentage of students are Proficient and above)? Graphic display of data, which Robert Marzano (2006) has found to be the second-most powerful factor in boosting achievement, is especially effective when teachers and administrators see the names of individual students and how each of them is doing.

The spreadsheet in Exhibit 6.1 shows the successive Fountas-Pinnell reading levels of a class of Boston third graders (names deleted) based on one-on-one assessments. The date of each assessment is noted, which shows which students are making progress and which are stuck. There is additional diagnostic information from the assessments, making it possible for teachers to discuss what's not working and find approaches that might be more effective.

Hold Candid Data Meetings and Plan for Follow-Up As noted, it's vital that discussions of interim assessment data take place as soon as possible after each round of tests in same-grade and same-subject teacher teams (or, in very small schools, in one-on-one meetings between teachers and principals or instructional coaches). To be effective, these meetings need to be hard-hitting, honest, test-in-hand, and low-stakes—celebrating successes and then looking at *what* students

Exhibit 6.1
Reading Level Results

One School's Third-grade Fountas-Pinnell Achievement Data

Names	aa	A	B	C	D	E	F	G	H	I	J	K	L	M	N	O	P	Q	R
Student 1						Sep-06	4/07 6/07 10/07		1/07 10/07	4/07 6/07									
Student 2			Sep-06		Jan-07														
Student 3											Oct-06	Jan-07	Apr-07	Jun-07	Oct-07				
Student 4			Sep-06				Jan-07			Apr-07	6/07 10/07								
Student 5			Sep-06									9/06 1/07	Apr-07	6/07 10/07					
Student 19											10/06 1/07			Apr-07	Jun-07	Oct-07			
Student 20				9/06 1/07		Oct-07													
Student 21													09/06 01/07	4/07 6/07 10/07					
Student 22					Sep-06				Jan-07					4/07 6/07		Oct-07			

didn't understand and figuring out *why*. Data meetings should bring teachers out of their isolation and get them working smart to solve common learning problems. Many schools have found that it's helpful to have data meetings facilitated by someone from outside the team; focused data conversations rarely happen without a guiding hand. Out of each meeting should come specific plans for next steps—each teacher's battle plan for whole-class re-teaching of concepts that were widely misunderstood, small-group explanations for pockets of confusion, tutorials and after-school work for students with multiple learning problems, and distributed before-class-work, mini-lesson, and homework topics in areas where most students need refreshers.

When principals attend interim assessment data meetings, they don't have to be content experts to plunge into the conversation. Any competent school leader can look at interim learning results with teacher teams and be a thought partner as teachers look for the items that caused students the most trouble, diagnose problems, brainstorm and share solutions, and decide how to follow up. This is good news for young principals, who are sometimes insecure about supervising teachers with many more miles on their odometers.

Instructional coaches, who are most often specialists in literacy or math, are ideal helpers in interim assessment data meetings. Their subject-area expertise is most powerful when they work with teams analyzing detailed student achievement results and planning strategies for improving student understanding. The sidebar on Camden County, Georgia's experience with interim assessments makes this very clear.

 One District's Use of Interim Assessments and Coaches

In 1997, the Camden County Schools in Georgia began giving interim assessments every nine weeks. By 2002, the district, whose per-pupil spending is among the lowest in the state (171st out of 180 school districts), raised its English language arts and math achievement into the top thirty districts on statewide rankings. Camden County gives much of the credit for this achievement to the implementation of interim assessments and the effective use of data by teacher teams in each school.

In an article in *Middle School Journal* (March 2005), three Camden County leaders described the process of introducing interim assessments (supported by instructional coaches) and the five stages that teachers went through, each phase lasting two to three months:

Phase 1: Confusion and Overload

At first, almost all teachers were overwhelmed and frustrated by the flood of numbers, columns, graphs, and percentages from the interim tests. "This is too much!" was a common reaction. "I can't understand any of it. I have enough to do. I was hired to teach, not do statistics." Teachers had a point: the reporting format for the interim assessments (designed by a consulting firm under contract to the district) used a completely different format from statewide tests. Lead teachers listened sympathetically to these concerns, helped simplify the reporting format, and walked teachers through the reports one subject at a time.

Phase 2: Feeling Inadequate and Distrustful

As teachers analyzed the test results in the early part of the year, they were alarmed at how poorly their students performed on material they had taught. Their first impulse was to blame the test: "How can two questions on a test possibly establish mastery of an objective? These questions are terrible! We don't use this format, vocabulary, terminology , etc. in our classes. I don't teach it that way! These scores can't be right. I taught this concept for a whole week. . . . Something is wrong." The lead teachers, sometimes feeling they needed to wear a suit of armor, listened as teachers vented—and began to see the glimmerings of a desire to investigate the cause of the low scores.

Phase 3: Challenging the Test

Teachers insisted on looking at copies of the actual tests, indicating "a need to avoid personal responsibility and to identify the test as the cause of the low scores." Sitting with their lead teachers, teams looked at items that most students had answered incorrectly, identifying the wording and "tricks" that had thrown their students. One English teacher said, "No wonder those items about business letters scored low; look at this test question. We don't use this word in class—'editing the letter for *publication*.' Publication? There's the reason right there for those low scores." The intrepid lead teachers asked, "Is this a problem with the test question or the instruction?"

Teachers continued to blame the test—but said that maybe they would start using the word *publication* in their lessons. With other test items, it was a different story. Looking at an item where the correct answer was *ears* and 30 percent of students picked *ear's,* teachers groaned, "But we've taught plurals and possessives." When the lead teacher asked, "Is this a test question problem?" teachers had to agree that it wasn't. In Phase 3, the lead teachers continued to listen, offer suggestions, and guide the discussion toward scrutinizing the data for insights about students' progress and confusions. It was clear that teachers had never before looked at test scores, test items, and their own teaching in such a detailed way.

Phase 4: Examining the Results Objectively and Looking for Causes

At this point in the year, teachers looked at their classes' test reports without the skepticism and resistance of the earlier phases. They searched for patterns in students' responses, examined similarities among the high-scoring items, and brainstormed possible causes for low-scoring items. "They looked at all the variables, such as the types of students in their classes, the time of day, the time of the week, the sports schedules, the number of attempts to reach parents, sibling rivalry, and their own teaching strategies." Teachers began to compare notes ("What are you doing with symmetry that gets those results?") and sharing teaching techniques that seemed to be working in some classrooms (for example, using geo-mirrors or having students write in a daily math journal). The threat level of the tests diminished as teachers stopped assuming that low scores reflected on their competence. Teachers began to use the interim tests to answer two questions:

- Which students need extra help and in what topic?

- Which topics do I need to re-teach in different ways?

Lead teachers kept the focus on data analysis by persistently asking, "What do these scores tell us?" In this phase, teachers accepted the value of the data for improving their teaching and realized that if students were not understanding, perhaps their teaching strategies needed to be improved. They began asking, Did the test measure the learning objective? If the test item was clear, how was my teaching? Did I teach the objectives in a manner that showed connections among the concepts and had relevance for these students? Did I give them enough opportunity, enough variety, to allow them to master the content? Was the content interesting to them?

Phase 5: Accepting Data as Useful Information, Seeking Solutions, and Modifying Instruction

By this point, teachers fully accepted the usefulness of the interim tests and spent almost all their time searching for more effective teaching strategies. Some teachers conferred with individual students and set SMART goals for the next benchmark test (Specific, Measurable, Achievable, Results-oriented, Time-bound), for example, raising a score from 50 percent to 70 percent. Others put together customized study packets. Others encouraged students to analyze their errors and examine their learning style. Teachers also wrote shorter interim tests and quizzes to keep track of students' learning between benchmarks.

Summing up the transformation that the interim assessments brought about, one lead teacher said, "Prior to implementation of formative assessments . . . teachers were shooting in the dark. They were standing at the goal line in a dark gymnasium taking aim at a hoop they could not see. Now, we can see the goal and have a much better chance of ringing the basket!"

Source: Trimble, Gay, & Matthews (2005), summarized in *Marshall Memo* 78.

Principals don't have to attend all data meetings, but they can help teams crystallize their thinking by asking for a *brief,* informal report on the key findings and action plans, with one additional question: How can I help? Figure 6.2 shows a team's report on the percent of students attaining proficiency in interim writing assessments in the baseline and the first two assessments. This is the sort of graph that a team might compile for its own use and to share with the principal, showing the percent of students proficient and above on the subject in question. It's crucial that team reports (whether they are delivered in person or in writing) be low-stakes, nonthreatening, and nonbureaucratic. Teams shouldn't be bogged down in paperwork and must feel they can be creative, try new things, admit mistakes, and engage in an informal give-and-take about what's working and what needs to be improved.

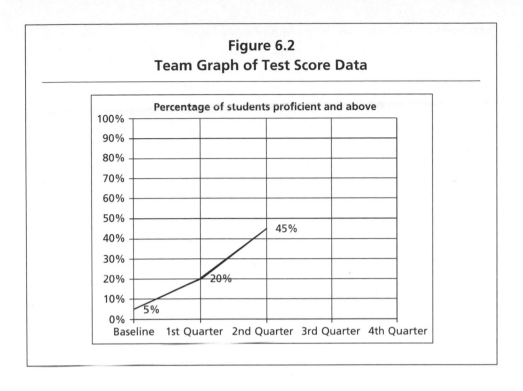

Figure 6.2
Team Graph of Test Score Data

Percentage of students proficient and above

(Graph showing percentage of students proficient and above, with y-axis from 0% to 100% and x-axis showing Baseline, 1st Quarter, 2nd Quarter, 3rd Quarter, 4th Quarter. Data points: 5% at Baseline, 20% at 1st Quarter, 45% at 2nd Quarter.)

Involve Students in the Process Curriculum goals and interim assessment data can have even greater impact when they are shared with students. Ideally, each child should know: What does proficiency look like? Where am I now compared to that goal? How am I going to close the gap? (Stiggins, 2007). In elementary and middle schools, it's very helpful for students to know their Fountas-Pinnell reading levels and have a target for the end of the year. (This leads them to ask, "How do I get to be a better reader?"—a question their teachers are ready to answer.) Middle- and high school students can conduct a postmortem on each interim assessment, listing which items they got wrong, whether their mistakes were careless or based on faulty understanding, and what their study strategy will be for the weeks ahead. Students at all levels should have copies of the rubrics used to assess their writing and become expert at self-evaluation, tracking their progress in each of the rubric domains, and continuously improving their writing. This can prevent a frequent and depressing scenario: the teacher spends hours grading writing assignments and students glance at the grade and throw their papers in the wastepaper basket. Teachers who get their students to use rubrics to assess their own writing before handing in final work are truly working smart.

Relentlessly Follow Up   Each interim assessment provides a wealth of information that needs to be put to strategic use in classrooms. Assessments are a waste of time if teachers don't implement their action plans for re-teaching (teaching things differently the second time around, not just louder and slower), follow up to see if students improve, and reflect on the data to improve their teaching. Richard DuFour and his colleagues have done some of the best work in the area of follow-up, describing schools that refuse to let students fail (*Whatever It Takes,* Solution Tree, 2004). The strategies they describe include "Do-Now" beginning-of-class work, mini-lessons, re-teaching to the whole class, tutorials, more effective use of outside tutors, peer tutoring, and parent work.

These ten keys to effective implementation of interim assessments are a formidable to-do list for a principal. It's clear that doing this right is a complex and demanding business, and it takes focused and determined leadership to get results. What's the most important element to success? If I could make only one visit to a school to assess its interim assessment process, I would ask to make unannounced visits to two or three teacher team meetings in which interim assessment results were being discussed. If I saw teachers with copies of spreadsheet reports and test items in front of them, drilling down on individual test items asking why students had difficulty, admitting frankly what didn't work, and sharing methods and materials that got results, mapping out specific action plans, pushing each other to find the best possible solutions to learning problems while maintaining an informal, collegial atmosphere, I would feel pretty confident that things were going well and the school was on the way to dramatic gains in student achievement.

TAKING STOCK

Most schools have a deeply embedded tendency to teach, test, and move on, driven by fear of high-stakes tests, the need to cover the curriculum, and beliefs about teaching and learning. The principal is the point person in helping teachers see the gap-widening effects of this pattern, empowering them to pause when students don't understand, and giving them the time and support they need to reflect with their colleagues on what's not working and fix learning problems before it's too late.

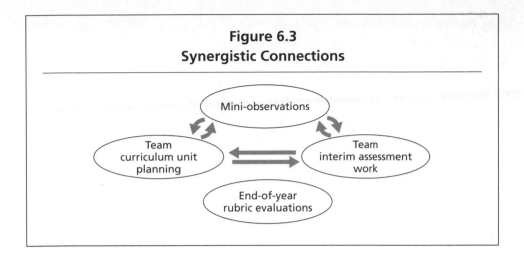

Figure 6.3
Synergistic Connections

Mini-observations

Team curriculum unit planning

Team interim assessment work

End-of-year rubric evaluations

Schools that have this engine of improvement running are no longer going through the motions or implementing "one right way" to teach: they are engaged in what F.D.R. called "bold, persistent experimentation"—trying new approaches, judging their success, discarding what didn't work, and continuously improving teaching and learning. The principal is in the best position to help teachers understand and trust this process and give it their all. Teacher investment is vital, because changes in classroom practices are deeper and more lasting when they come from within, as part of an a continuous, low-stakes, collegial dialogue about the best ways to get all students to high levels of achievement.

The effect of high-quality conversations about interim assessment data ripple out to all aspects of school improvement, helping teachers plan better, teach better, use on-the-spot assessments better, analyze what's working and what isn't, and follow up with struggling students. It also sharpens principals' vision when they visit classrooms, greatly improving the power of mini-observations. Figure 6.3 shows this three-way interaction.

 Teaching to the Test

Is it right for schools to "teach to the test"? If that means "test prep" —forcing students to do pages and pages of sample test items week after week—the answer is no; that's educational malpractice. If "teach to the test" means aligning the curriculum to state standards and paying particular attention to the standards that are tested, I see no problem—provided the standards are robust, the tests are high-quality, and teachers use good pedagogy to prepare their students.

Another caution: interim assessments don't need to be clones of state tests. To be sure, students should be familiar and comfortable with what state tests look like. When the big day arrives and they open up their high-stakes test, their reaction should be, *This is challenging stuff but it's what we've been learning, I'm used to answering questions like these, and I can handle it.* But interim assessments can also take the form of performance tasks, essays (even if the state doesn't test writing that year), and presentations. Members of the track team who specialize in sprints don't prepare for the 100-meter dash by doing nothing but 100-meter dashes. They run a variety of distances, do weight training, and eat a balanced diet. In the same way, students should be getting a variety of instructional and assessment approaches. This will produce the best possible performance on the narrower bandwidth of actual state tests—and prepare them for success in high school, college, and beyond.

Critics of high-stakes state testing complain that it narrows the curriculum. But as noted, Robert Marzano has calculated that American K–12 curriculum expectations are so overblown that it would take twenty-two years of schooling to cover them. For this reason, an intelligent paring-down of standards is a good thing—unless it means the elimination of art, music, physical education, and high-quality field trips. Students need a balanced curriculum to succeed in the twenty-first century; this is especially important for students who enter school with disadvantages.

Rubrics

Potent, Time-Efficient Evaluation Tools

*Most existing systems of teacher evaluation are taken seriously
by neither teachers nor administrators. They are based on
outmoded criteria, observations are conducted on the run by
poorly trained evaluators who are not sure what they should be
looking for, and virtually all teachers are rated at the top of
whatever scale is used.*

—Charlotte Danielson

Late one May evening in the latter part of my Boston principalship, I was sitting at my home computer writing yet another
teacher evaluation. It was a real struggle to come up with thoughtful comments in each of the categories of the district's evaluation
form (planning, classroom management, and the rest). Even though
I had done frequent mini-observations in this teacher's classroom
and followed up with informal chats, I'd seen less than 1 percent of
her teaching, knew very little about her dealings with parents and
colleagues, and had no data on how much her students were learning.
Suddenly my hands froze on the keyboard. "I'm faking it!" I said out
loud. "This is nonsense!" (Or words to that effect.)

It was a defining moment. All my accumulating doubts about teacher evaluation crystallized into a depressing argument:

- My verbiage wasn't giving teachers clear feedback on how they were doing in most of the evaluation criteria—and how they might improve.
- The Satisfactory/Unsatisfactory rating scale didn't allow me to make important judgments on different levels of proficiency.
- My evaluations were mostly superficial and often missed the target.
- It was no wonder teachers often ignored them and rarely changed anything based on what I wrote.
- Spending hours and hours on this process was not a good use of my time.

As this logic hit home, I shifted from being a Saint to a Cynic on the Saints /Cynics/Sinners scale presented in Chapter Two. In my remaining years as a principal, I did my write-ups as quickly and as close to the deadline as possible, sometimes with the help of a good stiff drink. This was not a productive dynamic—for me or for the teachers I evaluated.

Fellow principals with whom I shared these subversive thoughts often agreed. We ruefully observed that the evaluation process was an elaborate and largely empty ritual. Administrators observe. We do our write-ups and fill out the evaluation forms. Teachers sign them, sometimes with pro forma objections, usually with no comments at all. Occasionally we use evaluations to make a serious criticism, which may or may not be heeded. *Very* occasionally we use them to make the case for dismissing a chronically ineffective teacher. But most of the time, our evaluations are accepted with a shrug and have virtually no impact on student learning.

In a more benign era, this ritual didn't attract much attention. Some teachers may even have appreciated the fact that it kept principals busy and out of mischief. But now the stakes are higher. Educators are being held accountable for the achievement of every single child. Acutely conscious of the widening achievement gap, we can't avoid the conclusion that if our approach to teacher evaluation is chewing up large amounts of time and rarely producing improvement, it needs to be changed.

But how? Chapter Two explored two ideas—merit pay and more aggressive supervision and evaluation—and rejected both. This chapter will present a more promising solution: using rubrics to evaluate teachers.

Over the last decade, a number of districts and charter schools have experimented with rubrics. A major source of inspiration has been Charlotte Danielson's book, *Enhancing Professional Practice: A Framework for Teaching* (ASCD, 1996, 2007), which contains an extraordinarily thorough set of scoring guides and a rationale for using them for summative evaluation. Supporters of rubrics say that they address some of the most glaring problems of conventional teacher evaluation. Rubrics are more judgmental, giving teachers a clearer sense of where they stand, usually on a 4-3-2-1 scale. Rubrics explicitly describe the characteristics at each level of performance, giving mediocre and unsatisfactory teachers a road map for improvement. And rubrics are much less time-consuming for principals, since lengthy narratives and lesson descriptions are not required.

Great in theory—but as I collected and scrutinized rubrics from different schools and districts, I had concerns. Some, including Danielson's, are so long and detailed that they seem overwhelming to many teachers and administrators (Danielson's cover sixty-six criteria and are spread out over twenty-two pages). Others organize teaching in illogical ways and have gaps in their descriptions of teaching. And almost none are formatted in ways that are user-friendly.

CREATING A NEW SET OF RUBRICS

But these flaws are not fundamental. I was so impressed by the overall concept that I set about building a better mousetrap. My goal was to create rubrics that were compact, well-organized, and easy to use. What follows is a step-by-step description of how I decided on six domains of teaching, established a rating scale, synthesized hundreds of criteria into 10-point lists of proficient teaching within each domain, and then teased the lists into 4-3-2-1 rubrics. A number of schools and districts have used my rubrics successfully in recent years. I hope this description—and the rubrics themselves—will be helpful to educators involved in rethinking teacher evaluation. You are welcome to use or modify the rubrics in any way you see fit (see www.marshallmemo.com for a free electronic version—click on Kim Marshall Bio/Publications and scroll down).

Step One—Deciding on Domains

With any teacher evaluation instrument, the decision that needs to be made first is what "buckets" will be used to sort out the countless criteria of good teaching. Here are some recent categorizations:

Charlotte Danielson, Enhancing Professional Practice: A Framework for Teaching *(1996, 2007)*

1. Planning and Preparation
2. The Classroom Environment
3. Instruction
4. Professional Responsibilities

*Jon Saphier's short list (*How to Make Supervision and Evaluation Really Work *(1993)*

1. Classroom teaching
2. Contributing member of the staff
3. Communication with parents and community
4. Routine and administrative duties
5. Continuing professional growth and development

*Jon Saphier's "Areas of Performance"; (*The Skillful Teacher, *with Haley-Speca and Gower, 2008); these are an itemization of the "classroom teaching" category in the "short list" just cited:*

a. Attention
b. Momentum
c. Space
d. Time
e. Routines
f. Discipline
g. Clarity
h. Principles of learning
i. Models of teaching
j. Expectations
k. Personal relationship building
l. Classroom climate
m. Planning skills
n. Objectives

o. Learning experiences

p. Assessment

q. Curriculum design

r. Overarching objectives

North Star Academy Charter School, Newark (2004)

1. Planning and preparing instruction

2. Classroom management and classroom environment

3. Focus on student learning

   a. Engaging pedagogy

   b. Adapting instruction

   c. Assessment

   d. Delivering instruction

4. Concern for students

5. Professionalism and work habits

Boston Public Schools 2002 Revised Format

1. Knowledge of subject matter and currency in the curriculum

2. Setting the stage for learning

3. Classroom management

4. Effective teaching

5. Monitoring, assessment, and follow-up

6. Professional responsibilities outside the classroom:

   a. Collaboration with parents

   b. Collaboration with colleagues

   c. School responsibilities

   d. Professional growth

Santa Cruz Rubric, adopted as California Standards for the Teaching Profession (1997, 2004)

1. Engaging and supporting all students in learning

2. Creating and maintaining an effective environment for student learning

3. Understanding and organizing subject matter for student learning

4. Planning instruction and designing learning experiences for all students

5. Assessing student learning

6. Developing as a professional educator

Aspire Charter Schools, California (2003)

1. Commitment to students and learning

2. Knowledge of subject matter

3. Skill in the management of learning

4. Ability to reflect and improve

5. Collaboration with colleagues, parents, and community

Drawing on these and other ways of organizing the competencies of teaching, I came up with a new synthesis that I think is compact and yet comprehensive:

A. Planning and preparation for learning

B. Classroom management

C. Delivery of instruction

D. Monitoring, assessment, and follow-up

E. Family and community outreach

F. Professional responsibilities

Step Two—Deciding on a Rating Scale

Many different rating scales are used in schools, with anywhere from two to ten levels of proficiency and a variety of descriptive labels. Recently, four-point scales have emerged as the favorite because four is a simple, manageable number of levels for teachers and administrators—and four is an even number, clearly differentiating between proficient and less-than-proficient performance. Here are some recently developed scales:

Charlotte Danielson (1996, 2008):

4—Distinguished

3—Proficient

2—Basic

1—Unsatisfactory

Boston Public Schools Dimensions of Effective Teaching Rubric (2005):

4—Exceeding the standard

3—Meeting the standard

2—Progressing toward the standard

1—Beginning

North Star Academy Charter School, Newark (2004):

4—Advanced

3—Proficient

2—Working towards

1—Needs Improvement

Alexandria, Virginia (2003):

4—Exceeds expectations

3—Meets expectations

2—Needs improvement

1—Unsatisfactory

Conservatory Lab Charter School, Boston (2004):

4—Expert

3—Proficient

2—Developing

1—Novice

Santa Cruz (1997, 2004):

5—Innovating

4—Integrating

3—Applying

2—Emerging

1—Beginning

As I examined these and other scales, I began to clarify my own philosophy about the messages that teacher evaluation rubrics should send. I liked the way 4-3-2-1 scales created a clear division between the top two levels (good teaching) and the bottom two (below par), with no rating comparable to a "gentleman's C." I also noticed how rating labels communicate beliefs about what each level represents, which drives the way the criteria in that area are written. For example, using "novice" rather than "unsatisfactory" for the lowest level reflects a supportive, "not yet" approach to less-than-proficient performance. I wanted rubrics that supported improvement but would send a strong message about what unacceptable performance looked like and could be used to terminate a teacher after a reasonable chance to improve.

And what about performance at the top two levels? My sense was that they should contain professional characteristics that research indicates will improve student achievement and narrow the racial and economic performance gap. Teaching that is consistently rated at these two levels should be virtually guaranteed to bring about high achievement for all students—otherwise there is something wrong with the rubric. I also believed that teachers should be rated with respect to known standards, not compared to their colleagues; in other words, teachers should not be graded on a curve. All this translated into the following philosophy for each level:

Level 4 should be reserved for teachers who are truly exceptional, well above standards, superb. Making the top level a "high bar" addresses a perennial problem with teacher evaluation—grade inflation. The clear expectation would be that only truly extraordinary teachers would be rated at this level.

Level 3 should represent really solid professional work—the expected norm of performance—without the slightest suggestion of mediocrity. Teachers who are working at Level 3 should be able to hold their heads high (while still, perhaps, aspiring to reach the highest level).

Level 2 is barely passing and should convey the clear message that performance is not good enough and needs to be improved. No teacher should be comfortable with ratings at this level—it's not a "getting by" rating; it's mediocre and unacceptable. Educators would not want their own children to be in the classroom of a Level 2 teacher.

Level 1 is clearly unsatisfactory, below standards, unacceptable, and headed straight toward job termination unless improvements are made—but the label should avoid using a word that sounds terminal and inescapable. The rubrics have to hold out hope and push for improvement.

Applying this philosophy and choosing words very carefully, these are the labels I decided on:

4—Expert

3—Proficient

2—Needs Improvement

1—Does Not Meet Standards

Step Three—Sorting the Criteria

The most difficult part of constructing rubrics is deciding on the criteria that belong in each domain and writing them in clear, succinct language. I found that the best approach was to start by drafting the Proficient level for each domain and doing all the writing, editing, sorting, synthesizing, sequencing, and getting feedback from critical friends *before* teasing out the criteria for the other three levels. If you are thinking about tweaking these rubrics, I highly recommend getting the Proficient level right first. If you try to edit all four levels at once, you'll drive yourself crazy.

Educators and laypeople have been coming up with lists of desirable teacher qualities from time immemorial, and there are literally thousands to work with. I delved into the literature and the recent ideas from schools and districts, picked the best, and sorted them into the six buckets. I found a surprising amount of convergence on certain bedrock principles of good teaching, and began combining and consolidating. To my surprise, each domain boiled down to exactly ten criteria. Finally, I did some serious wordsmithing to reduce each descriptor to as few words as possible, based on the belief that brevity and succinctness increase the likelihood that the rubrics will be useful to principals and teachers).

You will note that there are no items in the rubrics directly assessing whether students have learned what's been taught. Why not? After all, isn't learning the "bottom line" of teaching? True, but as I argued in Chapter Two, there are several reasons why teacher evaluation isn't the best place for administrators to address student learning results. A better strategy, as described in Chapter Five, is for principals to create "professional learning communities" and hold same-subject and same-grade teachers accountable for the key processes involved: working toward common learning goals, giving frequent interim assessments (every four to nine weeks), and using the data from those assessments to continuously improve their teaching and help struggling students. I believe this "engine of improvement" will run most smoothly and powerfully in a low-stakes environment, with teacher teams owning data-driven improvement. My rubrics evaluate this research-based process for improving teaching, not the student achievement gains that should result.

My rubric-building steps produced the following list of criteria for proficient-level teaching:

Teacher Evaluation Criteria—Proficient Level

A. Planning and preparation for learning
- Knows the subject matter well and has a good grasp of child development and how students learn.
- Plans the year so students will meet state standards and be ready for external assessments.
- Plans most curriculum units backwards with standards, state tests, and some of Bloom's levels in mind.
- Plans on-the-spot and unit assessments to measure student learning.
- Anticipates misconceptions and confusions that students might have.
- Designs lessons focused on measurable outcomes aligned with unit goals and state standards.
- Designs lessons that are relevant, motivating, and likely to engage students in active learning.
- Designs lessons that use an effective, multicultural mix of materials.
- Designs lessons that target diverse learning needs, styles, and interests.
- Organizes classroom furniture, materials, and displays to support unit and lesson goals.

B. Classroom management
- Clearly communicates and consistently enforces high standards for student behavior.
- Is fair and respectful toward students and builds positive relationships.
- Commands respect and refuses to tolerate disruption.
- Fosters positive interactions among students and teaches useful social skills.
- Teaches routines and has students maintain them all year.
- Develops students' self-discipline and teaches them to take responsibility for their own actions.
- Has a repertoire of discipline moves and can capture and maintain students' attention.
- Maximizes academic learning time through coherence, lesson momentum, and smooth transitions.
- Is a confident, dynamic presence and nips most discipline problems in the bud.
- Uses incentives wisely to encourage and reinforce student cooperation.

C. Delivery of instruction
- Conveys to students, This is important, you can do it, and I'm not going to give up on you.
- Tells students that it's okay to make mistakes; effective effort, not innate ability, is the key.
- Gives students a clear sense of purpose by posting the unit's essential questions and the lesson's goals.
- Activates students' prior knowledge and hooks their interest in each unit and lesson.
- Uses clear explanations, appropriate language, and good examples to present material.

- Orchestrates effective strategies, materials, and classroom groupings to foster student learning.

- Has students actively think about, discuss, and use the ideas and skills being taught.

- Differentiates and scaffolds instruction to accommodate most students' learning needs.

- Is flexible about modifying lessons to take advantage of teachable moments.

- Has students sum up what they have learned and apply it in a different context.

D. Monitoring, assessment, and follow-up

- Posts clear criteria for proficiency, including rubrics and exemplars of student work.

- Diagnoses students' knowledge and skills up front and makes small adjustments based on the data.

- Frequently checks for understanding and gives students helpful information if they seem confused.

- Has students set goals, self-assess, and know where they stand academically at all times.

- Regularly posts students' work to make visible and celebrate their progress with respect to standards.

- Uses data from interim assessments to adjust teaching, re-teach, and follow up with failing students.

- Takes responsibility for students who are not succeeding and gives them extra help.

- When necessary, refers students for specialized diagnosis and extra help.

- Analyzes data from assessments, draws conclusions, and shares them appropriately.

- Reflects on the effectiveness of lessons and units and continuously works to improve them.

E. Family and community outreach

- Communicates respectfully with parents and is sensitive to different families' culture and values.

- Shows parents a genuine interest and belief in each child's ability to reach standards.

- Gives parents clear, succinct expectations for student learning and behavior for the year

- Promptly informs parents of behavior and learning problems, and also updates parents on good news.

- Updates parents on the unfolding curriculum and suggests ways to support learning at home.

- Assigns appropriate homework, holds students accountable for turning it in, and gives feedback.

- Responds promptly to parent concerns and makes parents feel welcome in the classroom.

- Uses conferences and report cards to give parents feedback on their children's progress.

- Tries to contact all parents and is tenacious in contacting hard-to-reach parents.

- Reaches out to families and community agencies to bring in volunteers and additional resources.

F. Professional responsibilities

- Has very good attendance.

- Is punctual and reliable with paperwork, duties, and assignments; keeps accurate records.

- Demonstrates professional demeanor and maintains appropriate boundaries.

- Is ethical and above-board, uses good judgment, and maintains confidentiality with student records.

- Shares responsibility for grade-level and schoolwide activities and volunteers to serve on committees.

- Is a positive team player and contributes ideas, expertise, and time to the overall mission of the school.

- Keeps the administration informed about concerns and asks for help when it's needed.

- Listens thoughtfully to other viewpoints and responds constructively to suggestions and criticism.

- Collaborates with colleagues to plan units, share teaching ideas, and look at student work.

- Seeks out effective teaching ideas from colleagues, supervisors, workshops, reading, and the Internet.

Step Four—Creating the Rubrics

The last step was teasing out these Proficient teaching criteria to the other three levels: Expert, Needs Improvement, and Does Not Meet Standards. This required some careful writing to reflect the philosophy behind the different performance levels, with the top rating reserved for truly exceptional performance, the third for marginal performance that clearly needs to change, and the bottom rating denoting unacceptable performance that will result in job action if it doesn't improve. I worked hard to capture the spirit of each level and fit each rubric onto one sheet of paper, creating a slim, user-friendly packet.

My original format had each descriptor running across the page. This approach lends itself to using a highlighter to swipe each chosen line, creating a vivid graphic display of the teacher's overall performance. But I was persuaded by feedback from principals to switch to a grid format with single-word tag-lines for each criterion, and that's the format presented in this chapter. This format makes it easier for the principal and teacher to look horizontally to see the gradations of performance for each criterion and then vertically to see the overall picture of performance.

What about written comments supplementing rubric scores? In both formats, there's very little space at the bottom of each page for written comments. This is intentional! Most of what a principal has to say to each teacher should be communicated in the choice of rubric levels, and any supplementary comments or commendations should be as succinct as possible. Principals can use a highlighter or, if the rubrics are in electronic form, fill in the chosen levels for a given teacher in a particular color.

The final step in creating the rubrics was writing a summary page that allows the principal to pull the overall ratings for each of the six domains together in one place so the teachers can each see a summary of their performance. There's also space for the principal and the teacher to write comments and for both to sign off on the evaluation (with the standard disclaimer that the teacher's signature doesn't necessarily denote agreement with the evaluation). The rubrics and the summary page are printed in full on the following pages (Table 7.1 A–F, followed by a summary evaluation page, Exhibit 7.1).

RUBRICS

Table 7.1 Teacher Evaluation Rubrics
A. Planning and Preparation for Learning

The Teacher:	4 Expert	3 Proficient	2 Needs Improvement	1 Does Not Meet Standards
a. Knowledge	Is expert in the subject area and has a cutting-edge grasp of child development and how students learn.	Knows the subject matter well and has a good grasp of child development and how students learn.	Is somewhat familiar with the subject and has a few ideas of ways students develop and learn.	Has little familiarity with the subject matter and few ideas on how to teach it and how students learn.
b. Strategy	Has a well-honed game plan for the year that is tightly aligned with state standards and assessments.	Plans the year so students will meet state standards and be ready for external assessments.	Has done some thinking about how to cover high standards and test requirements this year.	Plans lesson by lesson and has little familiarity with state standards and tests.
c. Alignment	Plans all units backwards, aligned with high standards, state assessments, and all of Bloom's levels.	Plans most curriculum units backwards with standards, state tests, and some of Bloom's levels in mind.	Plans lessons with some thought to larger goals and objectives and higher-order thinking skills.	Teaches on an ad hoc basis with little or no consideration for long-range curriculum goals.
d. Assessments	Prepares diagnostic, on-the-spot, interim, and summative assessments to monitor student learning.	Plans on-the-spot and unit assessments to measure student learning.	Drafts unit tests as instruction proceeds.	Writes final tests shortly before they are given.
e. Anticipation	Anticipates misconceptions that students are likely to have and plans how to overcome them.	Anticipates misconceptions and confusions that students might have.	Has a hunch about one or two ways that students might become confused with the content.	Proceeds without considering misconceptions that students might have about the material.

f. Lessons	Designs lessons with clear, measurable goals closely aligned with standards and unit outcomes.	Designs lessons focused on measurable outcomes aligned with unit goals and state standards.	Plans lessons with unit goals in mind.	Plans lessons aimed primarily at entertaining students or covering textbook chapters.
g. Engagement	Designs highly relevant lessons that will motivate all students and sweep them up in active learning.	Designs lessons that are relevant, motivating, and likely to engage students in active learning.	Plans lessons that will catch some students' interest and perhaps get a discussion going.	Plans lessons with very little likelihood of motivating or involving students.
h. Materials	Designs lessons involving an appropriate mix of top-notch, multicultural learning materials.	Designs lessons that use an effective, multicultural mix of materials.	Plans lessons that involve a mixture of good and mediocre learning materials.	Plans lessons that rely mainly on mediocre and low-quality textbooks, workbooks, or worksheets.
i. Differentiation	Designs lessons that break down complex tasks and address all learning needs, styles, and interests.	Designs lessons that target diverse learning needs, styles, and interests.	Plans lessons with some thought as to how to accommodate special needs students.	Plans lessons aimed at the middle of the class.
j. Environment	Artfully uses room arrangement, materials, and displays to maximize student learning of all material.	Organizes classroom furniture, materials, and displays to support unit and lesson goals.	Organizes furniture and materials to support the lesson, with only a few decorative displays.	Has a conventional furniture arrangement, hard-to-access materials, and few wall displays.

Overall rating: _____   Comments:

B. Classroom Management

The Teacher:	4 Expert	3 Proficient	2 Needs Improvement	1 Does Not Meet Standards
a. Expectations	Is direct, specific, consistent, and tenacious in communicating and enforcing very high expectations.	Clearly communicates and consistently enforces high standards for student behavior.	Announces and posts classroom rules and punishments.	Comes up with ad hoc rules and punishments as events unfold during the year.
b. Relationships	Shows warmth, caring, respect, and fairness for all students and builds strong relationships.	Is fair and respectful toward students and builds positive relationships.	Is fair and respectful toward most students and builds positive relationships with some.	Is sometimes unfair and disrespectful to the class; plays favorites.
c. Respect	Wins all students' respect and creates a climate in which disruption of learning is unthinkable.	Commands respect and refuses to tolerate disruption.	Wins the respect of some students but there are regular disruptions in the classroom.	Is not respected by students and the classroom is frequently chaotic and sometimes dangerous.
d. Social-Emotional	Implements a program that successfully develops positive interactions and social-emotional skills.	Fosters positive interactions among students and teaches useful social skills.	Often lectures students on the need for good behavior, and makes an example of "bad" students.	Publicly berates "bad" students, blaming them for their poor behavior.
e. Routines	Successfully inculcates class routines so that students maintain them throughout the year.	Teaches routines and has students maintain them all year.	Tries to train students in class routines but many of the routines are not maintained.	Does not teach routines and is constantly nagging, threatening, and punishing students.

f. Responsibility	Successfully develops students' self-discipline, self-confidence, and a sense of responsibility.	Develops students' self-discipline and teaches them to take responsibility for their own actions.	Tries to get students to be responsible for their actions, but many lack self-discipline.	Is unsuccessful in fostering self-discipline in students; they are dependent on the teacher to behave.
g. Repertoire	Has a highly effective discipline repertoire and can capture and hold students' attention any time.	Has a repertoire of discipline moves and can capture and maintain students' attention.	Has a limited disciplinary repertoire and students are frequently not paying attention.	Has few discipline moves and constantly struggles to get students' attention.
h. Efficiency	Uses coherence, lesson momentum, and silky-smooth transitions to get the most out of every minute.	Maximizes academic learning time through coherence, lesson momentum, and smooth transitions.	Sometimes loses teaching time due to lack of clarity, interruptions, and inefficient transitions.	Loses a great deal of instructional time because of confusion, interruptions, and ragged transitions.
i. Prevention	Is alert, poised, dynamic, and self-assured and nips virtually all discipline problems in the bud.	Is a confident, dynamic presence and nips most discipline problems in the bud.	Tries to prevent discipline problems but sometimes little things escalate into big problems.	Is unsuccessful at spotting and preventing discipline problems, and they frequently escalate.
j. Incentives	Gets students to buy in to a highly effective system of incentives linked to intrinsic rewards.	Uses incentives wisely to encourage and reinforce student cooperation.	Uses extrinsic rewards in an attempt to get students to cooperate and comply.	Gives away goodies (such as free time) without using it as a lever to improve behavior.

Overall rating: _____ Comments:

C. Delivery of Instruction

The Teacher:	4 Expert	3 Proficient	2 Needs Improvement	1 Does Not Meet Standards
a. Expectations	Exudes high expectations and determination and convinces all students that they will master the material.	Conveys to students: This is important, you can do it, and I'm not going to give up on you.	Tells students that the subject matter is important and they need to work hard.	Gives up on some students as hopeless.
b. Effort-Based	Teaches students to be risk-takers, learn from mistakes, and believe that through effective effort, they will get smarter.	Tells students it's okay to make mistakes; effective effort, not innate ability, is the key.	Tells students that making mistakes doesn't mean they're stupid; they can learn from errors.	Doesn't prevent many students from feeling embarrassed when they make mistakes in school.
c. Goals	Shows students exactly what's expected by posting essential questions, goals, rubrics, and exemplars.	Gives students a clear sense of purpose by posting the unit's essential questions and the lesson's goals.	Tells students the main learning objectives of each lesson.	Begins lessons without giving students a sense of where instruction is headed.
d. Connections	Always grabs students' interest and makes connections to prior knowledge, experience, and reading.	Activates students' prior knowledge and hooks their interest in each unit and lesson.	Tries to make the subject interesting and relate it to things students already know.	Rarely hooks students' interest or makes connections to their lives.
e. Clarity	Always presents material clearly and explicitly, with well-chosen examples and vivid and appropriate language.	Uses clear explanations, appropriate language, and good examples to present material.	Sometimes uses language and explanations that are fuzzy, confusing, or inappropriate.	Often presents material in a confusing way, using language that is inappropriate.

f. Repertoire	Orchestrates highly effective strategies, materials, and groupings to involve and motivate students.	Orchestrates effective strategies, materials, and classroom groupings to foster student learning.	Uses a limited range of classroom strategies, materials, and groupings with mixed success.	Uses only one or two teaching strategies and types of materials and fails to reach most students.
g. Engagement	Gets all students highly involved in focused work in which they are active learners and problem-solvers.	Has students actively think about, discuss, and use the ideas and skills being taught.	Attempts to get students actively involved but some students are disengaged.	Mostly lectures to passive students or has them plod through textbooks and worksheets.
h. Differentiation	Skillfully meets the learning needs and styles of all students by differentiating and scaffolding.	Differentiates and scaffolds instruction to accommodate most students' learning needs.	Attempts to accommodate students with special needs, with mixed success.	Fails to provide for differentiated instruction for students with special needs.
i. Nimbleness	Deftly adapts lessons and units to exploit teachable moments and correct misunderstandings.	Is flexible about modifying lessons to take advantage of teachable moments.	Is focused on implementing lesson plans and sometimes misses teachable moments.	Is rigid and inflexible with lesson plans and rarely takes advantage of teachable moments.
j. Application	Consistently has students summarize and internalize what they learn and apply it to real-life situations.	Has students sum up what they have learned and apply it in a different context.	Asks students to think about real-life applications for what they are studying.	Moves on at the end of each lesson and unit without having students summarize.

Overall rating: _____   Comments:

D. Monitoring, Assessment, and Follow-Up

The Teacher:	4 Expert	3 Proficient	2 Needs Improvement	1 Does Not Meet Standards
a. Criteria	Posts and reviews the criteria for proficient work, including rubrics and exemplars, and students internalize them.	Posts clear criteria for proficiency, including rubrics and exemplars of student work.	Tells students some of the qualities that their finished work should exhibit.	Expects students to know (or figure out) what it takes to get good grades.
b. Diagnosis	Gives students a well-constructed diagnostic assessment up front, and uses the information to fine-tune instruction.	Diagnoses students' knowledge and skills up front and makes small adjustments based on the data.	Does a quick K-W-L (Know, Want to Know, Learned) exercise before beginning a unit.	Begins instruction without diagnosing students' skills and knowledge.
c. On-The-Spot	Uses a variety of effective methods to check for understanding; immediately unscrambles confusion and clarifies.	Frequently checks for understanding and gives students helpful information if they seem confused.	Uses moderately effective methods (such as thumbs up, thumbs down) to check for understanding during instruction.	Uses ineffective methods ("Is everyone with me?") to check for understanding.
d. Self-Assessment	Has students set ambitious goals, continuously self-assess, and take responsibility for improving performance.	Has students set goals, self-assess, and know where they stand academically at all times.	Urges students to look over their work, see where they had trouble, and aim to improve those areas.	Allows students to move on without assessing and improving problems in their work.
e. Recognition	Frequently posts students' work with rubrics and commentary and uses it to motivate and direct effort.	Regularly posts students' work to make visible and celebrate their progress with respect to standards.	Posts some 'A' student work as an example to others.	Posts only a few samples of student work or none at all.

f. Interims	Works with colleagues to use interim assessment data, fine-tune teaching, re-teach, and help struggling students.	Uses data from interim assessments to adjust teaching, re-teach, and follow up with failing students.	Looks over students' tests to see if there is anything that needs to be re-taught.	Gives tests and moves on without analyzing them and following up with students.
g. Tenacity	Relentlessly follows up with struggling students with personal attention to reach proficiency.	Takes responsibility for students who are not succeeding and gives them extra help.	Offers students who fail tests some additional time to study and do re-takes.	Tells students that if they fail a test, that's it; the class has to move on to cover the curriculum.
h. Support	Makes sure that students who need specialized diagnosis and help receive appropriate services immediately.	When necessary, refers students for specialized diagnosis and extra help.	Sometimes doesn't refer students promptly for special help, or refers students who don't need it.	Fails to refer students for special services or refers students who do not need them.
i. Analysis	Works with colleagues to analyze and chart assessment data, draw action conclusions, and share them with others.	Analyzes data from assessments, draws conclusions, and shares them appropriately.	Records students' grades and notes some general patterns for future reference.	Records students' grades and moves on with the curriculum.
j. Reflection	Works with colleagues to reflect on what worked and what didn't and continuously improve instruction.	Reflects on the effectiveness of lessons and units and continuously works to improve them.	At the end of a teaching unit or semester, thinks about what might have been done better.	Does not draw lessons for the future when teaching is unsuccessful.

Overall rating: _____ Comments:

E. Family and Community Outreach

The Teacher:	4 Expert	3 Proficient	2 Needs Improvement	1 Does Not Meet Standards
a. Respect	Shows great sensitivity and respect for family and community culture, values, and beliefs.	Communicates respectfully with parents and is sensitive to different families' culture and values.	Tries to be sensitive to the culture and beliefs of students' families but sometimes has a tin ear.	Is often insensitive to the culture and beliefs of students' families.
b. Belief	Shows parents an in-depth knowledge of their children and a strong belief that they will meet or exceed standards.	Shows parents a genuine interest and belief in each child's ability to reach standards.	Tells parents that he or she cares about their children and wants the best for them.	Does not communicate to parents knowledge of individual children or concern about their future.
c. Expectations	Gives parents clear, user-friendly learning and behavior expectations and exemplars of proficient work.	Gives parents clear, succinct expectations for student learning and behavior for the year.	Sends home a list of classroom rules and the syllabus for the year.	Does not inform parents about learning and behavior expectations.
d. Communication	Makes sure parents hear positive news about their children first, and immediately flags any problems.	Promptly informs parents of behavior and learning problems, and also updates parents on good news.	Lets parents know about problems their children are having but rarely mentions positive news.	Seldom informs parents of concerns or positive news about their children.
e. Involving	Frequently involves parents in supporting and enriching the curriculum as it unfolds.	Updates parents on the unfolding curriculum and suggests ways to support learning at home.	Sends home occasional suggestions on how parents can help their children with schoolwork.	Rarely if ever communicates with parents on ways to help their children at home.

f. Homework	Assigns highly engaging homework, gets close to a 100% return, and provides rich feedback.	Assigns appropriate homework, holds students accountable for turning it in, and gives feedback.	Assigns homework, keeps track of compliance, but rarely follows up.	Assigns homework but is resigned to the fact that many students won't turn it in, and doesn't follow up.
g. Responsiveness	Deals immediately and successfully with parent concerns and makes parents feel welcome any time.	Responds promptly to parent concerns and makes parents feel welcome in the school.	Is slow to respond to some parent concerns and gives off an unwelcoming vibe.	Does not respond to parent concerns and makes parents feel unwelcome in the classroom.
h. Reporting	In conferences, report cards, and informal talks, gives parents detailed and helpful feedback on children's progress.	Uses conferences and report cards to give parents feedback on their children's progress.	Uses report card conferences to tell parents the areas in which their children can improve.	Gives out report cards and expects parents to deal with the areas that need improvement.
i. Outreach	Is successful in contacting and working with all parents, including those who are hard to reach.	Tries to contact all parents and is tenacious in contacting hard-to-reach parents.	Tries to contact all parents, but ends up talking mainly to the parents of high-achieving students.	Makes little or no effort to contact parents.
j. Resources	Successfully enlists classroom volunteers and extra resources from homes and the community.	Reaches out to families and community agencies to bring in volunteers and additional resources.	Asks parents to volunteer in the classroom and contribute extra resources.	Does not reach out for extra support from parents or the community.

Overall rating: _____ Comments:

F. Professional Responsibilities

The Teacher:	4 Expert	3 Proficient	2 Needs Improvement	1 Does Not Meet Standards
a. Attendance	Has perfect or near-perfect attendance.	Has very good attendance.	Has mediocre attendance.	Has poor attendance.
b. Reliability	Carries out assignments conscientiously and punctually, keeps meticulous records, and is never late.	Is punctual and reliable with paperwork, duties, and assignments; keeps accurate records.	Occasionally skips assignments, is late, makes errors in records, and misses paperwork deadlines.	Frequently skips assignments, is late, makes errors in records, and misses paperwork deadlines.
c. Professionalism	Presents as a consummate professional and always observes appropriate boundaries.	Demonstrates professional demeanor and maintains appropriate boundaries.	Occasionally acts and/or dresses in an unprofessional manner and violates boundaries.	Frequently acts and/or dresses in an unprofessional manner and violates boundaries.
d. Judgment	Is invariably ethical, honest, and above-board, uses impeccable judgment, and respects confidentiality.	Is ethical and above-board, uses good judgment, and maintains confidentiality with student records.	Sometimes uses questionable judgment, is less than completely honest, and discloses student information.	Acts in an ethically questionable manner, uses poor judgment, and/or discloses student information.
e. Teamwork	Is an important member of teacher teams and committees and frequently attends after-school activities.	Shares responsibility for grade-level and schoolwide activities and volunteers to serve on committees.	When asked, will serve on a committee and attend an after-school activity.	Declines invitations to serve on committees and attend after-school activities.

f. Contributions	Frequently contributes valuable ideas and expertise that further the school's mission.	Is a positive team player and contributes ideas, expertise, and time to the overall mission of the school.	Occasionally suggests an idea aimed at improving the school.	Rarely if ever contributes ideas that might help improve the school.
g. Communication	Informs the administration of any concerns and reaches out for help and suggestions when needed.	Keeps the administration informed about concerns and asks for help when it's needed.	Is reluctant to share concerns with the administration or ask for help.	Bottles up concerns or constantly complains, and is not open to help.
h. Openness	Actively seeks out feedback and suggestions and uses them to improve performance.	Listens thoughtfully to other viewpoints and responds constructively to suggestions and criticism.	Is somewhat defensive but does listen to feedback and suggestions.	Is very defensive about criticism and resistant to changing classroom practice.
i. Collaboration	Meets at least weekly with colleagues to plan units, share ideas, and analyze interim assessments.	Collaborates with colleagues to plan units, share teaching ideas, and look at student work.	Meets occasionally with colleagues to share ideas about teaching and students.	Meets infrequently with colleagues, and conversations lack educational substance.
j. Self-Improvement	Devours best practices from fellow professionals, workshops, reading, study groups, the Internet, and other sources.	Seeks out effective teaching ideas from supervisors, colleagues, workshops, reading, and the Internet.	Keeps an eye out for new ideas for improving teaching and learning.	Is not open to ideas for improving teaching and learning.

Overall rating: _____   Comments:

Exhibit 7.1
Evaluation Summary Page

Teacher's name: _____ School year: _____

School: _____ Subject area: _____

Evaluator: _____ Position: _____

RATINGS ON INDIVIDUAL RUBRICS:

A. *Planning and Preparation for Learning:*

    Expert   Proficient   Needs Improvement   Does Not Meet Standards

B. *Classroom Management:*

    Expert   Proficient   Needs Improvement   Does Not Meet Standards

C. *Delivery of Instruction:*

    Expert   Proficient   Needs Improvement   Does Not Meet Standards

D. *Monitoring, Assessment, and Follow-Up:*

    Expert   Proficient   Needs Improvement   Does Not Meet Standards

E. *Family and Community Outreach:*

    Expert   Proficient   Needs Improvement   Does Not Meet Standards

F. *Professional Responsibilities:*

    Expert   Proficient   Needs Improvement   Does Not Meet Standards

OVERALL RATING:

    Expert   Proficient   Needs Improvement   Does Not Meet Standards

OVERALL COMMENTS BY PRINCIPAL:

OVERALL COMMENTS BY TEACHER:

Principal's signature: _____ Date: _____

Teacher's signature: _____ Date: _____

(By signing, the teacher acknowledges having seen and discussed the evaluation; it does not necessarily denote agreement with the report.)

INTRODUCING AND USING THE RUBRICS

For principals presenting these rubrics to teachers for the first time, I have a suggestion. At first blush, the full set of rubrics can seem quite daunting. A gentler way to introduce them is the way they are rolled out in this chapter. First explain the rationale and history of teacher evaluation rubrics, then how the six domains were chosen and the rationale behind the rating scale, then the criteria for the Proficient level (a list only sixty items long), and finally how those were teased out to create the full six-page instrument. (In charter and private schools, where there might be more building-level discretion in shaping the rubrics, principals might want to ask teachers to make suggestions for tweaking the rubrics, which would foster a greater degree of ownership.)

These rubrics cover every aspect of a teacher's professional work and are designed for summative, end-of-year evaluation. As with any evaluation system, it's essential that at the beginning of every year, the rubrics are presented to the staff for review and sign-off by all teachers. The rubrics are the school's definition of good (and not-so-good) instruction, and it's important ethically and legally for all employees to have advance notice of the criteria by which they will be evaluated.

For principals to do a good job filling out such comprehensive rubrics, it's necessary to gather lots of information on each teacher. One approach that *won't* work is trying to complete the rubrics based on observing one or two lessons. These rubrics are not checklists for clinical supervision or mini-observations. They are best used to pull together all the impressions gathered in the course of a school year. If rubric scores are to be thorough and credible, principals need to be in classrooms, corridors, team meetings, professional development sessions, and other school events on a regular basis. As described in Chapter Three and Chapter Four, I believe the best way to make a fair appraisal of classroom performance—and to give teachers interim feedback as the year progresses—is frequent, unannounced mini-observations (ten to fifteen per teacher per year) with face-to-face follow-up conversations on each visit within twenty-four hours.

I have presented these rubrics to numerous groups of educators and am occasionally asked whether it's fair to hold first-year teachers to the same standard as their more experienced colleagues. Should the Needs Improvement level be an acceptable score for rookies, or should a less comprehensive set of rubrics be used? I think not. The best thing we can do with novice teachers is to give them a clear sense of the school's definition of good teaching and then provide lots of feedback and support as their first year unfolds. It's certainly understandable if a beginning teacher has fewer Proficient and Expert scores on the rubric, but receiving honest feedback on rigorous criteria is one of the best ways to get better—and mediocrity should never be accepted. Low scores are feedback, and as Ken Blanchard has said, "Feedback is the breakfast of champions."

Another implementation question with these rubrics is whether the six domains should be equally weighted when determining teachers' overall performance. Should Classroom Management and Delivery of Instruction, for example, be given more weight than the other four domains? The argument could be made that management and instruction are more central to a teacher's performance and tell the most about what students are experiencing day by day. The question, however, is whether it's important to know a teacher's overall score on the rubrics. What matters most, it seems to me, is providing all teachers with detailed feedback on their performance and deciding if job action—or commendation—is in order.

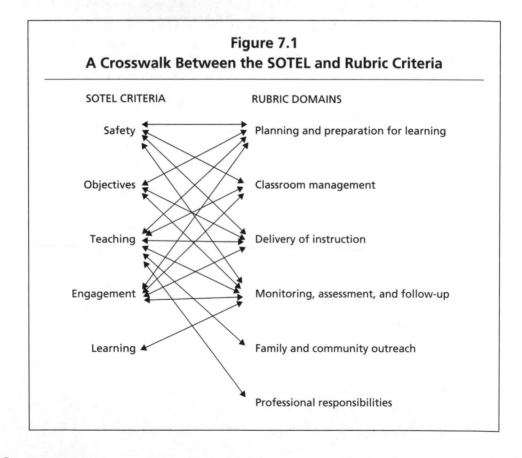

Figure 7.1
A Crosswalk Between the SOTEL and Rubric Criteria

SOTEL CRITERIA

RUBRIC DOMAINS

Safety

Objectives

Teaching

Engagement

Learning

Planning and preparation for learning

Classroom management

Delivery of instruction

Monitoring, assessment, and follow-up

Family and community outreach

Professional responsibilities

I'm not convinced that the overall scores on the rubrics need any more refinement. But this is a question that can be debated and decided within each district and school using the rubrics.

What is the relationship between the rubrics and the SOTEL mini-observation checklist suggested in Chapter Four? (That is, Safety, Objectives, Teaching, Engagement, and Learning.) SOTEL and these rubrics substantially overlap, but they have very different purposes—a quick overview of teaching in action versus a thorough end-of-year analysis of a teacher's overall performance. Figure 7.1 presents a crosswalk between the two, showing their commonalities—and also some gaps. Where SOTEL is weakest is in assessing parent and community outreach and professional responsibilities, which are rarely visible in classroom visits. These are the areas where principals need to do the most follow-up with teachers, and where teachers' input (either verbally or filling out the rubrics themselves) is most helpful.

TEACHERS SCORING BELOW PROFICIENT

What should principals do when teachers get overall scores of Needs Improvement on these rubrics? Performance at this level is mediocre at best, and none of us would want our own children (or our beloved nieces and nephews) in a classroom with this kind of teaching. But Needs Improvement isn't grounds for dismissal. Should these teachers be allowed to skate along year after year?

Obviously this is not in the best interests of children—or colleagues—and I have a suggestion. The school district could negotiate the following clause with the teachers' union:

> An overall rating of Needs Improvement must be followed up imme-
> diately by the teacher (setting goals geared to the evaluation), the
> principal (drafting an individual improvement plan for the teacher),
> and the leadership team (providing plenty of support tailored to the
> teacher's needs). A teacher who doesn't pull up the overall rating to
> Proficient or above the following year will face dismissal.

Teachers performing at the Does Not Meet Standards level need to get a formal heads-up on the areas that need improvement *well before the end of the year*. This is the one situation where the rubrics should be used during the year, following steps like these:

1. As soon as a teacher is identified as unsatisfactory by mini-observations, the principal does an evaluation using the full set of rubrics.

2. The principal writes a diagnosis and prescription with specific recommendations or mandates for remedial action—for example, attending a workshop on classroom management, visiting an exemplary colleague's classroom, or working with a literacy coach.

3. The principal gives the teacher a specified amount of time to improve (usually a month), and then returns for a second interim evaluation.

4. This cycle is repeated with the teacher getting clear direction and support each time.

5. Any teacher who still does not meet standards after a designated number of cycles is dismissed.

Exact procedures and an appeal process need to be worked out with the district's or school's legal counsel, as should the question of whether some of the six domains should carry more weight in dismissal decisions, for example, classroom management and delivery of instruction.

Providing struggling teachers with a detailed diagnosis and prescription and a chance to improve is an important ethical and legal responsibility. It's also very time-consuming. Principals in this mode have no choice but to spend a good deal of time visiting the teacher's classroom, conferring and providing support, and writing detailed improvement plans. In situations like this, using rubrics probably won't save the administrator much time compared to conventional evaluation instruments. But for teachers performing at Levels 2, 3, and 4, rubrics are *much* less onerous.

How are unions reacting to teacher evaluation rubrics? There isn't much of a track record so far, but in districts where unions have signed off on rubrics (Alexandria, Virginia, is one), the key factors are transparency with the criteria, input in the construction of the rubrics, clear advance notice to all teachers on the process, and administrative training. With those elements in place, there is no reason why rubrics can't be accepted as the new norm for teacher evaluation.

A few U.S. school districts are using Peer Assistance and Review (PAR), a union-approved process for freeing up top-notch teachers to support and make evaluation recommendations on novice teachers and others who are having difficulty in the classroom. The sidebar titled "Peer Assistance and Review" provides a detailed description of this approach.

Peer Assistance and Review

Peer Assistance and Review (PAR) was born in Toledo in 1981, the brainchild of Dal Lawrence, then president of the local AFT branch, and spread to a number of other districts, including Cincinnati, Columbus, Rochester, and Dade County. The basic idea is to free up highly effective educators to act as "consulting teachers" for two or three years and assign them to work with novice teachers and more experienced teachers who are having difficulty. Consulting teachers help their charges with lesson and unit planning, procure curriculum materials, observe and give feedback on classes, provide emotional support, and advocate for them with the principal. Consulting teachers report to a districtwide board composed of teachers and administrators, usually co-chaired by the union president and the director of human resources. At meetings of this board, members discuss individual cases and share ideas on effective coaching strategies. Each spring, the board makes recommendations on continued employment of certain teachers to the superintendent, who decides which names to pass along to the school board.

Here is how PAR addresses several common issues:

- *Giving teachers feedback:* A well-designed PAR program assigns a caseload of 12–15 teachers to each consulting teacher and ensures that they visit classrooms at least once a week (some visits unannounced) and give ongoing feedback. Consulting teachers are also available for consultation in impromptu meetings, phone calls, and e-mails. Data from PAR districts indicate that this kind of attention and support helps teacher retention. In Columbus, for example, 80 percent of new teachers are still in the district after five years, and in Rochester the retention rate is 85 percent.

- *Linking evaluation to professional development:* Consulting teachers are in and out of classrooms on a regular basis and have a real sense of how things are going. They can build trust, give their charges ongoing instructional feedback, create individual assistance plans, and draw on authoritative standards for good teaching.

- *Telling ineffective teachers the truth:* PAR pierces the isolation of many classrooms and gives teachers constant, honest feedback on their performance from a peer who speaks from personal knowledge. Equally important, consulting teachers are held accountable for their evaluations (by their review panel) in a way that principals are not. Principals who take part in the PAR process often learn a lot about observation and feedback. Clear standards of effective teaching help everyone get beyond the hackneyed "I know good teaching when I see it" and promote conversations based on real evidence of what's going on in classrooms.

- *The credibility of evaluations:* Consulting teachers working with principals and their review panels can produce evaluations with much more heft.

- *Firing ineffective teachers:* The joint union-management committee can recommend dismissal based on far more classroom evidence and bona fide opportunities for underperforming teachers to improve. Consulting teachers, who have double credibility by virtue of their status as teachers and the time they are spending in classrooms, are willing to recommend dismissal where a teacher is not improving despite intensive support. A California principal said: "I'm working collaboratively with the union. It's a whole different feel and there's a sense that the union and I agree that we need teachers who use best practice, and we're working together to have best practices occur, and we're not opposed in terms of keeping some person in there who is not utilizing best practice. I feel like we're all on the same team and it's about children and the kind of teaching they get."

Source: Based on *Marshall Memo* 254 summary of "Taking the Lead" by Jennifer Goldstein in *American Educator,* Fall 2008 (Vol. 32, #3, p. 4–11, 36–37); available online: www.aft.org/pubs-reports/american_educator/issues/fall2008 /goldstein.pdf.

THE BRIDGE TO CONTINUOUS IMPROVEMENT

When these rubrics are used in individual end-of-year evaluations of teachers, they can have a powerful impact on performance. Supplementing that process, there are five additional ways the rubrics can improve teaching and learning: spotlighting the specific rubric criteria that address "professional learning community" activities; having teachers set goals; encouraging teachers to self-assess and bring their thoughts to end-of-year evaluation conferences; getting input from parents and students; and charting the rubric scores of the whole faculty. Let's look at each of these in more detail.

Professional Learning Community

As I argued in Chapter Five and Chapter Six, one of the principal's most important jobs is getting teachers invested in a "professional learning community" process of continuous improvement, so that teacher teams are working collaboratively on planning and assessment and a "supervisory voice" is installed inside all teachers' heads, prodding them to think constantly about what students are learning and how teaching can be improved. Nine of the rubric criteria touch on this area, and they can be used to point teachers in the direction of taking more and more responsibility for improving teaching and learning themselves in the 99.9 percent of the time when the principal is not around. Here is the cluster of PLC-related rubric elements (taken from the Proficient level):

- Plans on-the-spot and unit assessments to measure student learning.
- Uses data from assessments to adjust teaching, re-teach, and follow up with failing students.
- Analyzes data from summative assessments, draws conclusions, and shares them appropriately.
- Reflects on the effectiveness of lessons and units and continuously works to improve them.
- Shares responsibility for grade-level and schoolwide activities and volunteers to serve on committees.
- Is a positive team player and contributes ideas, expertise, and time to the overall mission of the school.
- Listens thoughtfully to other viewpoints and responds constructively to suggestions and criticism.
- Collaborates with colleagues to plan units, share teaching ideas, and look at student work.
- Seeks out effective teaching ideas from supervisors, colleagues, workshops, reading, and the Internet.

When principals introduce the rubrics at the beginning of the each year, they might highlight these criteria and stress their importance to professional growth and learning—and offer support to maximize their development in the school.

Goal Setting

When teachers use the rubrics to self-evaluate at the beginning of the year, they have a clear idea of the highest-priority areas for improvement. These would naturally translate into specific, measurable goals for the year (for example, designing and implementing two UbD curriculum units, teaching a social-competency curriculum, and becoming expert in using several new kinds of on-the-spot assessments). Teachers would be quite likely to take these goals seriously and monitor them with their principal throughout the year—in marked contrast to the safe, often meaningless goals I have seen teachers setting in the past. (*I want to improve my bulletin boards.*) As Charlotte Danielson told me, "Teachers are highly motivated to improve their performance when they have, themselves, assessed it."

Self-Assessment

Shortly before meeting with the principal to discuss the end-of-year evaluation, teachers might be encouraged to fill out the rubrics themselves. In the meeting, teacher and supervisor can put each page side by side and compare their ratings. As this process unfolds, there may be differences of opinion. In some areas, the teacher may be able to fill in gaps in the principal's knowledge (especially relating to parent and community outreach and professional responsibilities). In other areas, teachers may be hard on themselves and the principal may be in the position of reassuring them and showing them that they deserve a higher rating. (*"Come on, you're being way too tough on yourself there! I've seen you doing that very effectively with your students."*) Some teachers, on the other hand, may be overly generous with Expert ratings, and the principal will have to gently challenge them. (*"Gee, that's not the impression I've had in my mini-observations; can you give me evidence that you're doing that with your students?"*) Of course the principal decides the final scores, but evaluations will be fairer and more credible if teachers have substantive input—and the principal really listens.

Advisory Input

Including parent and student input in the evaluation process is frowned upon by teacher unions, and they have a point; most parents don't have firsthand information on what's going on in classrooms, and students can be unfair in their assessments of strict and demanding teachers. But getting advisory input from parents and students can be highly informative for teachers. Besides, it's happening on websites like RateMyTeacher.com whether educators like it or not. Using online questionnaire services like Survey Monkey, principals can gather "customer satisfaction" data on the general running of the school, and teachers can tap into a rich lode of opinion that can inform their practice and help them improve.

Charting Faculty Results

Once a principal has given ratings to an entire faculty, it's possible to create a spreadsheet that can serve as a valuable guide for prioritizing professional development. Figure 7.2 pictures a chart showing the domain ratings for a hypothetical

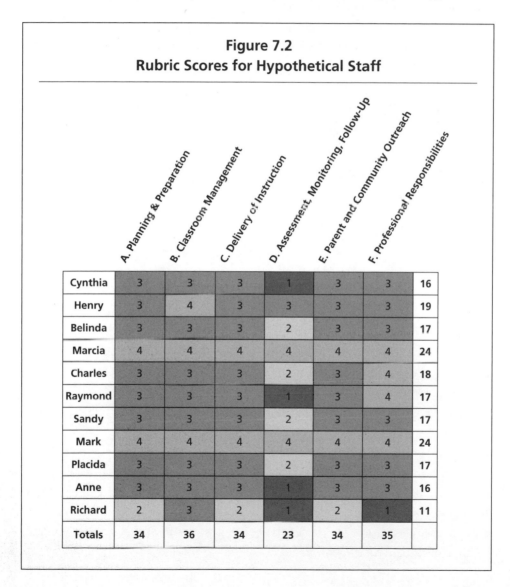

Figure 7.2
Rubric Scores for Hypothetical Staff

	A. Planning & Preparation	B. Classroom Management	C. Delivery of Instruction	D. Assessment, Monitoring, Follow-Up	E. Parent and Community Outreach	F. Professional Responsibilities	
Cynthia	3	3	3	1	3	3	16
Henry	3	4	3	3	3	3	19
Belinda	3	3	3	2	3	3	17
Marcia	4	4	4	4	4	4	24
Charles	3	3	3	2	3	4	18
Raymond	3	3	3	1	3	4	17
Sandy	3	3	3	2	3	3	17
Mark	4	4	4	4	4	4	24
Placida	3	3	3	2	3	3	17
Anne	3	3	3	1	3	3	16
Richard	2	3	2	1	2	1	11
Totals	34	36	34	23	34	35	

staff of eleven teachers. (In Excel, the cells can be color-coded to enhance the impact of the table, for example, blue for Expert ratings, green for Proficient, yellow for Needs Improvement, and red for Does Not Meet Standards.) Such a chart—which would, of course, be confidential to administrators—vividly highlights the highest priority area in a school—in this case, Assessment, Monitoring, and Follow-Up. It also reveals that two teachers—Marcia and Mark—are experts in this area, and could be very helpful to their colleagues. The principal could further refine the data, making a spreadsheet of teachers' ratings in the ten areas within Assessment, Monitoring, and Follow-Up and providing even more guidance on what kind of training and support would be most helpful to bring teachers up to speed and which teachers have expertise that could be shared with colleagues.

TAKING STOCK

Thinking back to my "This is nonsense" epiphany and its aftermath, I recall how uncomfortable I was with the cynical mode I adopted, and how deeply I resented the hours I spent writing teacher evaluations that didn't seem to be making a difference. I desperately needed a process that would allow me to give teachers clear, specific, and helpful feedback with as little paperwork as possible. And I needed all the time and the energy I was burning up on evaluation write-ups to deal with the heart of the matter—what was being taught, how well teacher teams were collaborating, whether students were learning, and how teaching could continuously improve. Looking back, I believe well-designed rubrics would have been the answer to my prayers. I envy principals who can use them today.

To be sure, rubrics are a relatively new phenomenon. It's still an open question how they will be received by districts, teachers, and unions across the country, and we don't have long-term data on their impact on student achievement. But the prospects for a positive impact on teaching and learning seem excellent. Good teacher evaluation rubrics lay out the standards for teaching excellence so that everyone knows what it takes to be proficient. Good rubrics give teachers detailed information on where they stand and provide clear direction for improvement. Most important, good rubrics allow principals to spend less time trying to document the *process* of teaching so they can spend more time focusing on *results*—on getting the "engine of improvement" running in their teacher teams and in every classroom. This is what's needed if we are to bring all of our students to high levels of achievement.

Rubrics interact with all the other elements recommended in earlier chapters, and this synergy can truly improve teaching and learning over time.

Summing up, here is a comparison of how a principal evaluates a teacher using the conventional model and the steps recommended here:

Conventional model	Proposed model
Pre-observation conference	Unit plan developed by teacher teams
Lesson plan	Common assessments written by teams
Lesson observation	Principal's feedback to teams on unit plans, assessments
Evaluation write-up	Teams meet to share ideas as each unit is taught
Post conference with teacher	Frequent principal mini-observations in all classrooms
Occasional classroom visits	Face-to-face feedback conversations with teachers
	Teams give common assessments
	Teams analyzes unit learning results, plan follow-up
	Teams discuss results with the principal
	The principal supports follow-up with students
	The principal uses rubrics for year-end evaluations

Time Management

Doing First Things First

*The reason most major goals are not achieved is that we spend
our time doing second things first.*

—Robert McKain

*The key is not to prioritize what's on your schedule, but to
schedule your priorities.*

—Stephen Covey

How can a dedicated principal work really, really hard and fail
to get significant gains in student achievement? The answer is
obvious: by spending too much time on the wrong things and
not enough time on the right things. That sounds pretty straight-
forward—but in my fifteen years as a principal, I wasn't clear enough
about the "right things" and often fell victim to HSPS—Hyperactive
Superficial Principal Syndrome. As a result, our students didn't do
nearly as well as they could have.

Over the years, I attacked the time management challenge in three ways. The
first was working *longer and harder*—finding ways to fit more into each day

and increasing my stamina and endurance. The second was working *smarter*— learning time-management tricks and steadily becoming more efficient. The third was working *deeper*—figuring out the research-based practices that were the best match for the unique circumstances of the Mather School. By the end of my principalship, I was beginning to figure out some best practices that would move student achievement, and we made some significant gains.

BEST OF BEST PRACTICES

Despite this progress, it was only after I left the Mather, immersed myself in the literature, and watched a variety of principals in action that I developed a more balanced understanding of these three layers. This chapter, addressed directly to principals, presents the following suggestions for working *deep* and working *smart* without working so hard that you burn out:

- Have a laser-like focus on student achievement and your strategic plan.
- Make sure all staff know exactly what is expected in terms of classroom instruction and discipline.
- Use a good personal planning system for the year, month, week, and day.
- Set up a schedule of meetings for key teams and make sure they happen.
- Use a good system for writing things down, prioritizing, and following up.
- Put competent people in key roles and delegate maximum responsibility to them.
- Get into classrooms and team meetings and give teachers feedback.
- Use good strategies to prevent or deflect time-wasting crises and activities.
- Take care of yourself, including family, health, exercise, sleep, and vacations.
- Regularly evaluate progress and work on continuous improvement.

These align with a rubric at the end of this chapter; you might want to use it to score yourself as you read.

Focus on Student Achievement

Have a laser-like focus on student achievement and your strategic plan.

For many principals, each day is driven by events rather than by long-range goals. All too often, the school's strategic plan, laboriously written and signed off on the year before, is a distant memory, lost in the hurly-burly of managing the school. What's a harried principal to do? Here's a step-by-step approach:

First, put student achievement data on the table and clarify the mission. The principal should ask colleagues if they are satisfied with the current level of achievement (the honest answer is almost invariably no), assert that the mission is preparing students for college success (which means getting them performing at the proficient level or above at each grade level), set a long-range target (for example, 85 percent of students achieving at proficient or above in literacy, math, and behavior in four years), and turn the discussion to how that goal will be achieved.

Second, take a big-picture look at the school and decide on the areas that need the most attention. To get results, every school needs to perform certain functions well:

- *Mission and strategy:* The entire school community is focused on high achievement for all students, research-based theories of action for producing it, long-range targets, and annual SMART goals and action plans for two or three "Big Rocks" (see discussion and sidebar later in this chapter).

- *Climate and culture:* The school is safe and humane and functions smoothly.

- *Curriculum alignment:* Teachers and students are crystal clear about year-end learning outcomes geared toward college success, unit goals, and aligned objectives for every lesson.

- *Resources:* Staff have the materials and tools needed to reach their goals.

- *Good instruction:* Hiring, supervision and evaluation, coaching, professional development, and "difficult conversations" all operate to ensure first-rate teaching for every child.

- *Interim assessments:* Teachers regularly check for understanding and use the insights they gain to fine-tune teaching and curriculum, re-teach, and follow up with struggling students.

- *Collaboration:* Teacher teams meet regularly to backwards-plan curriculum units, analyze interim assessment data and student work, share best practices, and strategize to support all students' success.

- *Safety nets:* Struggling students get prompt and effective help within and beyond the regular school day.

- *Parents:* Families are guided toward the most effective ways to support their children's achievement and future success.

Obviously all nine of these can't be top priorities, and the task is deciding which three or four most urgently need improvement. A thorough diagnosis—using surveys, interviews with key stakeholders, and perhaps focus groups—will identify those areas.

Third, craft two or three initiatives that will bring about major improvements in the priority areas. Each initiative (which can cover more than one priority) should have a research-based theory of action so there is a high level of confidence that it will work. Everyone in the school should be able to name the big projects of the year. Here are examples of initiatives adopted by a school with challenges in literacy and math achievement and student behavior (the school already has mini-observations and unit planning up and running):

- Initiative #1: A literacy push aimed at boosting all students' reading and writing achievement. It includes training of teachers in balanced literacy; interim assessments of writing every six weeks with all-hands-on-deck six-trait rubric scoring and data analysis; a full-time literacy coach to provide close-in coaching to grade-level teams and individual teachers linked to the interim assessment results; beefed-up leveled classroom libraries; and a book room stocked with leveled sets of books.

- Initiative #2: Math interim assessments five times during the year with twenty-four-hour turnaround of results using a new scanner and software; half-day data analysis meetings with teacher teams coached by the administrative team; and a scheduled follow-up three-day blitz with re-teaching for students who need it and enrichment activities for already-proficient students.

- Initiative #3: A radically improved advisory program using dramatic literature excerpts, clips from popular movies, and poetry to boost character education and the school's core values, coupled with lesson plans and staff training, all aimed at reducing bullying to near zero and building a positive, achievement-oriented culture in the school.

Fourth, develop an action plan and measurable goals for each initiative. The action plan should be short and sweet, with the theory of action for each initiative, measurable outcomes that are SMART (Specific, Measurable, Attainable, Results-oriented, and Time-bound), timelines, and a clear delineation of responsibility.

Mike Schmoker has argued (2004) that this compact document *is* a school's strategic plan.

Finally, make sure these priorities are on everyone's mind; shoehorn them into every day, week, and month of the year. This means downgrading or saying no to some other activities that are appealing and plausible but are not on the short list. In this regard, the "Big Rocks" story (see sidebar) is very helpful:

 ## The Big Rocks

One day an expert in time management was speaking to a group of business students and, to drive home a point, used an illustration those students will never forget. As he stood in front of the group of high-powered overachievers, he said, "Okay, time for a quiz."

He pulled out a one-gallon, wide-mouth mason jar and set it on the table in front of him. Then he produced about a dozen fist-sized rocks and carefully placed them, one at a time, into the jar. When the jar was filled to the top and no more rocks would fit inside, he asked, "Is this jar full?"

Everyone in the class said, "Yes."

"Really?" he said. He reached under the table and pulled out a bucket of gravel. He dumped some gravel in and shook the jar, causing pieces of gravel to work themselves down into the space between the big rocks.

He asked the group once more, "Is the jar full?" By this time, the class was on to him. "Probably not," one of them answered.

"Good," he replied. He reached under the table and brought out a bucket of sand. He started dumping the sand into the jar and it went into all the spaces left between the rocks and the gravel. Once more he asked the question, "Is the jar full?"

"No," the class shouted. Once again he said, "Good." He grabbed a pitcher of water and began to pour it in until the jar was filled to the brim.

Then he looked at the class and asked, "What is the point of this illustration?" One eager beaver raised a hand and said, "The point is, no matter how full your schedule is, if you try really hard you can always fit some more things into it!"

"No," the speaker replied, "that is not the point. The truth this illustration teaches us is that if you don't put the big rocks in first, you'll never get them in at all."

So tonight, or in the morning, when you are reflecting on this short story, ask yourself: What are the "big rocks" in my life? Time with my loved ones? My faith, my education, my dreams? A worthy cause? Teaching or mentoring others? Remember to put those BIG ROCKS in your jar first or you'll never get them in.

Source: Adapted from Covey, 1994.

The major initiatives are the school's big rocks, and they need to be put in first, claiming space that would otherwise be occupied by the time and human energy equivalents of gravel and sand and water in the school's "jar."

Putting first things first is the preeminent challenge of the principalship, and it's a daily struggle that school leaders never fully win. But there are ways of improving your average, and a higher average will make a big difference to the quality of teaching and learning. With the rocks clearly in mind, the principal can allocate time and resources, say "Sorry" to off-plan initiatives, be "present" for staff and students, and roll with the punches—because there will still be those days when everything goes wrong at once.

Clarify Expectations

Make sure staff know exactly what is expected in terms of classroom instruction and discipline.

This sounds obvious, but I'm amazed at how many teachers don't have a slim booklet that clearly states what students need to know and be able to do by the end of the year, basic classroom and schoolwide procedures and routines, and a list of the infractions that require a referral to the office (by implication, the teacher is responsible for handling everything else). Without these expectations in place, a principal will spend countless hours clarifying, reminding, and backfilling, which distracts teachers and administrators from the big rocks. (See Appendix A for a sample booklet of learning expectations.)

Plan Systematically

Use a good personal planning system for the year, month, week, and day.

A daily to-do list is not enough. Such lists often contain lots of little tasks that are easy to check off but don't address the big rocks. The tug of HSPS is so constant and so inexorable that principals need a foolproof ritual to bring year-end goals down to the daily level. For me, this was a two-hour planning block every weekend when I reviewed my targets for the year, broke them down into two-month chunks, and scheduled next steps in all key areas for the week ahead. An electronic calendar program (Outlook or Entourage, for example) is an important tool, regularly synched with a handheld device. In his excellent book, *Getting Things Done* (2001), David Allen says that the best way to reduce stress and avoid dropping the ball is to put all your professional and personal appointments, deadlines, and perennial events (for example, key birthdays and annual reminders) in one place. Long-range projects need to be broken down into concrete, manageable chunks that find their way into the calendar.

The daily to-do list is still important—as long as it reflects long-range priorities as well as all the little stuff principals must do. As principal, I tried a variety of calendars and organizational formats and finally designed and made copies of a customized sheet (see Exhibit 8.1) that I filled in as I prepared for each day. It had boxes for the seven periods of the day (to mesh my activities with teachers' and students' daily rhythm), for before- and after-school time (when there were fewer interruptions), for my weekly goals (which I copied over every day to keep them "in my face"), and a line for each homeroom (where I could jot student and staff birthdays and other reasons for classroom visits). As I filled in meetings, teacher conversations, and phone calls each day, I kept the master class schedule in front of me and was strategic about catching teachers during their free periods. At the end of most days, I was lucky if I had done half of the items on my list (hopefully I'd done the most important ones, which I highlighted with red stars). As I tore off each day's sheet and turned to a fresh one to plan for the next day, I thought hard about whether the items I hadn't done were really important. Then I either ditched them or copied them onto the next day's blank sheet along with a host of new items.

There are lots of other formats for keeping on task during a busy day. Some principals like Day-Timer calendars. Some print out their Outlook or Entourage calendar sheet for each day, put it on a clipboard, and use it to remember appointments and take notes. Some keep track on a PDA, BlackBerry, or iPhone. The key is to have a way of bringing big-picture goals down to the day-by-day level so the big rocks manage to grab a place the jar before it is filled up by other activities.

Exhibit 8.1
A Sample To-Do Format Geared to the Schedule and Homerooms of a School

Kim Marshall, Mather School 635-8757   Date:

Early-7:30	Room 1
	Room 2
	Room 3
	Room 4
Pre-9:30	Room 5
	Room 6
	Room 8
	Room 34
1-9:45	Room 36
	Room 9
	Room 10
	Room 11
2-10:30	Room 12
	Room 32
	Room 13
	Room 14
3-11:15	Room 15
	Room 16
	Room 17
	Room 18
4-12:00	Room 19
	Room 20
	Room 21
	Room 22
5-12:50	Room 23
	Room 24
	Room 25
	Room 26
6-1:40	Room 27
	Week goals:
7-2:25	
After-3:30	

Insist on Team Meetings

Set up a schedule of meetings for key teams and make sure they happen.

Unless team meetings are firmly set in people's calendars, they are easily canceled or ignored in the weekly hurly-burly. People are busy. Students are demanding. There's always too much to do, and many meetings are boring. But regular meetings of the leadership team, grade-level and subject-area teams (for unit planning, looking at interim assessment results, and sharing ideas), the student support team (for case conferences on high-risk students), and other teams are *vital* to long-range impact on students, and they deserve to have regular, scheduled times that are preempted only for genuine emergencies. Weekly meetings of same-subject, same-grade teacher teams are particularly important and deserve double blocks of uninterrupted time—a key priority for school programming. This is where the all-important "professional learning community" work of continuously improving teaching and learning can take place—but it won't happen unless the time is carved in stone in everyone's calendars and the principal monitors meetings closely.

Not Losing It

Use a good system for writing things down, prioritizing, and following up.

A quadruple challenge for principals is remembering and following up on the most important stuff, dealing with e-mail, having the right information at one's fingertips, and confronting the tendency to POUT (Put Off Unpleasant Tasks). Mastering the flow of information and being organized makes you credible and effective. But even principals with brilliant memories can't possibly retain all the information that floods in every day. I soon learned that when I lost track of things and failed to follow up, my credibility with teachers, students, and parents went out the window—and my blood pressure soared.

Most rookie principals quickly realize an ironclad rule: *you have to write things down.* But fashions conspire to prevent principals from carrying around the right equipment. Women's pants, shirts, and jackets rarely have pockets designed to hold pens, notepads, cell phones, and BlackBerrys—and a surprising number of men refuse to put a pen and piece of paper in their shirt pockets because when they were teenagers, kids who did this were mercilessly teased. So what's a principal to do? *Get over it!* Buy practical clothes, use your shirt pocket, carry around a clipboard, or use an electronic device clipped to your belt. Without ready access to a pen and paper (or a device with a stylus or a thumbpad), you're going to forget important things and earn a reputation as an unreliable flake.

When I first started as principal, I wrote down everything on various pieces of paper and then at the end of the day spent more than an hour unpacking my lists (sometimes finding it difficult to read notes I'd jotted on the fly). I finally developed a system of keeping several 3x5 note cards in my shirt pocket and writing incoming information onto one of several designated cards—one for immediate action items, one for e-mail I needed to send that afternoon, one for staff memo ideas, one for parent letter ideas. At the back of my slim stack I kept a few blank cards for random ideas. This system saved an hour a day because everything was already sorted: when I sat down to do e-mail, all the e-mail reminders were on one card; when I wrote the staff memo and the parent letter, all the ideas I needed to remember were right there. Miscellaneous ideas jotted on the blank cards could be popped straight into files in my office (for example, a quote that I could use at the next year's opening staff meeting or an idea for a different bell schedule).

One of the shibboleths of time management is that you should handle every piece of paper only once. This might work for people in high-level government and business positions with adequate support staff, but it absolutely won't work for school leaders. So what happens to all those notes and pink phone messages and U.S. mail and bits of *stuff* that flood in during the day? How can a principal be a *people person,* not a paper-pusher, in the heart of the school day? My system was to quickly scan the contents of my in-basket several times a day and use a fifteen-second rule: if an item couldn't be signed, delegated, or thrown away within fifteen seconds, it went onto my after-hours pile. In the late afternoon, when things quieted down, I began to make my way through this pile, and what didn't get finished, I took home—and what couldn't be finished in the evening went to the weekend pile (along the way, I ditched certain less-important items).

Another useful time-management tool is sorting incoming items into "bins" —metaphorical categories—and getting them off your mental desk and onto an organized list or into someone else's hands as quickly as possible. Like my pre-sorted 3x5 pocket cards, bins helped make sense of information and keep me sane. Here are some of the receptacles into which I sorted incoming stuff:

- Put in the weekly staff bulletin.
- Put in the weekly parent letter.
- Put on the agenda for the next faculty meeting.
- Suggest to grade-level teams.
- Delegate to the assistant principal.

- Delegate to the secretary.
- Delegate to the counselor.
- Have a face-to-face conversation with the person.
- Announce in the morning public-address program.
- Talk about in the weekly all-school assembly.
- Put on the agenda for the leadership team.
- Put on the late-afternoon paperwork pile.
- Politely say no.
- Discuss in a personal visit to a particular classroom.
- Write an individual note for a teacher's mailbox.
- Write and copy a group note to several members of a teacher team.
- Put on the tentative agenda for next year's beginning-of-the-year staff meeting.
- Put into the next Survey Monkey staff questionnaire.
- Drop everything and do now.

Sorting the hundreds of incoming bits of information into virtual bins like these is extraordinarily helpful in clearing your desk and being able to access the right information at the right time.

A regular staff memo—weekly seems to be most principals' choice—is an exceptionally valuable tool. It's a convenient bin for all sorts of information that the principal wants to pass along to colleagues, from the mundane to the inspirational: reminders of paperwork deadlines, fire drills, welcoming new staff members and bidding farewell to those who depart, recognizing colleagues for above-and-beyond contributions, staff and student birthdays, lost items, professional development opportunities, positive stories about teachers and students, seeking reactions to ideas, best practices and interesting research findings, good quotes, and reinforcement of the school's vision and mission. A brief, well-written memo gives everyone the same information at the same time, squashes rumors, allows the principal to deal with a lot of routine matters without taking up precious time in face-to-face meetings, and is an opportunity to bind the community together. In the memo that I published throughout my principalship (titled the *Mather Memo*), I regularly shared cartoons with an educational theme, bringing a smile to many of my colleagues' faces. Even serious principals need to lighten up occasionally!

E-mail is the next challenge. Most principals are assaulted by e-mail from sunup to sundown, often getting more than a hundred messages a day. There's a strong tendency to work on e-mail during the day to avoid a depressing build-up, but time management gurus are unanimous in saying that this is a huge mistake. Why? First, dealing with e-mail in dribs and drabs is inefficient because when we're rushed, we put aside messages that require time and thought and end up reading and thinking about them twice. E-mail should be tackled only when we have the time and concentration to deal decisively and thoroughly with all of it—that is, in the late afternoon, the evening, or the early morning. Second, constant interruptions keep leaders from focusing on the people, issues, and projects in front of them. Psychological research has shown that constant electronic distractions undermine concentration, high-level thinking, and retention (Begley, 2009). Third, doing e-mail (especially checking a hand-held device) is annoying—even insulting—to the people you're with because it makes them feel they are less important than this anonymous person who has commandeered your attention. And finally, it's much more satisfying and affirming to read and respond to a day's worth of e-mail in the late afternoon than to read messages one or two at a time. *(Is that all? Don't people love me?)* Here's how I suggest dealing with e-mail:

- If you haven't already done so, turn off the chime or beep or vibration that announces the arrival of new e-mail. An e-mail message is not like an incoming phone call; the beauty of e-mail is that it's *asynchronous*—you can answer at a time that's convenient for you (hopefully within twenty-four hours).

- Schedule one or two thirty-minute blocks (perhaps early morning and late afternoon) when you do your e-mail in concentrated, efficient bursts. It's amazing how quickly you can make your way through fifty or more e-mails.

- Let people know your e-mail philosophy so they don't expect you to respond instantly. An automatic reply message on your computer can say something like this: "I check e-mail each weekday afternoon after 3:00 PM. If your message is urgent, please call me on my cell phone, XXX-XXX-XXXX."

Okay, say you've developed an excellent system for writing things down and relegating paperwork and e-mail to blocks of times outside the heart of the school day. It's still possible to drop the ball on important matters if you fall victim to that all-too-common affliction, POUT. We all have things we hate to do—and are quite creative at putting off. Mine were financial planning and dealing with notes from angry people; I dreaded dealing with them and would handle any number of easier, lower-priority tasks before finally getting around to them, sometimes days later. Principal friends of mine confess to putting off writing teacher evaluations and the school improvement plan, scheduling, parent communication, or filing. As the 1950s cartoon character Pogo Possum said, "We have met the enemy and he is us."

So a key time management trick is having a clear sense of what your POUT demons are and developing a strategy to force yourself to deal with them in a timely manner. Eric Dawson, the head of Peace Games, hates working on the budget, so when it's time to finally do the dirty deed, he puts on a special hat so everyone in the office knows they need to leave him alone. Or maybe it's best to follow the old maxim, "Do the worst first."

Filing away paperwork is a chore many people avoid as long as possible. When paper and e-mail build up—on our desks or computers—we can't find important information when we really need it, sometimes with dire consequences. When I was principal, my pile built up inexorably, and every month or so, I would come in on a Saturday morning, put on some good music, and get it done. It was actually very satisfying, and I reaped the reward every time I was able to find something I needed.

On the question of whether to take work home, there are two distinct styles among principals I know. Some like to stay late at school, finish off as much as possible, go home in the early evening, and relax. Others like to go home in the late afternoon, take a break (exercise, watch some TV or other entertainment, spend time with family) and then do another two or three hours of work in the late evening. It's six of one, half a dozen of the other. The bottom line is getting the really important stuff done every day—and having a life.

Delegate Effectively

Put competent people in key roles and delegate maximum responsibility to them.

Some principals have a strong urge to do everything themselves, and are impatient when others don't do things just right. (I was one of those principals.) This tendency needs to be curbed! The reality is that principals can't inspire every child, observe every classroom, scrutinize every lesson plan, plan every unit, look through every student's portfolio, analyze the results of every test, lead every training workshop, and chair every team meeting. Far from it! Given the impossible number of academic challenges and the even more overwhelming number of operational demands, principals must empower teachers to do the bulk of this work—otherwise they will fall victim to HSPS and preside over a fragmented staff, abysmal student performance, and an ever-widening achievement gap.

The key to long-range sanity and effectiveness is hiring good people, nurturing them, and staying involved with their work—but refraining from micromanagement. For principals who have taken over schools with less-than-stellar staff members or have made hiring mistakes, it may be several years before optimal delegation is possible, but the goals are clear:

- Teachers handling instruction and all but the most serious discipline problems
- Teacher teams planning high-quality curriculum units and using interim assessment data to continuously improve teaching and learning
- Counselors preventing or dealing with students' emotional problems
- Custodians handling the physical plant
- Students taking increasing responsibility for their own behavior and learning
- The principal freed up to orchestrate the whole process and focus relentlessly on the big rocks (while occasionally picking up trash in the corridors)

Of course teachers and other staff members can't do their jobs when they are constantly pulled out for professional development and other meetings. I'm a big advocate of *time on task* for school staff—on the job 95 percent or more of the time. Airline pilots aren't trained while they are flying planes, and educators' professional development and administrative meetings should not encroach on contact time with students. The same goes for principals, who need to be in their buildings almost all the time (out for perhaps one meeting a month, optimally in another school where they can see exemplary instruction and leadership in action).

Delegation is essential to good time management, but there are certain things that I believe principals should do themselves. Among those are being out front to greet students as they enter school in the morning, wishing them well as they go home, being in the cafeteria during part of lunchtime, and attending key student and community events. In each of these situations, the principal's presence has great symbolic value, and principals can also use these occasions to take the pulse of the school and make themselves available for informal contact with students and staff. Visibility and accessibility really matter in this job.

It's also important that staff members know they have permission to tell the principal things that won't necessarily be pleasant to hear. Some of the worst management failures (the Space Shuttle *Challenger* disaster, for example) occur when leaders wall themselves off from honest feedback.

Observe the Work

Get into classrooms and team meetings and give teachers feedback.

As I argued in Chapter Two, conventional evaluation visits have these built-in flaws (among others): they don't give principals a very accurate picture of day-to-day instruction; they put a premium on pleasing the boss with a razzle-dazzle lesson as opposed to promoting real student learning; there is no research evidence that they improve teaching; and they are so daunting and time-consuming that they prevent principals from being in classrooms on a frequent basis. Except for gathering evidence to dismiss an ineffective teacher, conventional evaluation is a poor use of a principal's time.

Chapters Three and Four made the case for an alternative: mini-observations—frequent, unannounced visits to classrooms with prompt feedback to each teacher. Having a numerical target for a certain number of visits a day is a crucial time-management tool. Supervising a staff of forty-two teachers, my goal was five a day.

But as I said in Chapters Five and Six, it's not enough to get into classrooms and give feedback to individual teachers. Visits to team meetings are also crucial, both curriculum planning meetings and data analysis meetings. Principals don't have to sit in on all meetings, but they should drop in regularly, contribute the discussions, learn from their colleagues, and follow up with team leaders afterward.

Administer That Ounce of Prevention

Use good strategies to prevent or deflect time-wasting crises and activities.

Kenneth Freeston and Jonathan Costa (1998) believe that school leaders' work falls into three buckets: activities that add value by improving teaching and boosting achievement for all students; necessary activities that aren't sexy but keep the school running, such as ordering supplies and doing the budget; and activities that are a waste of time, like redoing things that weren't done right the first time. The principalship is a constant struggle to maximize value-added work and minimize waste work, while getting the necessary work done as efficiently as possible.

It's astonishing how much time a screw-up can consume. One morning I was walking briskly down a corridor to see a teacher, and as I passed an open classroom, I thought I heard another teacher utter the word *jackass* in front of a roomful of students. I was distracted by my immediate task and didn't focus on what he had said, but the next day, there was a huge ruckus on this corridor: a parent had stormed into the school, by-passed the office, and confronted the teacher outside his classroom for calling her daughter a jackass. There ensued a chain of events, starting with my physically separating the teacher and parent and coaxing her down to my office, that easily consumed twenty hours of my time. Had I been more attentive and promptly asked the teacher about his comment (his defense was that he told the girl that she was acting *like* a jackass) and phoned the mother immediately, the next few days would have been far more productive. Some crises can't be avoided, but anything we can do to prevent or deflect time-wasting activities saves precious energy that can be devoted to the real work.

There are lots of other ways to cut down on wasted time: meeting agendas and crisp closure with teacher teams and the faculty, multitasking (within reason), and spending very little time in your office—thus avoiding those frequent drop-ins that invariably start with the words, "Got a minute?" A sitting principal is a sitting duck!

But it is possible for principals to get so focused on being efficient that they lose sight of how they come across to their colleagues. In a charming *Phi Delta Kappan* article (2003), principal Autumn Tooms described how a visitor gently told her that she was charging around the halls of her school in a way that made her staff think she was angry. "Had I told anyone I was angry?" asked Tooms. "No. Had anyone ever asked if I was angry? No. Did it matter that my assistant principal walked the same way when she was on a mission? Again, no." Tooms realized that she needed to modulate her intensity, and she wrote "stroll" on the back of her office door and on her walkie-talkie. Tooms still got a lot done every day, but her staff no longer thought she was angry with them.

And of course there are also times when an event trumps time management—a child is seriously injured, a staff member's parent dies—and the most important thing is to drop everything and be a human being. This is perhaps the highest time-management skill: knowing when to shift gears and be there for people.

Get a Life

Take care of yourself, including family, health, exercise, sleep, and vacations.

The principalship is an intensely demanding job and there are no shortcuts; even skillful and strategic time managers are exhausted at the end of most weeks. But if you burn out, students and staff will be poorly served. Good time management includes knowing your limits, planning for the long haul, and finding ways to ways to maintain your personal energy level. Here are a few suggestions:

- Exercise faithfully (twenty minutes of vigorous exercise three times a week or thirty minutes of moderate exercise five times a week is the amount most doctors agree on).

- Eat the right foods (breakfast is the most important meal) and get enough sleep.

- Carve out regular time for relaxation and fun (one of my nonnegotiables was watching a good movie with my wife every Friday evening).

- Build a support system—friends who give you support and candid feedback, a mentor, and a sensitive and devoted Significant Other.

- Orchestrate small and large wins; there's nothing like success to produce an extra shot of optimism and energy.

Keep Improving

Regularly evaluate progress and work on continuous improvement.

Allocating time for reflection and self assessment is difficult (another time-management challenge!), but it's essential to getting better. There are a number of ways of monitoring progress and thinking about what's working and not working. I jotted notes in a personal diary every weekend, kept track of the number of classroom visits I was making, and regularly revisited my goals for the year, asking myself if I was putting my time and energy into the right activities. At the end of each year, I went through my diary and extracted twenty key words that described the most important events of the year. Over my fifteen years as principal, it was always fascinating to look back and remember the contours of each year.

I also suggest using the rubric at the end of the chapter, in Table 8.1, to score yourself now, highlighting the three strongest areas and the three that most need improvement. Develop a strategy for improving in your areas of need, and then (perhaps every three months) score yourself on the rubric again to see if you've made progress. The goal is to have all your ratings at the Proficient and Expert level. If you do, it means you're working smart and working deep, which should be a key part of being a successful principal.

TAKING STOCK

I recently did a time-and-motion study of the different ways of observing and evaluating what goes on in classrooms. Here is an estimate of the number of hours a year a principal might devote to each activity in a school with thirty-five teachers:

- Full-dress evaluations—*300 hours* (50 observations, 6 hours each)
- Mini-observations—*115 hours* (average of four a day, five minutes each, plus five-minute feedback conversations after each one)
- Showing the flag (a quick tour of all classrooms)—*80 hours* (half an hour a day most days)
- Lesson plan inspection—*70 hours* (2 hours of deskwork a week)
- Scoring rubrics and individual end-of-year principal and teacher evaluation conferences—*55 hours* (an hour per teacher to fill out rubrics, about a half-hour per teacher for conferences)
- Interim assessment monitoring—*50 hours* (5 cycles a year, 10 hours principal supervision of the process and meetings each)
- Curriculum planning—*40 hours* (6 teams, 6 times a year, 6 hours planning time each, principal there about an hour per meeting)
- Learning walks—*12 hours* a year (4 times, 2 hours for each walk-through, 1 hour to process)

Figure 8.1 is a graph showing these statistics.

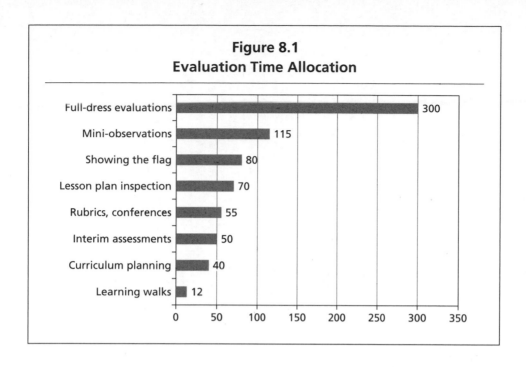

Figure 8.1
Evaluation Time Allocation

Activity	Hours
Full-dress evaluations	300
Mini-observations	115
Showing the flag	80
Lesson plan inspection	70
Rubrics, conferences	55
Interim assessments	50
Curriculum planning	40
Learning walks	12

With all the other things a principal must do, there aren't enough hours in the school year for all eight of these activities. A principal must *choose,* and a wise principal will focus time and energy on the activities that contribute the most to teaching and learning. I have argued that mini-observations, monitoring of curriculum planning and interim assessments, and using rubrics for end-of-year teacher evaluation are by far the most productive activities on the list. The time needed to do those four activities well—115 hours + 55 hours + 50 hours + 40 hours—totals 260 hours. If full-dress evaluations can be limited to those teachers in serious need of improvement—taking perhaps 40 hours of intensive classroom visits and follow-up meetings—the principal is spending the same amount of time as the conventional model (300 hours). But I believe the time is much better spent and far more likely to bring about real improvements in teaching and learning. This is a compelling argument for shifting time from unproductive conventional supervision and evaluation and focusing it on the high-gain activities described in this book. There would still be time for occasional learning walks, which can add some value to the overall school improvement effort.

Table 8.1　Principal's Time Management Rubric

	4 Expert	3 Proficient	2 Developing	1 Novice
a. Focus	I have a laser-like focus on student achievement and my strategic plan for the year.	I keep student achievement and my strategic plan in mind every day.	I periodically remind myself of my strategic plan and the goal of student achievement.	Each day is driven by events, not by my long-term goals.
b. Expectations	Staff know exactly what is expected of them in terms of classroom instruction and discipline.	Most of my staff know what is expected in terms of classroom instruction and discipline.	I often have to remind teachers of policies on instruction and discipline.	I am constantly reminding staff to use better procedures for instruction and discipline.
c. Planning	I have an effective personal planning system for the year, month, week, and day.	I write down a list of what I want to accomplish each week and day.	I come to work with a list of what I want to accomplish that day.	I have a list in my head of what I want to accomplish each day but sometimes lose track.
d. Meetings	All key teams (leadership, grade-level, student support, and others) are scheduled to meet on a regular basis.	Several key team meetings are scheduled to occur on a regular basis.	Each month I have to schedule key meetings because they are not in people's calendars.	I call grade-level, curriculum, and other meetings when there is a crisis or an immediate need.
e. Follow-up	I have a foolproof system for writing things down, prioritizing, and following up.	I almost always write important things down and follow up on the most critical ones.	I try to write things down but am swamped by events and sometimes don't follow up.	I trust my memory to retain important tasks, but I sometimes forget and drop the ball.

f. Delegation	I have highly competent people in key roles and delegate maximum responsibility to them.	I give key staff people plenty of responsibility for key items.	I have trouble letting go and delegating a number of key tasks.	I end up doing almost everything myself.
g. Supervision	I visit three to five classrooms a day and give face-to-face feedback to each teacher within twenty-four hours.	I get into some classrooms every day and give personal feedback to each teacher.	I try to get into classrooms as much as possible but many days I don't succeed.	I am so busy that I rarely visit classrooms.
h. Prevention	I have effective strategies for preventing or deflecting time-wasting crises and activities.	I am quite good at preventing or deflecting most time-wasting crises and activities.	I try to prevent them, but crises and time-wasters sometimes eat up large chunks of time.	Much of each day is consumed by crises and time-wasting activities.
i. Balance	I am sharp and fresh because I attend to family, friends, fun, exercise, nutrition, sleep, and vacations.	I am on top of my job because I mostly balance work demands with healthy habits and a life outside school.	I am sometimes unfocused because I'm not always attending to family, health, exercise, sleep, and vacations.	I am often unfocused and irascible because I neglect my family, rarely exercise, don't sleep enough, and am in poor health.
j. Self-assessment	I regularly evaluate progress toward my goals and work on continuous improvement.	I periodically review how I am doing on my weekly goals and try to do better.	I try to keep track of how I am doing on my goals.	I occasionally berate myself for not accomplishing my long-range goals.

Overall rating: _____ Comments:

Putting It All Together

*The core mission of formal education to not simply to ensure
that students are taught but to ensure that they learn.*

—Richard DuFour

This book tells the story from the ground up—my experience as a maverick teacher, my early struggles as a principal, some rookie missteps supervising and evaluating teachers, success with mini-observations, baby steps with curriculum planning and interim assessments, and then, after I left the Mather School, strengthening these pieces and adding time-efficient year-end teacher evaluation rubrics. I believe that these four elements support and enhance each other (see Figure 9.1), setting up a dynamic that continuously improves teaching and produces dramatic gains in student achievement—especially for students who enter school with disadvantages.

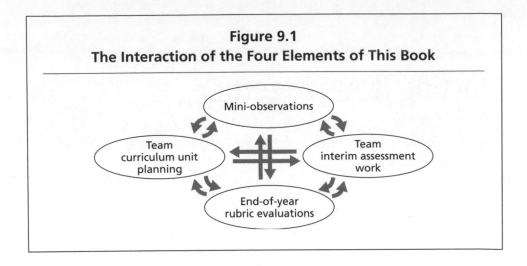

Figure 9.1
The Interaction of the Four Elements of This Book

Mini-observations

Team curriculum unit planning

Team interim assessment work

End-of-year rubric evaluations

SUPPORTING SCHOOL-LEVEL CHANGE

Is it possible for a school to get this process going on its own? In a few cases, yes, but support from outside really helps—starting in Washington. Federal funding, R&D on effective programs and practices, support for world-class standards and assessments, and strongly articulated beliefs about effective schools and student learning are key ingredients. At the state level, clear K–12 learning goals and high-quality assessments are essential, along with targeted assistance for effective programs and extended learning time. But most of the action is at the district, principal, and classroom level:

School Districts

As much as principals and teachers may grumble about the central office, effective leadership and support from the superintendent and key district officials are key. They include measures such as these:

- A clear vision and mission based on high achievement for all students.

- Adequate funding for salaries, staff support, facilities, security, and instructional materials.

- A collective bargaining agreement with the teachers' union that supports mini-observations and evaluation rubrics and provides professional time for teacher teams to meet on curriculum and assessments at the end of the summer, during the school year (ideally weekly), and right after students leave for the summer.

- Clear, manageable learning expectations for each grade aligned to state standards. If state standards are not robust enough to ensure that students graduate ready for success in college and careers, the district needs to supplement them.

- Support for teacher teams across the district on chunking the curriculum into units and creating backwards-designed UbD unit plans for general use.

- An interim assessment system with high-quality assessments, twenty-four– to forty-eight-hour turnaround time (which usually involves school-based scanning), and teacher-friendly data reports.

- Training and support for principals and teachers on mini-observations, rubrics, backwards curriculum unit planning, and effective use of interim assessment data.

- Critical appraisals of textbooks and other instructional materials to ensure high quality and alignment with state standards and assessments.

- Monitoring of school data, with targeted assistance where it's needed.

Principals

The principal is in the ideal position to inspire, explain, and support improvements in teaching and learning. Principals don't need to be experts in every subject area and micromanage every detail, but they do need to get three things right: foster teacher ownership for the school's mission (after all, teachers are alone with their classes 99.9 percent of the time); get teachers working with their grade- and subject-area colleagues (isolation makes it much more difficult to have effective teaching in every classroom); and relentlessly keep the whole school community focused on student achievement (no more *teach, test, and move on*). These translate into the following actions:

- Actively promoting a vision and mission focused on student proficiency at each grade level and eventual success in college and career.

- Juxtaposing the vision with an unflinching look at current data and getting ownership for a plan to close the gap.

- Getting the whole school community focused on two or three well-developed "big rock" projects that address the school's most urgent needs.

- Hiring top-notch people to fill every vacancy.

- Providing teacher teams with clear learning expectations for each grade level, accompanied by exemplars of proficient student work.

- Making sure teachers know what's required for students to do well on state tests. They should receive a clear message that the best form of test preparation is high-quality, well-aligned teaching every day, not the "junk food" of test prep.
- Working with staff to create a detailed calendar of curriculum units, assessments, and teacher team meetings for the year.
- Providing training and support for teacher teams to design curriculum units. The goal should be all units schoolwide being backwards-planned within two or three years.
- Monitoring and contributing to the interim assessment process. If the district's program is faulty, find ways to improve or supplant it.
- Actively supervising all teachers through mini-observations and follow-up conversations.
- Getting expert coaching and professional development for all teachers and teacher teams.
- In one-on-one conversations and team meetings, acting as a cross-pollinator of ideas and best practices from inside and outside the school.
- Sharing pertinent research and best practices from the wider world.
- Using rubrics to craft candid and helpful year-end evaluations of teachers, with struggling teachers evaluated earlier, provided with support, and, if necessary, dismissed.

Teachers

The real work of schools, of course, is done in classrooms. Key elements in effective instruction include

- Collaborating with grade-level colleagues to align teaching with end-of-year learning expectations, assessment criteria, and a broader sense of what will produce long-range student success.
- Taking personal and collective responsibility for getting all students over the bar.
- Collaboratively crafting curriculum units and common assessments.
- Planning the best possible instruction and learning experiences for students every day.

- Continuously monitoring students' learning with on-the-spot assessments and using insights to modify teaching and follow up with students who are not doing well.

- Looking at interim assessment results with same-grade and same-subject colleagues.

- Using data and insights from colleagues, professional development, and research to continuously improve teaching and follow up with struggling students.

EFFECTIVE SUPERVISION AND EVALUATION

Think back to the logic model of how supervision and evaluation might work under ideal conditions. When this model was presented in Chapter Two, you probably saw a number of ways that it breaks down in schools and thought it was mostly pie in the sky. But if this book's recommendations were implemented, could the model work? The logic model is in italics, followed by my commentary:

1. *Principals and teachers have a shared understanding of what good teaching looks like.* The teacher evaluation rubrics presented in Chapter Seven provide a clear description of teaching at four levels of quality. If the rubrics are shared and discussed at the beginning of each year and if teachers self-assess, there should be no doubt about what's expected in the classroom.

2. *Principals get into classrooms and see typical teaching in action.* Unannounced mini-observations (described in Chapter Three and Chapter Four) give principals a true sense of how teachers are working with students on a day-to-day basis, especially if principals use good time-management techniques (as suggested in Chapter Eight) and get into classrooms on a systematic basis. Feedback conversations after each mini-observation allow teachers to fill in the gaps and give their perspective in a two-way discussion about teaching and learning that maximizes adult—and student—learning.

3. *Principals capture and remember key points from their classroom visits.* Whether or not the principal takes notes during visits, the key is having a short, comprehensive mental checklist (SOTEL was suggested in Chapter Four) that provides hooks for remembering the most important information during visits.

4. *Principals give teachers feedback on what's effective and what needs to be improved.* Prompt, face-to-face conversations are essential to closing the loop with teachers. They allow for more information sharing and greater candor—and sensitivity—than written feedback. These conversations are even more substantive when principals are at least occasionally present in curriculum planning and interim-assessment results meetings (as recommended in Chapter Five and Chapter Six). Then they know what students are supposed to be learning—and how well they are actually learning—and can be part of robust, ongoing conversation about improving results. Finally, teacher evaluation rubrics (presented in Chapter Seven) give teachers crisp, comprehensive feedback and a clear road map for improvement.

5. *Teachers understand and accept the feedback.* The principal's suggestions and criticisms, week by week and in the year-end evaluation rubrics, are more likely to be understood and accepted if they are based on actual data from unannounced mini-observations. Principals gain additional credibility when they participate in the curriculum planning and interim assessment process and can pass along best practices and student learning from other classrooms in the school.

6. *Teachers use the feedback to improve their classroom practice.* If teachers are invested with their team colleagues in curriculum planning and interim assessment analysis, they are constantly thinking about ways they can be more successful with their students, and a principal's suggestions (delivered in a low-key, collegial spirit) will fall on fertile ground.

7. *As a result, student achievement improves.* Thoughtful curriculum planning, collaboration (with colleagues sharing ideas and looking at interim assessments results), feedback from mini-observations, rubric evaluation at the end of each year, and a constant process of experimentation and data analysis—all this greatly increases the likelihood of significant gains in student learning.

In short, I believe the logic model has been transformed into a powerful and practical statement of how supervision and evaluation can and should work—and a final line could be added: principals and teachers are *partners* in bringing first-rate instruction to every child. And the twelve problems with conventional supervision and evaluation presented in Chapter Two have all been solved:

- ☑ The principal sees only a tiny fraction of teaching time.
- ☑ Teachers often put on a dog-and-pony show.
- ☑ The principal's presence changes classroom dynamics.
- ☑ Doing good lesson write-ups takes skill and training.
- ☑ Detailed write-ups of lessons can miss the bigger picture.
- ☑ Many evaluation instruments are cumbersome and legalistic.
- ☑ Ratings lack bite, don't guide improvement.
- ☑ Criticism can shut down adult learning or be shrugged off.
- ☑ Evaluations can feed teacher isolation and jealousy.
- ☑ Some principals don't confront bad and mediocre teaching.
- ☑ Principals are too busy to do effective evaluations.
- ☑ Focus is on pleasing the principal, not student learning.

WORKING TOGETHER TO CLOSE THE ACHIEVEMENT GAP

Do you recall the vignette in Chapter Two about the teacher who began to cry in an evaluation conference when told she had mixed up mean, median, and mode in a math lesson? It's a true story, and I was her principal. Since then, I've done a lot of thinking about what went wrong.

The teacher was clearly putting on a special lesson for my formal observation, and although she had done a lot of preparation, an important mathematical error had crept into the lesson plan. She may have been more focused on impressing me with a razzle-dazzle hands-on activity than on the quality of her students' learning. In fairness to her, she had been working in isolation from other teachers at her grade level and had not been exposed to high-quality professional development. Her nervousness about the high-stakes meeting in my office undoubtedly contributed to her being devastated when (in her view) I played gotcha. Her take-away from my criticism—"Never to take a risk"—seems defensive and wrong, but given the supervision and evaluation process we were using, it was understandable.

If we could time-shift this teacher to a contemporary American school implementing the four key components advocated in this book, how might things be different? For starters, she and her teammates would be operating in a standards-based environment and know that their students were going to take rigorous state math tests. They would collaboratively backwards-design the math unit, clarifying their big ideas and essential questions, the important facts and concepts to be learned, and the way student learning would be assessed at the end of the unit. In this process, they would probably catch this teacher's misconception about mean, median, and mode and figure out a classroom strategy to teach the concept, anticipating students' likely misconceptions.

As she began to teach the unit in her classroom, the teacher would probably be less concerned about what I would think if I happened to drop in than about whether her students were getting it and how they would do on their unit assessment and on the state test at the end of the year. If I did catch a teaching error during a mini-observation, I would correct it in an informal follow-up chat. And if students did well on the end-of-unit or interim assessment, the team would report the results to me and their colleagues with real pride in a job well done. The teacher's year-end rubric evaluation would probably end up being mostly Proficient, and our meeting would be a candid and businesslike sharing of commendations and suggestions.

This is a far better scenario than the kind of tense confrontation I described—better for teachers, better for students, and better for the whole school community. But for it to become a reality, we have to rethink conventional teacher supervision and evaluation. Principals need to go beyond classroom inspection and actively supervise curriculum planning, interim assessment analysis, and follow-up, with student learning at the center of every conversation. With this expanded portfolio, principals can spot-check classrooms with mini-observations while orchestrating a creative, low-stakes, collegial process that gets teacher teams deeply invested in continuously improving their teaching and their students' success. What fuels this engine of improvement is constantly experimenting, analyzing what's working and what isn't, refusing to let students fail. Teams must work with the realization that there isn't one right way to teach, and effective teaching must be tuned to the unique circumstances of every classroom: the teacher, the students, the subject matter, and the moment.

What would we look for in a school that has this engine running? First, that there is effective teaching in all classrooms, relentlessly focused on results. Dylan Wiliam and Ian Beatty put it best, in an e-mail they wrote me early in 2009:

> Agile teaching,
>
> responsive to student learning minute by minute,
>
> day by day,
>
> month by month.

Second, that teacher teams are designing curriculum units and assessments with the end in sight and continuously improving instruction down to the individual lesson. Third, that teacher teams meet periodically to analyze interim assessment results, candidly discussing what isn't working, pushing each other to develop the best possible practices, and making plans to follow up and get all students on track.

And at the center we would see a principal with a firm grasp on all these elements, very well-informed about what is happening in classrooms, skillfully juggling the myriad events and interruptions inherent in the job, and keeping the focus on the ultimate goal—all students graduating with the skills and knowledge they need to take the next step toward college and career success.

A Slim Curriculum Expectations Booklet

Atlantic Elementary School

Grade 4 Learning Expectations

September 2009

TABLE OF CONTENTS

Note: *This table of contents illustrates the paging the learning expectations would have as a separate publication. I include it here mainly to emphasize that this is a* slim *booklet.*

Much of this booklet is drawn from a draft created by the staff of the Cornerstone Academy for Social Action, (CASA) a New York City elementary school. The material in the mission, theory of action, report card expectations, and social development/effective effort sections is not from CASA.

MISSION

The goal of Atlantic Elementary School is proficiency in academics and character for all students. We aim to get every child to the proficient level or above on rigorous state assessments and on our own measures of effective effort and conduct. Graduates of Atlantic School should be able to earn a place on the honor roll in any middle school and be well on the way to success in college and life.

OUR THEORY OF ACTION

To get all students to proficiency or above, we all need to work hard and work smart. Here are the key elements:

- Skillful teaching in all classrooms, using balanced literacy and the best math, science, and social studies approaches
- Teachers working in teams to bring the best practices to all students, constantly assess how they are doing, and give students feedback and support that helps them grow and develop and become increasingly confident and self-reliant
- Teachers working closely with parents and other family members to boost each child's achievement
- Students building their vocabulary and content knowledge across all subject areas
- Students reading a wide variety of books and other materials, most at the "just right" level of difficulty
- Students doing a lot of writing and constantly self-assessing, editing, and improving what they write
- Students having a positive attitude toward reading, writing, math, and other subjects and believing that if they work hard, they can get smarter and smarter
- Students knowing where they stand in each subject (especially their Fountas-Pinnell reading level), setting goals, and having a plan for getting there

INTRODUCTION TO THE LEARNING EXPECTATIONS

Based on New York State standards, this document is designed to make clear what each child should know and be able to do by the end of fourth grade, so as to have a solid foundation for success in subsequent grades. This guide includes exemplars of work children should be able to complete by the end of the grade and the reading level that is expected. We understand that not all children are at the same level at any given point in the year, but we hope that high expectations will bring parents and teachers together to help close the achievement gap that exists in many New York State schools.

This guide is a work in progress. During the 2009–2010 school year, we will continue to evaluate the guide and adapt it as necessary, and appreciate your comments and suggestions.

READING

By the end of the school year, all fourth-grade students should be able to do the following:

- ☑ Independently read and understand passages at level S or above on the Fountas-Pinnell scale.
- ☑ Silently read print and electronic literary texts every day.
- ☑ Set personal reading goals and reflect on changes in reading patterns.
- ☑ Recognize how authors use literary devices such as simile and metaphor.
- ☑ Evaluate content by identifying important and unimportant details, themes across works, and different perspectives (such as cultural, ethnic, and historical).

Units of Study:

1. Fiction (realistic and fantasy)
2. Nonfiction
3. Author study
4. Reading of short texts (testing as a genre)
5. Memoir
6. Biography and autobiography and primary source document
7. Poetry
8. Historical fiction
9. Multicultural studies
10. Why do we read? Reflection and setting goals for summer reading

Reading report card grades will be broken down as follows:

- Reads with fluency and accuracy
- Understands what is read
- Reads a variety of material

Sources for grades:

- Reading log (an ongoing record of titles read independently)
- Class participation
- Independent and group work
- Fountas-Pinnell Benchmark Assessment System
- Curriculum unit outcomes
- Rubrics and checklists
- Reading responses
- Notebooks and folders
- Projects
- Homework
- Acuity interim assessment
- Participation in goal setting, as well as progress, reflection, revision, and accomplishment

Curriculum approach used:

- Reader's Workshop
- Balanced literacy
- Leveled libraries
- Good Habits, Great Readers (supplemental program)
- Teacher-created materials
- Fountas & Pinnell Benchmark kits

Sample Reading Passage

The following is a passage *From the Mixed-Up Files of Mrs. Basil E. Frankweiler* by E.L. Konigsburg, Atheneum, 1967 (page 28). This is the level that students should be able to read with good comprehension by the end of the fourth grade. Other fourth-grade books include *The Hundred Penny Box, The Legend of Sleepy Hollow, Chang's Paper Pony, Beezus and Ramona, Tales of a Fourth Grade Nothing*, and *The Witch of Banneker School*.

As soon as they reached the sidewalk, Jamie made his first decision as treasurer. "We'll walk from here to the museum."

"Walk?" Claudia asked. "Do you realize that it is over forty blocks from here?"

"Well, how much does the bus cost?"

"The bus!" Claudia exclaimed. "Who said anything about taking a bus? I want to take a taxi."

"Claudia," Jamie said, "you are quietly out of your mind. How can you even think of a taxi? We have no more allowance. No more income. You can't be extravagant any longer. It's not my money we're spending. It's *our* money. We're in this together, remember?"

"You're right," Claudia answered. "A taxi is expensive. The bus is cheaper. It's only twenty cents each. We'll take the bus."

"Only twenty cents each. That's forty cents total. No bus. We'll walk."

"We'll wear out forty cents worth of shoe leather," Claudia mumbled. "You're sure we have to walk?"

"Positive," Jamie answered. "Which way do we go?"

"Sure you won't change your mind?" The look on Jamie's face gave her the answer. She sighed. No wonder Jamie had more than twenty-four dollars; he was a gambler and a cheapskate. It that's the way he wants it, she thought, I'll never again ask him for bus fare; I'll suffer and never, never let him know about it. But he'll regret it when I simply collapse from exhaustion. I'll collapse quietly.

"We'd better walk up Madison Avenue," she told her brother. "I'll see too many ways to spend *our* precious money if we walk on Fifth Avenue. All those gorgeous stores."

These are examples of the four types of questions students should be asked to address, each based on the quoted passage:

- *Right there* (literal; the answer is right in the text, usually found in one sentence):
  How did Jamie persuade his sister to walk instead of taking the bus or a taxi?

- *Think and search* (inferential; students need to search the passage and connect ideas):
  Why did Claudia try so hard to persuade Jamie that they shouldn't walk?

- *On your own* (evaluative; using information in the passage and background knowledge):
  What piece of information in this passage tells us that it was written decades ago?

- *Word meaning*
  In the fifth paragraph, what does the word *extravagant* mean?

WRITING

By the end of the school year, all fourth-grade students should be able to do the following:

- ☑ Use organizational structures such as compare and contrast, cause and effect, and chronological order.
- ☑ Produce imaginative stories and personal narratives that show insight, logical progression, organization, and effective language.
- ☑ Produce a variety of original nonfiction writing, such as school reports.
- ☑ Recognize the perspective of others, distinguishing among fact, opinion, and exaggeration.
- ☑ Ask clarifying questions, summarize, and explain a line of reasoning.
- ☑ Review own writing to edit for grade-level spelling, punctuation, and consistency in verb tense.

Writing Tasks:

1. Literary essay (five paragraphs)
2. Nonfiction feature article—science content
3. Persuasive letter
4. Biographical report
5. Memoir
6. Poetry
7. Research report (two or more sources) with timeline—social studies content
8. Summary

Writing report card grades will be broken down as follows (based on the 6-Trait Rubric):

- Ideas
- Organization
- Voice
- Word choice
- Sentence fluency
- Conventions (spelling, grammar, syntax, and presentation)

Sources for grades:

- Meeting publishing deadlines
- Ability to write independently in a variety of genres
- Class participation
- Independent and group work
- Unit outcomes
- Rubrics and checklists
- Writing responses
- Notebooks and folders
- Projects
- Homework
- Interim assessments (acuity)
- Participation in goal setting, as well as progress, reflection, revision, and accomplishments

Curriculum approach used:

- Writer's Workshop
- 6-Trait writing assessment (see rubric on following page)
- Good Habits, Great Writers (supplemental program)
- Teacher-created materials

Grade 4 Writing Rubric

STUDENT: _____ CLASS: _____ TEACHER: _____

ASSESSMENT 1: DATE _____ YELLOW ASSESSMENT 2: DATE _____ ASSESSMENT 3: DATE _____ PINK BLUE

ASSESSMENT 4: DATE _____ GREEN ASSESSMENT 5: DATE _____ ORANGE

	1 Well Below Grade Level	2 Approaching Grade Level	3 On Grade Level	4 Above Grade Level
IDEAS	Shows little shaping of ideas for specific effect or purpose Shows little elaboration	Shows attempts at shaping of ideas for specific effect or purpose Shows some evidence of elaboration of ideas	Has a context created for the reader Includes reflective comments and elaboration of big ideas	Has content and ideas selected and shaped for specific audiences and purposes Shows evidence of elaboration of ideas to convey coherent meaning
ORGANIZATION	Is not planned Is not focused Shows little ordering of text to clarify meaning May order ideas chronologically and begin to link ideas	Shows some evidence of planning Shows attempts to organize information to keep the writing focused Uses a partial organizational framework, that is, provides simple orientation and story development paragraphs Shows some evidence of changes in sequence and addition of new ideas during revision	Shows evidence of planning to organize ideas Has a clear focus using a structure that is well organized and detailed Has sentences containing related information grouped into paragraphs Shows evidence of sentences or paragraphs rearranged to improve or clarify meaning	Shows evidence of organizing ideas using a variety of planning strategies Has an increasing sense of coherence and wholeness Has well-organized paragraphs that logically form a cohesive text Arrangement of sentences and paragraphs adds to the understanding and enjoyment of the text
VOICE	Shows little evidence of a personal style	Indicates the beginnings of personal involvement by the writer	Shows evidence of a developing personal style	Indicates a sense of personal involvement by the writer
WORD CHOICE	Shows little control of language and awareness of the subtleties of language Makes little use of figurative language	Shows some control of language and an awareness of the subtleties of language Makes some use of figurative language	Employs a wide vocabulary, using adjectives, adverbs, or synonyms for effect Makes effective use of figurative language	Uses a wide range of vocabulary to suit different audiences and purposes Makes effective use of figurative language to amplify content or engage the reader

	Identifies likely audiences and adjusts language and structure to achieve impact. Independently uses strategies such as dialog, tension, and suspense in narrative. Shows evidence of the writer's regular and accurate use of a dictionary and thesaurus	Uses varied language to suit the purpose and topic. With support, uses strategies such as dialog, tension, and suspense in narrative. Shows evidence of the writer's regular use of a dictionary or thesaurus, or both	Includes vocabulary that precisely conveys meaning. Begins to use dialog to help tell a story and develop characters in narrative. Little evidence of the writer's use of a dictionary or thesaurus, or both	At most, shows the beginning of selecting specific vocabulary. Includes little or no dialogue in narratives. No evidence of the writer's use of a dictionary or thesaurus, or both
SENTENCE FLUENCY	Uses a variety of sentence structures, beginnings, and lengths for effect. Shows reordering of texts to clarify meaning, that is, of moving words, phrases, and clauses. Oral reading is pleasurable and entertaining	Includes complex sentences with embedded clauses or phrases. Shows evidence of words and sentences rearranged to improve or clarify meaning. Oral reading is effortless	Shows some variation in sentence structures, beginnings, and lengths. Shows some reordering of text to clarify meaning, that is, of moving words, phrases, and clauses. Oral reading is possible	Shows little variation in sentence structures and beginnings. No evidence of reordering text to clarify meaning, that is, of moving words, phrases, and clauses. Oral reading is difficult
CONVENTIONS	Shows confident control of the conventions of writing. Has accurate spelling and punctuation. Shows accurate editing and proofreading. Grammar and usage are correct. Paragraphing is correct. Handwriting is legible and uniform. Good balance of space and text. Overall appearance is pleasing	Shows control of the conventions of writing. Punctuation and capitalization usually correct; has accurate spelling of all high-frequency words. Work is routinely edited and proofread. Grammar and usage are mostly correct. Paragraphing is mostly correct. Handwriting is mostly legible. Spacing improves clarity. Overall appearance is acceptable	Shows control of most of the conventions of writing. Work is mostly accurately spelled and punctuated. Shows some evidence of editing for accuracy, consistency, and clarity with necessary changes made. Grammar and usage are sometimes correct. Paragraphing is sometimes correct. Handwriting is poor but decipherable. Some thought is given to spacing. Overall appearance is distracting	Shows some control of the conventions of writing. Has some accurate spelling and punctuation. Shows little evidence of editing. Grammar and usage are mostly incorrect. Paragraphing mostly incorrect. Handwriting is unreadable. Spacing is random, or there is no spacing. Overall appearance is unacceptable

Writing Exemplar

<u>My Free Time</u>

Tip tap tat tit, My sister is the best person to play with in your free time. We play lots of wonderful games. We play with lots and lots of cute and fabulous dolls. I like playing with my sister because she is no ordinary sister. She is funny, cute, and friendly. The story all began with one little sister.

Me and my sister were up very early in the morning on a Sunday. My sister and I decided to play together. We went in her room because she has the most toys. Then we started playing a random game with her dolls. We got so into the game we played for hours and hours.

Our Mom and Dad woke up. They said that we had to go to Church. We said "NO!" We said we finally have free time to play with each other. But we had to go to church. So we went.

Right when we got home we tried to play the game. We forgot we went to the store and bought stuff. We had to help carry it in. After that it was lunch time. It went on and on. Finally we had free time!

We played and played till the game was over. After finishing the game we decided when ever we have free time we usualy would spend it together. Also we would try to find more free time. You sould try playing with my sister and see what she can make you do. That was a very valuble day with my sister.

MATH

By the end of the school year, all fourth-grade students should be able to do the following:

- ☑ Read and write whole numbers through 10,000.
- ☑ Round numbers to the nearest 10 (for example, round 878 to 880) and to the nearest 100 (for example, round 446 to 400).
- ☑ Understand that a decimal is part of a whole. For example, Sarah has two dimes and two pennies. This amount can be represented as $0.22. Recognize benchmark fractions (halves, thirds, fourths, fifths, sixths, and tenths), and identify equivalent fractions (for example $1/2 = 2/4$) using visual models.
- ☑ Know the names of polygons such as *triangle, pentagon,* and *octagon.* know that the names of polygons are related to the number of sides and angles. For example, a triangle has three sides and three angles.
- ☑ Find the perimeter of a polygon by adding the lengths of its sides.
- ☑ Classify angles as acute (less than 90 degrees), obtuse (greater than 90 degrees), right (exactly 90 degrees), and straight (180 degrees).
- ☑ Use data to develop insight and make predictions.
- ☑ Use observations, surveys, and experiments to collect and record data. Show the data using tables, bar graphs, and pictographs.
- ☑ Figure out whether a mathematical statement is true or false and explain why.
- ☑ Solve problems at the *proficient* level across the strands and units of study. (*Note:* This refers to a Math rubric that is still under development.)

Units of Study:

1. Naming and constructing geometric figures
2. Using numbers and organizing data
3. Multiplication and division; number sentences and algebra
4. Decimals and their uses
5. Big Numbers, estimation, and computation
6. Division; map reference frames; measurement of angles
7. Fractions and their uses; chance and probability
8. Perimeter and area
9. Fractions, decimals, and percentages
10. Reflection and symmetry
11. 3-D shapes, weight, volume, and capacity
12. Rates

Math report card grades will be broken down as follows:

- Understands and uses numbers
- Solves and explains problems
- Uses geometry, measuring, graphs, and other techniques listed in *Everyday Math*
- Teacher-made tests and trimester math tests
- A math notebook in which students record important learnings throughout the year

Sources for grades:

- Teacher-made tests and trimester math tests
- A math notebook in which students record important learnings throughout the year
- Facility for solving and explaining solutions
- Class participation
- Independent and group work
- Unit outcomes

- Rubrics and checklists
- Math journal responses or exit slips
- Recognizing Student Achievement (RSA)
- Notebooks and folders
- Projects
- Homework
- Quizzes and end-of-unit tests
- Interim assessments (acuity)
- Participation in goal setting, as well as progress, reflection, revision, and accomplishment

Curriculum approach used:

- Everyday Math curriculum program
- Teacher-made materials
- Trade books

SCIENCE

By the end of the school year, all fourth-grade students should be able to do the following:

- ☑ Explore how plants and animals make food by using air, water, and energy from the sun.
- ☑ Describe how conditions in the environment—such as the amount of available food, water, air, space, shelter, heat, and sunlight—can affect how living things develop and grow.
- ☑ Understand that magnetism is a force that attracts or repels certain materials.
- ☑ Observe, describe, and explore the physical properties of water.
- ☑ Test objects to determine whether they sink or float.
- ☑ Observe different substances, such as oil or liquid soap, to see how they mix with water.
- ☑ Study and describe how matter transforms from one state to another, for example, from solid (ice) to liquid (water) to gas (water vapor).
- ☑ Describe how erosion changes the surface of land.
- ☑ Describe how water is recycled on earth through the natural processes of precipitation, condensation, and evaporation.
- ☑ Explore the effects—both negative and positive—that a hurricane, forest fire, or other extreme natural event can have on living things.
- ☑ Show evidence of understanding science concepts and processes at the *proficient* level and above. (*Note:* This refers to a Science rubric that is still under development.)

Units of Study:

1. Animals and plants in their environment
2. Electricity and magnetism
3. Properties of water
4. Interactions of air, water, and land

Science report card grades will be broken down as follows:

- Written work and knowledge
- Projects and experiments

Sources for grades:

- Understanding of the scientific method
- Experiments and participation in science fair
- Independent and group work
- Class participation
- Curriculum unit outcomes
- Field trip participation
- Rubrics and checklists
- Science journal responses, notebooks, and folders
- Projects
- Homework
- Interim assessments
- Participation in goal setting, as well as progress, reflection, revision, and accomplishments

Curriculum approach used:

- Full Option Science System Program (FOSS)
- Teacher-made materials
- Trade books
- New York Scope and Sequence

SOCIAL STUDIES

By the end of the school year, all fourth-grade students should be able to do the following:

☑ Know and understand basic ideas about how our nation, state, and city developed, including early Native American Indian life in New York State; the Colonial and Revolutionary War periods; and the growth of industry, cities, and governments.

☑ Use skills that help get information and form opinions about social studies topics. For example, take notes to gather and organize information, to identify points of view, to work together to create group presentations, and to summarize current events and issues.

☑ Research and make presentations on various topics in social studies, such as geography, history, government, and economics, related to New York and American history.

☑ Understand and describe the sequence of events that led to the Revolutionary War, including economic factors such as taxes and resources.

☑ Understand and explain how the location of New York City was important in the development of industry, New York State, and the United States.

☑ Research and learn about the many immigrant groups that settled in New York City past and present.

☑ Know the important founding documents of the United States, such as the Declaration of Independence, the Constitution, and the Bill of Rights, and how they help us understand the role of government in a democracy.

☑ Compare and contrast the duties of local, state, and federal governments.

☑ Appreciate the importance of citizenship and active participation in government.

Units of Study:

1. Native Americans: first inhabitants of New York State
2. Three worlds meet
3. Colonial and Revolutionary periods
4. The new nation
5. Growth and expansion
6. Local and state government

Social studies report card grades will be broken down as follows:

- History
- Geography

Sources for grades:

- Responses to document-based questions
- Independent and group work
- Quizzes and tests
- Class participation
- Field trip participation
- Rubrics and checklists
- Notebooks and folders
- Reports and projects
- Homework
- Participation in goal setting, as well as progress, reflection, revision, and accomplishment

Curriculum approach used:

- Teacher-made materials
- New York Scope and Sequence

SOCIAL DEVELOPMENT AND EFFECTIVE EFFORT

Expectations throughout the year: Students can meet high standards in reading, writing, math, science, and social studies when they have developed their social skills, know the conduct that is expected of them in school, and apply effective effort. These are the standards on which we grade students on their report cards in December, March, and June:

Social Development and Conduct

- Observes classroom and school rules
- Shows self-control
- Respects the rights and opinions of others
- Respects cultural differences
- Works cooperatively with peers
- Accepts suggestions and learns from mistakes

Effective Effort

- Works hard; strives for excellence
- Pays attention in class
- Actively participates in discussions
- Follows written and oral directions
- Is able to work independently
- Knows where to find information
- Gets help when necessary
- Organizes workspace and materials
- Completes work on time
- Turns in neat, legible work
- Homework is consistently done (60 minutes every day and 20 minutes of personal reading)

Other Subjects

Some students will get subject, conduct, and effort grades from special education teachers.

Students have art, computer, library, music, and physical education classes every week. Report card grades in these subjects combine work, effort, and conduct in a single grade.

Principal Evaluation Rubrics

Rationale and suggestions for implementation:

1. These rubrics are organized around six domains covering all aspects of a principal's job performance:

   A. Diagnosis and planning

   B. Priority management and communication

   C. Curriculum and data

   D. Supervision and professional development

   E. Discipline and parent involvement

   F. Management and external relations

   The rubrics use a four-level rating scale with the following labels:

   4—Expert

   3—Proficient

   2—Needs Improvement

   1—Does Not Meet Standards

2. The rubrics are designed to give principals an end-of-year assessment of where they stand in all performance areas—and detailed guidance for improvement. They are not checklists for school visits.

These rubrics are a much-edited extension of the Principal Leadership Competencies developed by New Leaders for New Schools in 2004. Kim Marshall was a lead author of that document. Special thanks to Jon Saphier, Charlotte Danielson, Douglas Reeves, and Paul Bambrick-Santoyo for ideas and inspiration.

To knowledgeably fill out the rubrics, a principal's supervisor needs to have been in the school frequently throughout the year; it is irresponsible to fill out the rubrics based on one visit and without ongoing dialogue.

3. The *Proficient* level describes solid, expected professional performance; any principal should be pleased with scores at this level. The *Expert* level is reserved for truly outstanding leadership as described by very demanding criteria; there will be relatively few scores at this level. *Needs Improvement* indicates that performance has real deficiencies; it's not a "gentleman's C" and principals should be uncomfortable with scores at this level. And performance at the *Does Not Meet Standards* level is clearly unacceptable and needs to be changed immediately.

4. To score, read across the four levels of performance for each criterion, find the level that best describes the principal's performance, and circle or highlight it. On each page, this will create a clear graphic display of overall performance, areas for commendation, and areas that need work. Write the overall score at the bottom of each page with brief comments, and then record all the scores and overall comments on the summary page.

5. Evaluation conferences are greatly enhanced if the supervisor and principal fill out the rubrics in advance and then meet and compare scores one page at a time. Of course, the supervisor has the final say, but the discussion should aim for consensus based on actual evidence of the most accurate score for each criterion. Supervisors should go into the evaluation process with some humility since they can't possibly know everything about a principal's complex world. Similarly, principals should be open to feedback from someone with an outside perspective—all revolving around whether the school is producing learning gains for all students. Note that student achievement is not explicitly included in these rubrics, but clearly it's directly linked to a principal's leadership. The role of student results in evaluation is for each district or governing board to decide.

6. Resist the temptation to sugar-coat criticism and give inflated scores for fear of hurting feelings. This does not help principals improve. The kindest thing a supervisor can do for an underperforming principal is give candid, evidence-based feedback and robust follow-up support. Honest scores for all the principals in a district can be aggregated into a spreadsheet that can give an overview of leadership development needs for the district.

RUBRICS

Table B.1 Principal Evaluation Rubrics
A. Diagnosis and Planning

The Principal:	4 Expert	3 Proficient	2 Needs Improvement	1 Does Not Meet Standards
a. Team	Recruits a strong leadership team and develops its skills and commitment to a high level.	Recruits and develops a leadership team with a balance of skills.	Enlists one or two like-minded colleagues to provide advice and support.	Is a Lone Ranger working with little or no support from colleagues.
b. Diagnosis	Involves stakeholders in a comprehensive diagnosis of the school's strengths and weaknesses.	Carefully assesses the school's strengths and areas for development.	Makes a quick assessment of the school's strengths and weaknesses.	Is unable to gather much information on the school's strong and weak points.
c. Gap	Challenges colleagues by presenting the gap between current student data and a vision for college success.	Motivates colleagues by comparing students' current achievement with rigorous expectations.	Presents data without a vision or a vision without data.	Bemoans students' low achievement and shows fatalism about bringing about significant change.
d. Mission	Writes a succinct, inspiring, results-oriented mission statement that wins staff and student buy-in.	Writes a memorable, succinct, results-oriented mission statement that's known by all staff.	Distributes a boilerplate mission statement that few colleagues remember.	Does not share a mission statement.
e. Target	Gets strong staff commitment on a bold, ambitious 3–4-year student achievement target.	Builds staff support for a 3–4-year student achievement target.	Expresses confidence that student achievement will improve each year through hard work.	Takes one year at a time, urging teachers to improve their students' achievement.

f. Theory	Wins staff ownership for a robust, research-based theory of action for improving achievement.	Researches and writes a convincing theory of action for improving achievement.	Accepts colleagues' current notions of how student achievement is improved.	Says that hard work improves achievement—but appears to doubt that progress can be made.
g. Strategy	Collaboratively crafts a lean, comprehensive, results-oriented strategic plan with annual goals.	Gets input and writes a comprehensive, measurable strategic plan for the current year.	Writes a cumbersome, non-accountable strategic plan.	Recycles the previous year's cumbersome, non-accountable strategic plan.
h. Support	Fosters a sense of urgency and responsibility among all stakeholders for achieving annual goals.	Builds ownership and support among stakeholders for achieving annual goals.	Presents the annual plan to stakeholders and asks them to support it.	Gets the necessary signatures for the annual plan, but there is little ownership or support.
i. Enlisting	Masterfully wins over resistant staff members who feared change, harbored low expectations, or both.	Manages resistance, low expectations, and fear of change.	Works on persuading resistant staff members to get on board with the plan.	Is discouraged and immobilized by staff resistance, fear of change, and low expectations.
j. Tweaking	Regularly tracks progress, gives and takes feedback, and continuously improves performance.	Periodically measures progress, listens to feedback, and tweaks the strategic plan.	Occasionally focuses on key data points and prods colleagues to improve.	Is too caught up in daily crises to focus on emerging data.

Overall rating: _____   Comments:

B. Priority Management and Communication

The Principal:	4 Expert	3 Proficient	2 Needs Improvement	1 Does Not Meet Standards
a. Planning	Plans for the year, month, week, and day, relentlessly getting the highest-leverage activities done.	Plans for the year, month, week, and day, keeping the highest-leverage activities front and center.	Comes to work with a list of what needs to be accomplished that day but is often distracted from it.	Has a mental list of tasks to be accomplished each day, but often loses track.
b. Communication	Skillfully and eloquently communicates goals to all constituencies using a variety of channels.	Uses a variety of means (such as, face-to-face, newsletters, websites) to communicate goals to others.	Has a limited communication repertoire and some key stakeholders are not aware of school goals.	Is not an effective communicator, and others are often left guessing about policies and direction.
c. Outreach	Frequently solicits and uses feedback and help from staff, students, parents, and external partners.	Regularly reaches out to staff, students, parents, and external partners for feedback and help.	Occasionally asks staff, students, parents, or external partners for feedback.	Never reaches out to others for feedback or help.
d. Follow-Up	Has a foolproof system for capturing key information, remembering, prioritizing, and following up.	Writes down important information, remembers, prioritizes, and almost always follows up.	Writes things down but is swamped by events and sometimes doesn't follow up.	Trusts to memory to retain important information, but often forgets and drops the ball.
e. Expectations	Has total staff buy-in on exactly what is expected for management procedures and discipline.	Makes sure staff know what is expected for management procedures and discipline.	Periodically reminds teachers of policies on management procedures and discipline.	Is constantly reminding staff what they should be doing in management and discipline.

f. Delegation	Has highly competent people in all key roles and is able to entrust them with maximum responsibility.	Delegates appropriate tasks to competent staff members and checks on progress.	Doesn't delegate some tasks that should be done by others.	Does almost everything personally.
g. Meetings	All key teams meet on a regular basis and take responsibility for productive agendas.	Ensures that key teams (leadership, grade-level, student support) meet regularly.	Needs to call key team meetings each month because they are not in people's calendars.	Convenes grade-level, leadership, and other teams only when there is a crisis or an immediate need.
h. Prevention	Takes the initiative so that time-wasting activities and crises are almost always prevented or deflected.	Is effective at preventing or deflecting many time-wasting crises and activities.	Tries to prevent them, but crises and time-wasters sometimes eat up lots of time.	Finds that large portions of each day are consumed by crises and time-wasting activities.
i. Efficiency	Deals quickly and decisively with the highest-priority e-mail and paperwork, delegating the rest.	Has a system for dealing with e-mail, paperwork, and administrative chores.	Tries to stay on top of e-mail, paperwork, and administrative chores but is often behind.	Is way behind on e-mail, paperwork, and administrative chores, to the detriment of the school's mission.
j. Balance	Remains sharp and fresh by tending to family, friends, fun, exercise, nutrition, sleep, and vacations.	Is healthy and focused by balancing work demands with healthy habits.	Is sometimes unfocused and inattentive because of fatigue.	Is unproductive and irascible because of fatigue and stress.

Overall rating: _____ Comments:

C. Curriculum and Data

The Principal:	4 Expert	3 Proficient	2 Needs Improvement	1 Does Not Meet Standards
a. Expectations	Gets all teachers to buy in to clear, manageable, standards-aligned grade-level goals with exemplars of proficient work.	Tells teachers exactly what students should know and be able to do by the end of each grade level.	Refers teachers to district or national scope-and-sequence documents for curriculum direction.	Leaves teachers without clear direction on student learning outcomes for each grade level.
b. Baselines	Ensures that all teams use summative data from the year before and fresh diagnostic data to plan instruction.	Provides teacher teams with previous-year test data and asks them to assess students' current levels.	Refers teachers to previous-year test data as a baseline for current-year instruction.	Does not provide historical test data to teachers.
c. Targets	Gets each grade-level and subject team invested in reaching measurable, results-oriented year-end goals.	Works with grade-level and subject-area teams to set measurable student goals for the current year.	Urges grade-level and subject teams to set measurable student learning goals for the current year.	Urges teachers to improve student achievement, but without measurable outcome goals.
d. Materials	Ensures that all teachers have top-notch curriculum materials and training on how to use them.	Gets the best possible literacy, math, science, and social studies materials into teachers' hands.	Works to procure good curriculum materials in literacy and math.	Leaves teachers to fend for themselves with curriculum materials.
e. Interims	Ensures that high-quality, aligned, common interim assessments are given by all teacher teams at least four times each year.	Orchestrates common interim assessments to monitor student learning several times a year.	Suggests that teacher teams give common interim assessments to check on student learning.	Doesn't insist on common interim assessments, allowing teachers to use their own classroom tests.

f. Analysis	Orchestrates high-quality low-stakes data and action team meetings after each round of assessments.	Monitors teacher teams as they analyze interim assessment results and formulate action plans.	Suggests that teacher teams work together to draw lessons from the tests they give.	Does not see the value of analyzing tests given during the year.
g. Causes	Gets data meetings engaged in a no-blame, test-in-hand search for root causes and in hypothesis testing.	Asks that data meetings go beyond what students got wrong and delve into why.	Suggests that teachers focus on the areas in which students had the most difficulty.	Does not exercise leadership in looking for underlying causes of student difficulties.
h. Follow-up	Gets teams invested in following up assessments with effective re-teaching, tutoring, and other interventions.	Insists that teams follow up each interim assessment with re-teaching and remediation.	Suggests that teachers use interim assessment data to help struggling students.	Does not provide time or leadership for follow-up after tests.
i. Monitoring	Uses data on grades, attendance, behavior, and other variables to monitor and drive continuous improvement toward goals.	Monitors data in several key areas and uses them to inform improvement efforts.	Monitors attendance and discipline data to inform decisions.	Keeps an eye on attendance and suspension rates.
j. Celebration	Boosts morale and a sense of efficacy by getting colleagues to celebrate and own measurable student gains.	Shares student, classroom, and schoolwide successes and gives credit where credit is due.	Congratulates staff on "small wins" and other successes.	Takes credit for improvements in school performance.

Overall rating: _____ Comments:

D. Supervision and Professional Development

The Principal:	4 Expert	3 Proficient	2 Needs Improvement	1 Does Not Meet Standards
a. Meetings	In all-staff meetings, has teachers discuss results, learn best strategies, and build trust and respect.	Uses all-staff meetings to get teachers sharing strategies and becoming more cohesive as a group.	Uses staff meetings primarily to announce decisions, clarify policies, and listen to staff concerns.	Rarely convenes staff members and uses meetings for one-way lectures on policies.
b. Ideas	Ensures that the whole staff is current on professional literature and constantly explores best practices.	Reads and shares research and fosters an ongoing schoolwide discussion of best practices.	Occasionally passes along interesting articles and ideas to colleagues.	Rarely reads professional literature or discusses best practices.
c. Development	Orchestrates aligned, high-quality coaching, workshops, school visits, and other professional learning tuned to staff needs.	Organizes aligned, ongoing coaching and training that builds classroom proficiency.	Provides conventional staff development workshops to teachers.	Provides occasional workshops, leaving teachers mostly on their own in terms of professional development.
d. Empowerment	Gets teams to take ownership for using data and student work to drive constant refinement of teaching.	Orchestrates regular teacher team meetings as the prime locus for professional learning.	Suggests that teacher teams work together to address students' learning problems.	Does not emphasize teamwork and teachers work mostly in isolation from colleagues.
e. Support	Gives teacher teams the training, facilitation, and resources they need to make their meetings highly effective.	Provides teacher teams with facilitators so meetings are focused and substantive.	Has teacher teams appoint a leader to chair meetings and file reports.	Leaves teacher teams to fend for themselves in terms of leadership and direction.

f. Units	Ensures that teachers backwards-design high-quality, aligned units and provides feedback on drafts.	Asks teacher teams to cooperatively plan curriculum units following a common format.	Occasionally reviews teachers' lesson plans but not unit plans.	Does not review lesson or unit plans.
g. Supervision	Visits 3–5 classrooms a day and gives helpful, face-to-face feedback to each teacher within 24 hours.	Makes unannounced visits to a few classrooms every day and gives helpful feedback to teachers.	Tries to get into classrooms but is often distracted by other events and rarely provides feedback.	Only observes teachers in formal observation visits once or twice a year.
h. Criticism	Courageously engages in difficult conversations with below-proficient teachers, helping them improve.	Provides redirection and support to teachers who are less than proficient.	Criticizes struggling teachers but does not give them much help improving their performance.	Shies away from giving honest feedback and redirection to teachers who are not performing well.
i. Housecleaning	Counsels out or dismisses all ineffective teachers, scrupulously following contractual requirements.	Counsels out or dismisses most ineffective teachers, carefully following contractual requirements.	Tries to dismiss one or two ineffective teachers, but is stymied by procedural errors.	Does not initiate dismissal procedures, despite evidence that some teachers are ineffective.
j. Hiring	Recruits, hires, and supports highly effective teachers who share the school's vision.	Recruits and hires effective teachers who share the school's mission.	Hires teachers who seem to fit the principal's own philosophy of teaching.	Makes last-minute appointments to teaching vacancies based on candidates who are available.

Overall rating: _____ Comments:

E. Discipline and Family Involvement

The Principal:	4 Expert	3 Proficient	2 Needs Improvement	1 Does Not Meet Standards
a. Expectations	Gets staff buy-in for clear, schoolwide student behavior standards, routines, and consequences.	Sets expectations for student behavior and establishes schoolwide routines and consequences.	Urges staff to demand good student behavior, but allows different standards in different classrooms.	Often tolerates discipline violations and enforces the rules inconsistently.
b. Effectiveness	Deals effectively with any disruptions to teaching and learning, analyzes patterns, and works on prevention.	Deals quickly with disruptions to learning and looks for underlying causes.	Deals firmly with students who are disruptive in classrooms, but doesn't get to the root causes.	Tries to deal with disruptive students but is swamped by the number of problems.
c. Celebration	Publicly celebrates kindness, effort, and improvement and builds students' pride in their school.	Praises student achievement and works to build school spirit.	Praises well-behaved students and good grades.	Rarely praises students and fails to build school pride.
d. Training	Ensures that staff are skilled in positive discipline and sensitive handling of student issues.	Organizes workshops and suggests articles and books on classroom management.	Urges teachers to get better at classroom management.	Does little to build teachers' skills in classroom management.
e. Support	Is highly effective at getting counseling, mentoring, and other support for high-need students.	Identifies struggling students and works to get support services to meet their needs.	Tries to get crisis counseling for highly disruptive and troubled students.	Focuses mainly on discipline and punishment with highly disruptive and troubled students.

f. Openness	Makes families feel welcome and respected, responds to concerns, and gets a number of them actively involved in the school.	Makes parents feel welcome, listens to their concerns, and tries to get them involved.	Reaches out to parents and tries to understand when they are critical.	Makes little effort to reach out to families and is defensive when parents express concerns.
g. Curriculum	Informs parents of monthly learning expectations and specific ways they can support their children's learning.	Sends home information on the grade-level learning expectations and ways parents can help at home.	Sends home an annual list of grade-level learning expectations.	Does not send home the school's learning expectations.
h. Conferences	Orchestrates productive parent/teacher report card conferences in which parents and students get specific suggestions on next steps.	Works to maximize the number of face-to-face parent/teacher report card conferences.	Makes sure that report cards are filled out correctly and provided to all parents.	Provides little or no monitoring of the report card process.
i. Communication	Sends home a weekly school newsletter, gets all teachers sending substantive updates, and organizes a user-friendly electronic grading program.	Sends home a periodic school newsletter and asks teachers to have regular channels of communication of their own.	Suggests that teachers communicate regularly with parents.	Leaves parent contact and communication up to individual teachers.
j. Backstopping	Provides effective safety-net programs for all students with inadequate home support.	Provides safety-net programs for most students whose parents do not provide adequate support.	Provides ad hoc, occasional support for students who are not adequately supported at home.	Does not provide assistance for students with inadequate home support.

Overall rating: _____   Comments:

F. Management and External Relations

The Principal:	4 Expert	3 Proficient	2 Needs Improvement	1 Does Not Meet Standards
a. Strategies	Implements proven macro strategies (such as looping or class size reduction) that boost student learning.	Suggests effective macro strategies (such as looping or team teaching) to improve student learning.	Explores macro strategies that might improve achievement.	Sticks with the status quo for fear of alienating key stakeholders.
b. Scheduling	Creates an equitable schedule that maximizes learning, teacher collaboration, and smooth transitions.	Creates a schedule that provides meeting times for all key teams.	Creates a schedule with some flaws and few opportunities for team meetings.	Creates a schedule with inequities, technical flaws, and little time for teacher teams to meet.
c. Movement	Ensures smooth, friendly student entry, dismissal, meal times, transitions, and recesses every day.	Supervises orderly student entry, dismissal, meals, class transitions, and recesses.	Intermittently supervises student entry, dismissal, transitions, and meal times.	Rarely supervises student entry, dismissal, and common spaces, and problems are frequent.
d. Custodians	Leads staff to ensure effective, creative use of space and a clean, safe, and inviting campus.	Supervises staff to keep the campus clean, attractive, and safe.	Works with custodial staff to keep the campus clean and safe, but there are occasional lapses.	Leaves campus cleanliness and safety to custodial staff, and lapses are frequent.
e. Transparency	Makes sure people understand how and why decisions were made, involving stakeholders whenever possible.	Ensures that staff members know how and why decisions are being made.	Tries to be open about decision making, but stakeholders sometimes feel shut out.	Makes decisions with little or no consultation, causing frequent resentment and morale problems.

f. Bureaucracy	Deftly handles bureaucratic, contractual, and legal issues so that they never detract from, and sometimes contribute to, teaching and learning.	Manages bureaucratic, contractual, and legal issues efficiently and effectively.	Sometimes allows bureaucratic, contractual, and legal issues to distract teachers from their work.	Frequently mishandles bureaucratic, contractual, and legal issues in ways that disrupt teaching and learning.
g. Budget	Skillfully manages the budget and finances to maximize student achievement and staff growth.	Manages the school's budget and finances to support the strategic plan.	Manages budget and finances with few errors, but misses opportunities to support the strategic plan.	Makes errors in managing the budget and finances and misses opportunities to further the mission.
h. Compliance	Fulfills all compliance and reporting requirements and creates new opportunities to support learning.	Fulfills compliance and reporting responsibilities to the district and beyond.	Meets minimum compliance and reporting responsibilities with occasional lapses.	Has difficulty keeping the school in compliance and district and other external requirements.
i. Schmoozing	Builds strong relationships with key district and external personnel and gets them excited about the school's mission.	Builds relationships with district and external staffers so they will be helpful with paperwork and process.	Is correct and professional with district and external staff but does not enlist their active support.	Neglects relationship-building with district and external staff and doesn't have their support to get things done.
j. Resources	Taps all possible human and financial resources to support the school's mission and strategic plan.	Is effective in bringing additional human and financial resources into the school.	Occasionally raises additional funds or finds volunteers to help out.	Is resigned to working with the standard school budget, which doesn't seem adequate.

Overall rating: _____ Comments:

Exhibit B.1
Evaluation Summary Page

Principal's name: _____ School year: _____

School: _____

Evaluator: _____ Position: _____

RATINGS ON INDIVIDUAL RUBRICS:

A. Diagnosis and Planning:

    Expert   Proficient   Needs Improvement   Does Not Meet Standards

B. Priority Management and Communication:

    Expert   Proficient   Needs Improvement   Does Not Meet Standards

C. Curriculum and Data:

    Expert   Proficient   Needs Improvement   Does Not Meet Standards

D. Supervision and Professional Development:

    Expert   Proficient   Needs Improvement   Does Not Meet Standards

E. Discipline and Parent Involvement:

    Expert   Proficient   Needs Improvement   Does Not Meet Standards

F. Management and External Relations:

    Expert   Proficient   Needs Improvement   Does Not Meet Standards

OVERALL RATING:

    Expert   Proficient   Needs Improvement   Does Not Meet Standards

OVERALL COMMENTS BY SUPERVISOR:

OVERALL COMMENTS BY PRINCIPAL:

Supervisor's signature: _____ Date: _____

Principal's signature: _____ Date: _____

(By signing, the principal acknowledges having seen and discussed the evaluation; it does not necessarily denote agreement with the report.)

BIBLIOGRAPHY

Allen, D. (2001). *Getting things done.* New York: Penguin.

Begley, S. (2009, February 16). Will the BlackBerry sink the presidency? *Newsweek,* p. 37.

Ben-Hur, M. (1998). Mediation of cognitive competencies for students in need, *Phi Delta Kappan, 79*(9), 661–666.

Black, P., & Wiliam, D. (1998). Inside the black box. *Phi Delta Kappan, 80*(2), 139–148.

Blanchard, K. (1982). *The one-minute manager.* New York: William Murrow.

Bloom, B. (1984, May). "The Search for Methods of Group Instruction as Effective as One-to-One Tutoring," *Educational Leadership, 41*(8), 4–17.

Boudett, K. P., Murnane, R. J., & City, E. A. (2005). *Data wise: A step-by-step guide to using assessment results to improve teaching and learning.* Cambridge, MA: Harvard Education Press.

Boudett, K. P., & Steele, J. L. (2007). *Data wise in action: Stories of schools using data to improve teaching and learning.* Cambridge, MA: Harvard Education Press.

Boyd-Zaharias, J., & Pate-Bain, H. (2008). Class matters: In and out of school. *Phi Delta Kappan, 90*(1), 41–44.

Bracey, G. (2004). "Value-added assessment findings: Poor kids get poor teachers." *Phi Delta Kappan, 86*(4).

Brown-Chidsey, R. (2007, October). No more waiting to fail. *Educational Leadership, 65*(2), 40–46.

Buck, F. (2008). *Get organized! Time management for school leaders.* Larchmont, NY: Eye on Education.

Chenoweth, K. (2007). *It's being done.* Cambridge, MA: Harvard Education Press.

Clotfelter, C., Ladd, H., & Vigdor, J. (2007, December). Teacher credentials and student achievement: Longitudinal analysis with student fixed effects. *Economics of Education Review,* pp. 673–682.

Covey, S. (1994). *First things first: To live, to love, to learn, to leave a legacy.* New York: Simon & Schuster.

Covey, S. (2004). *The seven habits of highly effective people.* New York: Simon & Schuster.

Danielson, C. (1996). *Enhancing professional practice: A framework for teaching.* Alexandria, VA: ASCD.

Danielson, C. (2001, February). New trends in teacher evaluation. *Educational Leadership, 58*(5).

Danielson, C. (2007). *Enhancing professional practice: A framework for teaching* (2nd ed.). Alexandria, VA: ASCD.

Danielson, C. (2008). *The handbook for enhancing professional practice.* Alexandria, VA: ASCD.

Danielson, C. (2009). *Talk about teaching.* Thousand Oaks, CA: Corwin Press.

Danielson, C., & McGreal, T. (2000). *Teacher evaluation to enhance professional practice.* Alexandria, VA: ASCD.

Daresh, J. (2006). *Leading and supervising instruction.* Thousand Oaks, CA: Corwin Press.

Darling-Hammond, L. (2000). How teacher education matters, *Journal of Teacher Education, 51*(3), 166–173.

Downey, C., Steffy, B., English, F., Frase, L., & Poston, W. (2004). *The three-minute classroom walk-through.* Thousand Oaks, CA: Corwin Press.

DuFour, R. (2004) What is a "professional learning community"? *Educational Leadership, 61*(8), 6–11.

DuFour, R., DuFour, R., & Eaker, R. (2008). *Revisiting professional learning communities at work.* Bloomington, IN: Solution Tree.

DuFour, R., DuFour, R., Eaker, R., & Karhanek, G. (2004). *Whatever it takes: How professional learning communities respond when kids don't learn.* Bloomington, IN: Solution Tree.

DuFour, R., & Marzano, R. (2009). High-leverage strategies for principal development. *Educational Leadership, 66*(5), 62–68.

Edmonds, R. (1979, October). Effective schools for the urban poor. *Educational Leadership,* pp. 15–24.

Ferguson, R., & Ladd, F. (1996). Additional evidence on how and why money matters: A production function analysis of Alabama schools, in Helen F. Ladd (Ed.), *Holding Schools Accountable: Performance-Based Reform in Education.* Washington, DC: Brookings Institution Press.

Fisher, D., & Frey, N. (2007). *Checking for understanding.* Alexandria, VA: ASCD.

Freeston, K., & Costa, J. (1998). Making time for valuable work, *Educational Leadership, 55*(7), 50–52.

Glenn, D. (2007). "You will be tested on this." *Chronicle of Higher Education, 53*(40), A14.

Grubb, N. (2007). Dynamic inequality and intervention: Lessons from a small country. *Phi Delta Kappan, 89*(2), 105–114.

Guskey, T. (2005, September). A historical perspective on closing achievement gaps. *NAASP Bulletin, 89*(644), 76–89.

Hattie, J. (2002, September/October). The relation between research productivity and teaching effectiveness: Complementary, antagonistic, or independent constructs? *Journal of Higher Education,* pp. 603–641.

Haycock, K. (1998). Good teaching matters . . . a lot. *Thinking K–16,* 3, 3–14.

Heath, C., & Heath, D. (2007). *Made to stick: Why some ideas survive and others die.* New York: Random House.

Howard, J. "Proficiency now! A rallying cry for all black folks in the 21st century." In J. Kamara and T. M. Van Der Meer, Eds. *State of the Race: Creating Our 21st Century: Where Do We Go From Here?* Boston: Diaspora Press, 2004, pp. 253–265.

Joint Committee on Standards for Educational Evaluation, Arlen Gullickson, Chair. (2009). *The personnel evaluation standards* (2nd ed.). Thousand Oaks, CA: Corwin Press.

Kotter, J., & Cohen, D. (2002). *The heart of change: Real-life stories of how people changed their organizations.* Boston: Harvard Business Press.

Levy, S. (2007, June 11). When bloggers say no to a simple chat. *Newsweek.* Retrieved from www.newsweek.com/id/34223/page/1, July 17, 2009.

Marshall, K. (1970, September). "Law and order in grade 6E," *Harvard Bulletin, 73*(1), 32–41.

Marshall, K. (1996). How I confronted HSPS (hyperactive superficial principal syndrome) and began to deal with the heart of the matter. *Phi Delta Kappan, 77*(5), 336–345.

Marshall, K. (2003a). A principal looks back: Standards matter. In D. T. Gordon (Ed.), *A nation reformed?* (pp. 53–68). Cambridge, MA: Harvard Education Press.

Marshall, K. (2003b). Recovering from HSPS (hyperactive superficial principal syndrome): A progress report. *Phi Delta Kappan, 84*(9), 701–709.

Marshall, K. (2008a). Interim assessments: A user's guide. *Phi Delta Kappan, 90*(1), 64–68.

Marshall, K. (2008b). Is supervising the heck out of teachers the answer? *Education Week, 27*(36), 23, 25.

Marzano, R. J. (2003). *What works in schools.* Alexandria, VA: ASCD.

Marzano, R. J. (2006). *Classroom assessment and grading that work.* Alexandria, VA: ASCD.

Marzano, R. J. (2007). *The art and science of teaching.* Alexandria, VA: ASCD.

Marzano, R. J., Waters, T., & McNulty, B. A. (2005). *School leadership that works.* Alexandria, VA, & Denver: ASCD & McREL.

Mazur, E. (1997). *Peer instruction: A user's manual.* Upper Saddle River, NJ: Pearson Prentice Hall.

McTighe, J., Seif, E., & Wiggins, G. (2004, September). You can teach for meaning. *Educational Leadership, 62*(1), 26–30.

Mishra, A. K. "Organisational responses to crisis: the centrality of trust." In R. Kramer and T. Tyler, Eds. *Trust in Organisations*. Thousand Oaks: Sage. 1996: pp. 261–287.

Moir, E., Freeman, S., Petrock, L., & Baron, W. (1997), revised by Stobbe, C., & St. John, L. (2004). *Continuum of Teacher Development Formative Assessment System from Professional Teaching Standards, California Standards for the Teaching Profession.* Santa Cruz: New Teacher Center at the University of California.

Mooney, N., & Mausbach, A. (2008). *Align the design.* Alexandria, VA: ASCD

Nuthall, G. (2004, Fall). Relating classroom teaching to student learning: A critical analysis of why research has failed to bridge the theory-practice gap. *Harvard Educational Review, 74*(3), 273–306.

Nye, B., Hedges, L., & Konstantopoulos, S. (2004, November). How large are teacher effects? *Educational Evaluation and Policy Analysis,* p. 94.

O'Neill, J., & Conzemius, A. (2005). *The power of SMART goals.* Bloomington, IN: Solution Tree.

Pickering, D. J., & Pollock, J. E. (2001). *Classroom instruction that works.* Alexandria, VA: ASCD.

Platt, A. D., Tripp, C. E., Fraser, R., Warnock, J., & Curtis, R. (2008). *The skillful leader II: Confronting conditions that undermine learning.* Acton, MA: Ready About Press.

Platt A. D., Tripp, C. E., Ogden, W. R., & Fraser, R. G. (2000). *The skillful leader: Confronting mediocre teaching.* Acton, MA: Ready About Press.

Pollock, J. (2007). *Improving student learning one teacher at a time.* Alexandria, VA: ASCD.

Popham, J. (2004a, November). A game without winners. *Educational Leadership, 62*(3), 46–50.

Popham, J. (2004b, November). "Teaching to the test": An expression to eliminate. *Educational Leadership, 62*(3), 82–83.

Popham, J. Defining and enhancing formative assessment (2006). A special paper for the Council of Chief State School Officers.

Reeves, D. (2000). *Accountability in action.* Englewood, CO: Advanced Learning Press.

Reeves, D. (2004). *Making standards work* (2nd ed.). Englewood, CO: Advanced Learning Press.

Ribas, W. (2005). *Teacher evaluation that works!!* Westwood, MA, & Lanham, MD: Ribas Publications and Rowman & Littlefield Education.

Rice, J. (2003). *Teacher quality: Understanding the effectiveness of teacher attributes.* Washington, DC: Economic Policy Institute.

Rivkin, S., Hanuschek, E., & Kain, J. (2005, March). Teachers, schools, and academic achievement. *Econometrica,* pp. 471–458.

Rutter, M., et al. (1979). *Fifteen thousand hours: Secondary schools and their effects on children.* Cambridge, MA: Harvard University Press.

Saginor, N. (2008). *Diagnostic classroom observation: Moving beyond best practice.* Thousand Oaks, CA: Corwin Press.

Sanders, W. L., & Rivers, J. C. (1996). *Cumulative and residual effects of teachers on future student academic achievement.* Knoxville: University of Tennessee Value-Added Research and Assessment Center.

Saphier, J. (1993). *How to make supervision and evaluation really work.* Acton, MA: Research for Better Teaching.

Saphier J. (2005). *John Adams' promise: How to have good schools for all our children, not just for some.* Acton, MA: Research for Better Teaching.

Saphier, J., Haley-Speca, M. A., & Gower, R. (2008). *The skillful teacher.* Acton, MA: Research for Better Teaching.

Saphier, J., & Marshall, K. (2008). Jon Saphier and Kim Marshall on supervision and evaluation: Many areas of agreement, a few areas of disagreement. *Marshall Memo.* Retrieved from www.marshallmemo.com/articles/Saphier%20Marshall%20 confluence%202008.pdf, May 24, 2009.

Sato, M., & Lensmire, T. (2009). Poverty and Payne: Supporting Teachers to work with children of poverty. *Phi Delta Kappan, 90*(5), 365–370.

Schmoker, M. (1992, May 13). What schools can learn from Toyota of America. *Education Week.*

Schmoker, M. (1999). *Results: The key to continuous school improvement* (2nd ed.). Alexandria, VA: ASCD.

Schmoker, M. (2001). *The results fieldbook: Practical strategies from dramatically improved schools.* Alexandria, VA: ASCD.

Schmoker, M. (2004). Tipping point: From feckless reform to substantive instructional improvement. *Phi Delta Kappan, 85*(6), 424–432.

Schmoker, M. (2006). *Results now: How we can achieve unprecedented improvements in teaching and learning.* Alexandria, VA: ASCD.

Schmoker, M., & Marzano, R. (1999). Realizing the promise of standards-based education, *Educational Leadership, 56*(6), 17–21.

Stiggins, R. (2007). Assessments through the student's eyes, *Educational Leadership, 64*(8), 22–26.

Stiggins, R., Arter, J., Chappuis, J., & Chappuis, S. (2006). *Classroom assessment for student learning.* Princeton, NJ: Educational Testing Service.

Stigler, J., & Hiebert, J. (1999). *The teaching gap.* New York: Free Press.

Stronge, J. H. (2002). *Qualities of effective teachers.* Alexandria, VA: ASCD.

Sullivan, S., & Glanz, J. (2005). *Supervision that improves teaching.* Thousand Oaks, CA: Corwin Press.

Toch, T., & Rothman, R. (2008). *Rush to judgment.* Washington, DC: Education Sector.

Tooms, A. (2003). The rookie's playbook: Insights and dirt for new principals. *Phi Delta Kappan, 84*(7), 530–533.

Tough, P. (2006). What it takes to make a student. *New York Times Magazine,* November 26, 2006, pp. 44–51, 69–72, 77.

Trimble, S., Gay, A., & Matthews, J. (2005, March). Using test score data to focus instruction. *Middle School Journal, 36*(4), 26–32.

Weisberg, D., Sexton, S., Mulhern, J., & Keeling, D. (2009). The widget effect: Our national failure to acknowledge and act on differences in teacher effectiveness. New Teacher Project. Retrieved from http://widgeteffect.org/downloads /TheWidgetEffect.pdf, July 13, 2009.

Whitehurst, G. (2002, March 5). Scientifically Based Research on Teacher Quality: Research on Teacher Preparation and Professional Development. White House Conference on Preparing Tomorrow's Teachers.

Wiggins, G. (1998). *Educative assessment.* San Francisco: Jossey-Bass.

Wiggins, G. (2006). Healthier testing made easy. *Edutopia, 2*(3), 48–51.

Wiggins, G., & McTighe, J. (2005). *Understanding by design* (2nd ed.). Alexandria, VA: ASCD.

Wiggins, G., & McTighe, J. (2007). *Schooling by design.* Alexandria, VA: ASCD.

Wiliam, D. (2007/2008). Changing Classroom Practice, *Educational Leadership, 65*(4), 36–41.

Wiliam, D. (2007). Content then process: Teacher learning communities in the service of formative assessment. In D. B. Reeves (Ed.), *Ahead of the curve: The power of assessment to transform teaching and learning* (pp. 183–204). Bloomington, IN: Solution Tree.

Wilkerson, J., & Lang, W. S. (2007). *Assessing teacher dispositions.* Thousand Oaks, CA: Corwin Press.

Williams, J. (2005). On the positive side: Bloomberg and Klein seek to repair a failure factory, *Education Next, 5*(4), 17–21.

RUBRIC SOURCES

The rubrics presented in Chapter Seven were developed after referring to a number of similar efforts in schools and districts:

Alexandria Public Schools (Virginia) performance evaluation rubrics (2003)

Aspire Charter Schools, California teacher evaluation rubrics (2003)

Boston Public Schools Performance Evaluation Instrument (1997)

City on a Hill Charter School (Boston) performance evaluation rubrics (2004)

Conservatory Lab Charter School (Boston) performance evaluation rubrics (2004)

Enhancing Professional Practice: A Framework for Teaching by Charlotte Danielson (ASCD, 1996)

"Indicators of Teaching for Understanding" by Jay McTighe and Eliot Seif (unpublished paper, 2005)

Linking Teacher Evaluation and Student Learning by Pamela Tucker and James Stronge (ASCD, 2005)

North Star Academy Charter School of Newark: Teaching Standards (2004–05)

Roxbury Preparatory Charter School, Boston: Criteria for Outstanding Teaching (2004–05)

The Skillful Teacher by Jon Saphier, Mary Ann Haley-Speca, and Robert Gower (Research for Better Teaching, 2008)

The Three Big Rocks of Educational Reform by Jon Saphier (Research for Better Teaching, 2005)

Vaughn Next Century Learning Center, Chicago performance evaluation rubric (2004)

What Works in Schools: Translating Research into Action by Robert Marzano (ASCD, 2003)

THE AUTHOR

Kim Marshall was a teacher, central office administrator, and principal in the Boston public schools for thirty-two years. He now advises and coaches new principals, working with New Leaders for New Schools; teaches courses and leads workshops on instructional leadership; and publishes a weekly newsletter, the Marshall Memo, which summarizes ideas and research from forty-four publications (www.marshallmemo.com). Kim has written several books and numerous articles on teaching and school leadership. He is married and has two children; both are high-school teachers, one in Boston, the other in California.

INDEX

Do-your-own-thing curriculum ethos, 10–11
Dog-and-pony shows, 60, 62
Downey, C., 61
DuFour, R., xi–xii, 199

E

E-mail, 188
Edmonds, R., 3–4, 16–17
Education coordinator, role of, 3
Effective teaching: and hiring, xvi; irreducible elements of, 73
Effective teaching, achieving, xiii–xv
Electronic audience response devices, 75
E-mail, 188
English, F., 61
Enhancing Professional Practice: A Framework for Teaching (Danielson), 142
Evaluation: rubrics, 139–150; taking stock, 112, time allocations (chart), 195
Evaluation forms, 27–29; example of, 28–29
Evaluation summary page (form), 164, 238
Evaluations, 5–7, 203–205, *See also* Supervision; Boston Public Schools evaluation checklist, 42; communication difficulties, 25; conventional, analyzing the failure of, 21–37; critical, 31–32; defined, 21; during-the-year supervisory write-ups, 41–42; end-of-year, 42; focus of, 36–37; intensifying, 39; limited point of view, 22–23; logical model, 21–37; natural resistance, 31–32; observer effects, 24–25; real-life scenarios, 19–20; stage dressing, 23–24; and standardized tests, 37–39; and supervision, 19–40; and teacher defensiveness, 32–33; tension,

fostering of, 33; test scores, using, 37–39; unhelpful ratings, 30–31
Exit cards, 75
Expectations, 6–7; clarifying, 181–182; grade-level learning expectations, and curriculum, 95; year-end learning expectations, 97
Expert level, SOTEL, 73–74

F

Feedback, 56–58, 204; delivering, 80–82; goal of, 84
Fifteen Thousand Hours (Harvard University Press), 3
Filing paperwork, 189
Finland, approach to assessment, 125–126
Fisher, D., 76
Follow-up: to interim assessments, 129–131, 136
Formative assessments, *See* On-the-spot assessments
Forms, and evaluations, 27–29
Frase, L., 61
Freeston, K., 191
Frey, N., 76
Full-dress evaluations, 194–195
Full-lesson observations, orchestrating, 84–86

G

"Gang of Six," 7
Gay, A., 134
Getting Things Done (Allen), 183
Glasbergen, Randy, 34
Glenn, D., 76
Goals: goal setting, and rubrics, 172; for initiatives, 180–181
Good teaching, 25; curriculum design, 89–112; importance of, xii–xviii; mental checklist of essentials of, 72; path to, 110; and student achievement, 179
Gower, R., 25, 142

Grade inflation, 30

Grade-level learning expectations, and curriculum, 95

Grading criteria, 12–13

Great aims, and good teaching, 72

Greater Newark Academy, scheduling time for assessments, 128

Grievance, losing, 42

Grubb, N., 126

H

Haley-Speca, M. A., 25, 142

Hanuschek, E., xii

Hattie, J., xii

Haycock, K., xii

Heath, C., 111

Heath, D., 111

Hedges, L., xii

Hiebert, J., 86

High-stakes testing, 14, 95, 107–110, 136; impact of, 107; pressure of, 110; state testing, 138

Hiring, and effective teaching, xvi

How to Make Supervision and Evaluation Really Work (Saphier), 142

Howard, J., 6–7, 16, 120

Hyperactive Superficial Principal Syndrome (HSPS), 34, 44, 47, 53, 177

I

Incoming items, sorting into bins, 186–187

Independent practice, and good teaching, 72

Initiatives: crafting, 180; measurable goals for, 180–181

"Inside the Black Box" (Black/Wiliam), 74

Instructional coaches, 85, 131

Interim assessments, xvii, 113–150, 201; benefits of, 121–122; commercial,

127–128; compared to state tests, 119; computerized tests, 120; data meetings, 129–131; design of, 119–120; detractors, 120; display data, 129; example of a district's use of, 131–134; follow-up, 129–131, 136; get teachers involved in making sense of, 129; high-quality conversations about, effect of, 137; high-quality tests, obtaining, 126–127; immediate follow-up, 128; implementation of, 122–124, 136; involving students in the process, 135; learning outcomes, clarifying, 126; mistakes made in implementing, 122–124; monitoring, 194; proponents, 120; purchase of, 120; Response to Intervention (RTI), 125–126; scheduling time for, 128; and SMART goals, 126; and state tests, 138; and student achievement, 179; taking stock, 136–137; understanding/trust, building, 124–125

J

Journal-writing sessions, 75

K

K-12 articulation, and curriculum, 95

Kain, J., xii

Keeling, D., 30

Klein, Joel, 1, 37

Konstantopoulos, S., xii

Kotter, J., 65

L

Ladd, F., xii

Ladd, H., xii

Laptop computers, providing for every student, xv

Lawrence, D., 169

Learning, lack of focus on, 13–14

Understanding by Design (UbD), 102–106; first use of, 105–106; framing the big ideas of a curriculum unit, 104–105; key steps for principal and leadership team, 104; and principal, 103–104; team unit planning time, 106; unit planning, 103, 106; unit-planning meetings, 103–104; writing matching essential questions, 104–105

Unit plans, 26; curriculum, 102–106

V

Videotaping lessons/teaching, 85

Vigdor, J., xii

Visits: capturing/remembering information from, 77–79; classroom observation time, 66–69; and depth, 53; keeping track of, 52–53, length vs. frequency of, 69; unannounced, xvi, 87, 191

W

Walkthroughs, 61–62

Weisberg, D., 30

Whatever It Takes (DuFour et. al), 136

Whitehurst, G., xii

Wiggins, G., xvi, 12, 89, 93, 102, 103–106, 113, 120

Wiliam, D., 74, 75, 116, 120, 127, 207

Wilson, Laval, 4

Y

Year-end learning expectations, 96–100; national standards, 98–100; state standards, 96–97

Year-end test scores, as assessment, 117–118